THE ROUGH
Vintage
London

www.roughguides.com

Credits

The Rough Guide to Vintage London

Editing: Ian Blenkinsop, Matthew Milton, Joe Staines
Design: Diana Jarvis
Additional Design: Dan May, Ed Wright
Cover Design: Scott Stickland
Cartography: Ed Wright
Proofreading: Jason Freeman
Production: Charlotte Cade, Liz Cherry

Additional Contributions:
Emma Sudall, Serena Wilson (HemingwayDesign),
Andrew Lockett, Matthew Milton, Joe Staines
(Rough Guides), Lucy Ryder Richardson, Petra
Curtis (www.modernshows.com),
Leona Baker (www.thrift-ola.com).

Rough Guides Reference

Editors: Kate Berens, Ian Blenkinsop,
Tom Cabot, Tracy Hopkins,
Matthew Milton, Joe Staines
Director: Andrew Lockett

Publishing Information

This first edition published May 2013 by
Rough Guides Ltd, 80 Strand, London WC2R 0RL
11 Community Centre, Panchsheel Park, New Delhi 110017, India
Email: mail@roughguides.com

Distributed by the Penguin Group:
Penguin Books Ltd, 80 Strand, London WC2R 0RL
Penguin Group (USA), 375 Hudson Street, NY 10014, USA
Penguin Group (Australia), 250 Camberwell Road, Camberwell, Victoria 3124, Australia
Penguin Group (New Zealand), 67 Apollo Drive, Rosedale, Auckland 0632, New Zealand
Rough Guides is represented in Canada by Tourmaline Editions Inc.,
662 King Street West, Suite 304, Toronto

Printed in Malaysia by Vivar Printing Sdn. Bhd.

The publishers and authors have done their best to ensure the accuracy and currency of all information in
The Rough Guide to Vintage London; however they can accept no responsibility for any loss or inconvenience
sustained by anyone as a result of its information and advice. Contact details for organizations and website
addresses frequently change: those included in this book were correct to the best of our knowledge at the
time of printing.

No part of this book may be reproduced in any form without permission from the publisher except for
the quotation of brief passages in reviews.

Main text © Frances Ambler, Emily Bick, Samantha Cook, Nicholas Jones and Lara Kavanagh 2013

Additional contributions to Lifestyle section © Hem Des LLP 2013 & Rough Guides Ltd

Foreword © Wayne Hemingway 2013

Maps © Rough Guides
Contains Ordnance Survey data © Crown copyright and database rights 2013

224 pages; includes index

A catalogue record for this book is available from the British Library.

ISBN 13: 978-1-40932-536-9

1 3 5 7 9 8 6 4 2

THE ROUGH GUIDE to

Vintage London

**CONSULTANT EDITOR:
WAYNE HEMINGWAY** MBE

by Frances Ambler, Emily Bick, Samantha Cook,
Nicholas Jones and Lara Kavanagh

www.roughguides.com

CONTENTS

FOREWORD

Vintage is a word that has entered the popular vocabulary in the past few years. From being something that was pretty underground, the concept is now widespread and flourishing in London. When, over thirty years ago, Gerardine and I emptied our wardrobes of second-hand clothes, shoes and accessories onto a tiny stall on Camden Market, little did we know that within a matter of weeks

this would grow into a dozen stalls attracting cool club kids from around the world, all eager to buy the second-hand treasures we were finding at every charity shop, jumble sale and textile recycling yard that we visited. The 50s printed frocks, CC41 granddad shirts, tonic suits, sturdy demob shoes, 60s canvas pumps and Tootal scarves we were unearthing were striking a chord with a crowd who understood that great design stands the test of time and is so much cooler than ephemeral high street trends. Two decades later, our second-hand revolution became known as vintage, and vintage is now accepted as part of the discerning design landscape.

Growing up wearing second-hand clothes to soul clubs and punk gigs, later adapting second-hand finds to create a New Romantic aesthetic, and now as collectors, vintage has always been important to us. Vintage plays a big part in how we approach many aspects of our life together, extending way beyond just the way we dress. Though we designed and built our own very modern house, the vast majority of items we've put in it are things we've found and upcycled ourselves. We don't slavishly follow fashion and trends, and we feel that this is what allows us to be creative. Vintage is about looking at timeless elements of design and finding and creating an enduring style. Great design can be totally timeless. On a macro scale the Southbank's magnificent Royal Festival Hall still looks as great today as it did when it was constructed for the Festival of Britain in 1951. This is partly a result of good design thinking in the first place, complemented by judicious updating and modern interventions.

One of my favourite rooms in our house is the "snug". This has a long, mid-century modern-inspired coffee table (bought from a young Czech designer exhibiting at Designers Bloc), a couple of mid-century modern bucket chairs from Portobello Road market (with loose covers we made ourselves) and a back-lit 60s cabinet (bought from Oxfam) that contains a quadraphonic stereo system, and wheel-out bar! The art on the wall is from our Land of Lost Content collection and – if we say so ourselves – is a modern way of treating an iconic Tretchikoff print. You can still pick up this kind of item from one of London's car boot sales, if you're lucky; there again you may need to pay a bit more when visiting somewhere like the wonderful Alfie's Antique Market in Marylebone.

While for many of us vintage is part of our everyday lives, you can, if you so desire, go even further and live a one hundred percent vintage lifestyle. *The Rough Guide to Vintage London* shows you how to do it. Whether it's useful tips on where to get your precious 1950s brogues brought back to life like polished chestnuts or the best places to take tea, watch a vintage film, dance to timeless Northern Soul or hire a classic car to get you round town, it's all here waiting for you. And it's happening in the UK's capital, the world's most creative city – one that has vintage running through its arteries.

Wayne Hemingway MBE
London, 2012

KEY TO SYMBOLS

 Menswear

 Womenswear

 Children's

 Markets

 Furniture

 Homeware and bric-a-brac

 Records and music

Books and comics

Cafés and tearooms

Bars and pubs

Restaurants

HOW TO USE THE GUIDE

The Rough Guide to Vintage London is divided into two parts: Shopping, Eating and Drinking, and Lifestyle. The first focuses on London's best and most prominent vintage fashion stores and other vintage outlets along with a sprinkling of bars, cafés and pubs. It is organized by geographical area (central, east, north, south and west) with all the entries listed alphabetically so, for example, the first chapter of Central London opens with an entry on "Ain't Nothin' But...", a blues bar in Kingly Street. All entries are highlighted on the maps at the beginning of each area chapter as well as being listed in the index.

The second section, Lifestyle, casts the net rather wider in order to convey the sheer range of products and services now available to the vintage enthusiast. Laid out as an alphabetical directory, this tells you – among many other things – where to hire (or buy) the ideal classic car, who can give you the perfect 1940s haircut, where to get your Fender Stratocaster repaired, or how to find a wedding dress like the one your nan wore. Venues, such as the amazing Wilton's Music Hall, are also included, as are special events like the Blitz Party or the eccentric Chap Olympiad, plus those museums, hotels and lidos that might inspire the retro-minded. Entries with stars next to them indicate enterprises that we feel are outstanding or leaders in their particular field.

Vintage is a fast-moving phenomenon (despite some dealers having been around a long time) and we've included several businesses that only operate online or at occasional vintage fairs or markets. Indeed, such is the speed of development of the vintage scene that it is inevitable we've missed some new openings or existing stores that may have moved. You can alert us to these or any other vintage news by writing to mail@uk.roughguides.com, including *The Rough Guide to Vintage London* in the header.

Vintage London represents a different city to the one presented in our normal London guide. This is not the world of Harrods and Buckingham Palace but a parallel one: more fashion-conscious, cooler and with the East End, rather than the West End, at the centre of the action. Our team have been surprised by the enthusiasm, vitality and range of the vintage scene and hope that newcomers and even veterans will be too.

Has there ever been a better time to go vintage? We think not and hope that this book enables you to live whatever vintage life you want to the full.

PART ONE

SHOPPING EATING& DRINKING

CENTRAL
LONDON

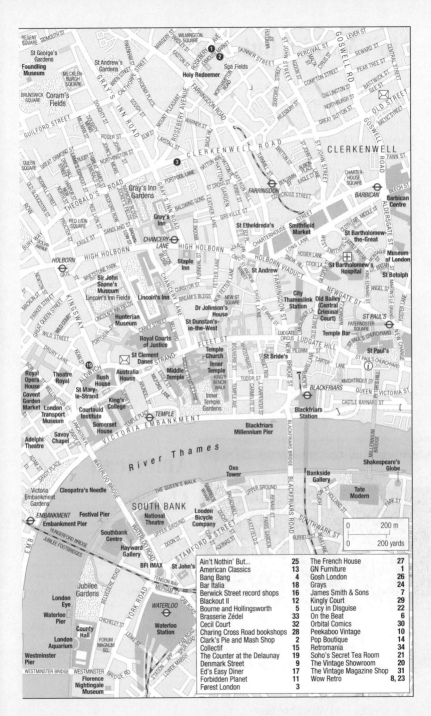

Ain't Nothin' But...	25	The French House	27
American Classics	13	GN Furniture	1
Bang Bang	4	Gosh London	26
Bar Italia	18	Grays	24
Berwick Street record shops	16	James Smith & Sons	7
Blackout II	12	Kingly Court	29
Bourne and Hollingsworth	5	Lucy in Disguise	22
Brasserie Zédel	33	On the Beat	6
Cecil Court	32	Orbital Comics	30
Charing Cross Road bookshops	28	Peekaboo Vintage	10
Clark's Pie and Mash Shop	2	Pop Boutique	14
Collectif	15	Retromania	34
The Counter at the Delaunay	19	Soho's Secret Tea Room	21
Denmark Street	9	The Vintage Showroom	20
Ed's Easy Diner	17	The Vintage Magazine Shop	31
Forbidden Planet	11	Wow Retro	8, 23
Forest London	3		

Ain't Nothin' But... 🍸 🍴

Ⓐ 20 Kingly Street W1B 5PZ Ⓣ 020 7287 0514 Ⓦ www.aintnothingbut.co.uk
Ⓞ Mon–Thurs 5pm–1am, Fri 5pm–2.30am, Sat 3pm–2.30am, Sun 3pm–midnight

In terms of retro-flavoured late night drinking holes, the boozy bohemian atmosphere of Ain't Nothin' But... is hard to beat. Live music aficionados, night hawks who fancy a tipple after the pubs have kicked out and those eager to try and forget what day of the week it is, all hang out at this friendly – and a little rough around the edges – blues joint.

The bar puts on live music every night from a mixture of prominent blues artists and a roster of regulars, as well as hosting jam sessions and open mic nights. Even on weekdays it's lively enough with free entry but, come the weekend, the party atmosphere (and a cover charge) really kicks in.

The decor is simple and delightfully scuffed. It's a basic strip of a bar with standing room only, which leads onto an only marginally larger seating area containing the stage. The walls are decorated with music memorabilia, while striking murals depicting blues greats such as Muddy Waters and Bo Diddley enliven the route to the loos. The simple wooden benches and tables and the seemingly requisite sticky floors further enhance the old time vibe.

With a clientele that will try and talk you into joining in, if not grab you off your seat for a dance, there's no room for pretensions at Ain't Nothin' But... Elbow your way to the bar, order yourself something from their large whisky collection and settle in for a good old-fashioned time.

American Classics 👤

Ⓐ 20 Endell Street WC2H 9BD
Ⓣ 020 7831 1210 Ⓦ www.
facebook.com/pages/American-
Classics-London Ⓞ Mon–Sat 11am–
6.30pm, Sun 12.30pm–5.30pm

American Classics started in the 1970s as one of London's first specialist importers of vintage

Levis, fuelled by the booming trade in a James Dean inspired, kitschily romantic version of 1950s Americana.

These days, they deal strictly in repro, claiming all of the good denim stock from the 1940s–60s is unwearable now, having been worn to death by the buttocks of all the generations that have passed since then. American Classics stocks brands that replicate the original denim detail for detail, though using similar finishes, stiffer weaves and stitch-for-stitch selvedge patterns as their predecessors. Not all the stock is American: it comes from Japan and Europe, depending on who stocks the most faithful copies. "Big E" brand Levi reproductions run from £140–215, and a pair of Lee 101 zip-front jeans is £210.

The rest of the shop is full of the hard-wearing, classic and timeless outdoor gear sported by bearded hipsters from Brooklyn to Shoreditch, or by similarly bearded lumberjacks thirty years ago. Down-filled vests and jackets start at £149, and Dockers cords are £89. Army sweatshirts complete the surplus look. This is also a top stockist for Red Wing shoes, the thick-soled, hard-wearing work boots (£179–270) from wintry Minnesota, US, that last for decades and keep feet warm while walking miles down icy roads.

Bang Bang

Ⓐ 21 Goodge Street W1T 2PJ Ⓣ 020 7631 4191
Ⓦ www.bangbangclothingexchange.co.uk Ⓞ
Mon–Fri 10am–6.30pm, Sat 11am–6pm

A fashion insider's secret, Bang Bang is the choosiest clothes exchange in central London: funkier than those in Knightsbridge or Marylebone, but friendlier than the Retro Man and Woman shops in Notting Hill. Everyone from students to stylists comes here to upgrade their wardrobes, and after London Fashion Week, it's not unusual to find catwalk and press samples in store. The proportion of vintage to recent (within the last five to ten years) designer wear is about 1:2, but the third of the store that is vintage will be some of the most colourful, distinctive, and aligned with recent trends. 1970s Chloe silk skirts, Quorum (early Ossie Clark) robe-like crepe gowns, and wildly patterned Bill Gibb knits have all popped up from time to time, and there always seems to be some 1990s Galliano or even earlier Westwood on the rails. Sometimes the best bits are unsigned: touile-de-jouy printed 1980s jumpsuits, or 1970s belts with buckles made of fist-sized quartz crystals. Prices range from £20–£30 for nondesigner items, to £200 and more for very rare designer vintage, and are similar to what you'll find on eBay.

For the girl who wants to breathe new life into a vintage wardrobe (or just wants more wardrobe space and a bit of cash) Bang Bang should be the first port of call. Sellers are offered store credit or two thirds of that in cash, and few take just the cash. Tips for anyone exchanging their clothes: think quality materials, colour and detailing--and phone first if you have more than one bag's worth. (Two more branches, including a menswear exchange, are in Soho.)

Bar Italia 🧁

Ⓐ 22 Frith Street W I D 4RF **☎** 020 7437 4520 **Ⓦ** www.baritaliasoho.co.uk **Ⓞ** Daily 7am–5am

Possibly Soho's, if not London's most famous classic café, Bar Italia's reputation has been formidable since its opening in 1949. In popular culture it'll probably be remembered as the place "where other broken people go", thanks to Pulp's song in its honour from the mid-90s. Today, as well as the broken people, its stools are populated by Italian expats, mod revivalists, media workers, and revellers for whom a night out has tipped over into morning.

Bar Italia advertises its *raison d'être*, caffe espresso, on its neon clock sign. It's a rare surviving example of the coffee shops that sprang up in London after the World War II and, in turn, fuelled the mod movement with one of their drugs of choice: caffeine. There is still always a fine selection of scooters parked close by.

Inside, despite its widescreen TV, you can almost imagine how exotic and exciting the café must have looked in grey war-weary Britain. Joints of meat and cycling shirts are hung up next to the Italian flags and boxing memorabilia covers the walls. Perch on a stool at the Formica bar to enjoy your espresso and you're sure to witness a few of its colourful and devoted clientele.

While alcohol is only served until 11pm (making its name slightly misleading), come at any hour for Italian style sandwiches and cakes and enough strong coffee to get you through the day, to its 5am closing time, or all the way through to the 7am re-opening and legendary breakfast. Whatever time you choose to drop by, Bar Italia remains a fascinating place to sit and watch the world go by.

Berwick Street record shops

A W1, Nearest tubes: Tottenham Court Road and Oxford Circus

Berwick Street is one of Soho's liveliest, grungiest stretches, preserving an older and untidier Soho, and is famous for its music shops. Counting the others on neighbouring streets, there's a decent number of these and a proper sense of a hub. **SISTER RAY** (nos.34–35) rolls away into the gloom of the storage behind the tills, and pursues the same eclectic principles that all of these shops believe in: rock and pop, blues, jazz... "all those are just labels; we know that music is music." Front-of-house you'll find a selection with detailed, loving recommendations written by the staff. Also look out for the "Sister Ray Hall of Fame" with its ever-changing selection of classics.

RECKLESS (no.30) has that air of concentration and high seriousness, punctured by a knowing sense of humour, that is distinctive to these places. Pushing through its racks it's impossible to guess what treasures you might be about to unearth. More expensive rarities line the walls, attesting to the finest discrimination between alternative versions of history. The **MUSIC AND VIDEO EXCHANGE** (no.95), across the sea of the market filling the street, is the most ragged and informal of Berwick Street's record stores, but with the same shared spirit of openness to all music, all periods and forms. Bargains are easy to find and there's a high chance that you'll spot some classic that you've always been meaning to buy.

Around the corner, at no.7 Broadwick Street, you'll find **SOUNDS OF THE UNIVERSE**, two floors of charismatic collision between hip-hop, jazz, soul, funk, electronica and so forth. A very easy place to beguile the hours.

Blackout II

A 51 Endell Street **T** 020 7240 5006 **W** www.blackout2.com **O** Mon–Fri 11.00am–7.00pm, Sat 11.30am–6.30pm, Sun noon–5pm

Blackout II's sign features an Art Nouveau woman peering out of an exploding cornucopia, which gives you some idea of what you'll find inside the shop. The crinoline and taffeta skirts of 1950s frocks burst forth as soon as you enter the door; signs warning away overeager hands, to protect the fabric, are the next thing you'll notice. Even more precious 1930s gowns are kept behind the till. They are sourced and sold as a labour of love by Roz, the owner, who has made Blackout II something of a vintage institution over the past 25 years.

The basement feels like a walk-in dressing room shared by a clutch of movie stars. All tastes are catered for, from Doris Day-styled two piece skirt suits in forest green to silky, louder-than-Pucci hostess flares. An almost endless supply of unworn vintage Joseph Rose heels from the 1950s and 60s can complete any look: here are silver mary janes with low block heels and stripy melon-coloured raw silk stilettoes. All kinds of coats line the outside racks, from simple wool princess styles in Hitchcock-heroine beiges and greys to a shaggy monkey-style fun fur to make Barbarella swoon. The inner racks are labelled by decade, and

the occasional Ossie Clark, Biba or Dior frock lurks within. One warning: don't come down here at the end of a day's shopping – there's not enough room to accommodate bulging carrier bags, and you'll need both hands to push apart the clothes and reach for all the things that will catch your eye. There's also a small, but well-chosen, selection of menswear.

Bourne and Hollingsworth

A 28 Rathbone Place W1T 1JF **T** 020 7636 8228 **W** www.bourneandhollingsworth.com **O** Mon–Wed 5.30pm–12.30am, Thurs–Sat 5pm–1am

A Dark'n'Stormy in a jam jar or a Chimp's Tea in a chintzy china teacup; as might be expected from a bar run by the people behind the Blitz Party and the Prohibition event, Bourne and Hollingsworth serve up their cocktails in real vintage style. Though its imitators have taken some of the edge off its quirkiness, this bar remains a favourite.

Bourne and Hollingsworth is inspired by the prettiest idea of what a secret drinking den should look like. Entrance to the bar is down a metal staircase, with only a black-and-white shop photograph indicating its location. Inside the tiny space looks like a genteelly deteriorating front room, complete with fading floral wallpaper, shabby chic chairs and granny-style floor lamps. The bar, literally a hole in the wall, adds to the illicit feel. And you'll need to book ahead if you want a table, as it's usually as packed as you'd expect a speakeasy to be.

The drinks menu serves up 25 different cocktails, a mixture of the classics and their own concoctions, served in all kinds of vessels including the jam jars and the teacups. A Storm in a Mug cocktail comes, naturally, in a mug, an enamel utilitarian number, perfect for secretive swigging.

While a few of its trappings may be too sickly sweet for some, there's no denying the devotion of Bourne and Hollingsworth fans. So much so that its owners set up The Fourth Wall. An exact replica of the bar, this portable and even more secretive version pops up at different locations round London. Sign up at Ⓦ www.whereisthefourthwall.com, to track it down.

Brasserie Zédel 🍴 🍸

Ⓐ 20 Sherwood Street W1F 7ED Ⓣ 020 7734 4888 Ⓦ www.brasseriezedel.com
Ⓞ Mon–Sun noon–midnight (Brasserie Zédel), Mon–Sun 4.30pm–midnight (Bar Américain)

Brasserie Zédel is the place to head if you've a longing for the style of the Fitzgeralds but can't quite match their finances. Situated off an unassuming street near Piccadilly Circus, descend the grand staircase to the *réception* and be instantly transported into another, more glamorous world. The classic bistro food is reasonable enough at reasonable prices but it's the atmosphere and surroundings that make a visit worthwhile.

This basement space was once part of the Regent Palace Hotel which, in the 1930s, remodelled the rooms that now house Brasserie Zédel in stunning Art Deco style. Zédel's sympathetic update showcases this original decor to its full advantage: diners eat amidst marble columns and rich gilding, overlooked by a grand, Parisian-style clock, although the price happily belies such opulent surroundings (the prix fixe for three courses is only £11.25). The Bar Américain retains its original luxurious birch veneer walls and has been gently enhanced with sympathetic period lighting and a fantastic 1930s style aeroplane wallpaper to create a very *Casablanca* feel. Or step into the Crazy Coqs, an intimate performance venue in what was once a billiard room. Performances mix cabaret and jazz and are on most nights; tickets are usually around £20 and need to be booked separately.

The Deco feel is maintained throughout, from the typography on the menus to the beautiful loos. The cocktail menu serves up a selection of classics like Manhattans and Martinis alongside a number of 1930s-style house cocktails that will help an evening to slip happily by. It's the perfect place for an intimate tête-à-tête with a lover or for a gossipy catch up while maintaining stylistic standards. Brasserie Zédel offers that rare combination of being hospitable, reasonably priced and wonderful to look at.

Cecil Court 📖

Ⓐ WC2, nearest tube: Leicester Square **Ⓦ** www.cecilcourt.co.uk

Cecil Court is a delightful pedestrianized street running between Charing Cross Road and St Martin's Lane, concentrating a wonderful variety of shops specializing in the past. Protected by their location, and perhaps achieving safety in numbers, these miniature storehouses of history preserve treasures ranging from music hall memorabilia to vintage children's books. First editions of 20th-century fiction are a particular specialism of many of the shops – **GOLDSBORO, STEPHEN POOLE, PETER ELLIS, TINDLEY AND CHAPMAN** and others – and the covers of mid-century and post-war classic writers such as Evelyn Waugh and Graham Greene set the tone for the street, with all the fresh strangeness of their disappeared aesthetics. It's a pleasure just to inspect these vanished styles in artwork and typography.

What follows is just a selection: Cecil Court is very manageable and you can see everything easily; the website gives a swift introduction to each of the shops.

DAVID DRUMMOND is crammed with treasures from pop culture and the performing arts – showbiz, theatre, cinema, opera, popular music: the window was dominated by The Beatles and Bond at the time of writing. Like many places along Cecil Court the riches that are stocked in a small space are remarkable. Besides books you'll find posters, programmes and other memorabilia, fixing the unique events they describe for the perpetual pleasure of the aficionado.

MOTOR BOOKS is a great example of Cecil Court specialization. There isn't a great deal else here besides books about cars but nevertheless, if you want the BMW 5 series collected service manuals for 1982–1988 then this is the place.

TRAVIS AND EMERY sells sheet music, orchestral scores, books on music and a great deal else – the past feels as though it's especially thickly clustered because so many of these things are packed onto the shelves and can't be identified from their anonymous spines.

MARCHPANE sells collectable children's books: entering the shop is an intense pleasure as you'll instantly see things that remind you of your own childhood, or perhaps of the shadowy volumes that belonged to your parents in their childhood and that lingered (unread).

Charing Cross Road bookshops 📖

Ⓐ WC2, nearest tubes: Leicester Square and Tottenham Court Road

Close to the northern end of Charing Cross Road the blackened exteriors of York Mansions and Clifton Mansions, on the west side of St Giles High Street, together with the line of idiosyncratic shops and restaurants at their base, give a sense of how this area must have looked when vintage tastes were contemporary fashion. Immediately to the right of the view the massive crossrail works (Europe's largest engineering project, cutting a swathe through the middle of the city), promises an acceleration of the change to Charing Cross Road and its tributaries. Many of the smaller bookshops have already disappeared (unable to afford the recent rent increases), and in their place the familiar chains – clothing and restaurants – have established themselves. But still it retains its special feeling, and the bookshops that have survived are central to this. What will be their fate when crossrail connects the street to the rest of the world in minutes and hours?

In some ways Charing Cross Road has always been an anomaly. Right at the centre of things, an integral feature of London's imaginary map carried around in millions of heads, it's always somehow managed to feel as though it's hidden away, with louder and glitzier streets distracting the focus – attention pulled away to Soho in one direction and Covent Garden in the other, leaving Charing Cross Road as a boundary to be stepped across or hurried along. The bookshops have pulled themselves into the shadows of this long and narrow fissure between glittering districts, and although only half a dozen or so are surviving today, it's still enough to rescue the street from accusations of blandness. **CLAIRE**

DE ROUEN at no.125 is the first bookshop that you'll come across if you start at the top of the street. It's a specialist fashion and photography bookshop, hidden away up a staircase and above a betting shop. David Bailey, no less, has called it "maybe the best photography bookshop in the world." Next door, in **SOHO ORIGINAL BOOKS**, alongside the erotic material (reminding you that Charing Cross Road is Soho's eastern border), you'll find general books, including music titles with a focus on famous names from the 1960s onwards. **FOYLES** (nos.113–119) is next: the most celebrated name in London bookselling; a vast bookstore with a fantastic collection encompassing many harder-to-find titles besides the more familiar stock, and still preserving something of the joyful confusion for which it used to be famous. It's difficult to beat for the latest editions of vintage 20th-century writing. Further along at no.100 is **BLACKWELLS**, another general bookshop, but with a focus on academic titles (and despite the shelves of general fiction and so on it always feels like a very serious place). The slightly seedy-looking **LOVEJOY'S** sells remaindered books and a selection of classic movie DVDs that you are unlikely to find elsewhere. **THE PHOENIX ARTIST CLUB** is a good place

to stop for a drink. It's hidden away underneath the Phoenix Theatre, and has a unique interior with old posters and theatrical trappings. A little further down is **MACARI'S**, a music store that's been selling mostly guitars and other plucked instruments here since 1958. A definite aura of the past somehow still lingers in these old buildings.

South of Cambridge Circus the road used to be devoted to bookselling. These days there are no bookshops on the western side of the road any longer, and there is a sense that the remaining shops are besieged: and yet the special character of the street is still obvious and the shops are as bustling and vital as ever. No.80 on the corner of Litchfield Street was once the site of Zwemmer, London's most famous art bookshop, which closed over ten years ago. The premises are now occupied by **KOENIG BOOKS**, also an art bookshop covering mostly modern art and design, and with a substantial remaindered section in the basement. **QUINTO** is the first of the classic second-hand bookshops that you'll come to if you continue southwards. When will its collection of hefty volumes in *The Oxford History of the County of Staffordshire* be bought? If you're lucky they'll still be there; and perhaps they are meant as a set of ramparts defending a tradition, and cannot be removed from the shelves. **HENRY PORDES** and **ANY AMOUNT OF BOOKS** seem to divide a common experience between them: multiple, rambling floors, with a stock covering everything, mixing immortal classics with forgotten ephemera. Bargains abound.

The spirit of the street endures. Glance along Litchfield Street for another glimpse of the past: Agatha Christie's play *The Mousetrap* is still playing at the St Martin's Theatre, and is now in its sixtieth year (at the time of writing).

Clark's Pie and Mash Shop 🍴

Ⓐ 46 Exmouth Market EC1R 4QE ☎ 020 7837 1974 Ⓞ Mon–Sat 10.30am–5.30pm

It's Friday lunchtime and, despite the rain, a queue is forming in Exmouth Market. It's made up of school kids, construction workers and bespectacled workers from nearby design agencies. A family tumble out from a taxi and join the queue. The draw? Traditional pie and mash served with liquor. Clark's has been serving up pie and mash since 1910. Its menu is straightforward, starting at £3.75 for a small pie and mash, moving to a large pie and mash, then two pies and mash, and so on. Traditionally eaten by the working class in south and east London, the pie is made from mince beef (dwindling stocks meant eel was ousted as the standard filling, though jellied eels are still available at Clark's) encased in flaky pastry. The two scoops of mash are standard school-dinner stuff flavoured with parsley. Then comes the liquor, over which pie and mash loyalties are fought. It's a watery mixture flavoured with parsley, which, despite the name, contains absolutely no alcohol. For those not raised on the stuff, it's hard to believe this is what has people queuing out the door.

Take a seat in one of the café's wooden booths for the full experience. The interior retains many original fittings including the white tiles typical of traditional pie and mash shops. A visit, however, is as much about the chat as the food or the decor. Regulars are known by name (if not, a simple "darlin' " suffices), locals catch up with their neighbours and families, as agency directors cut deals over their pies. Among the many other cuisines on offer at Exmouth Market, it's reassuring to have a very British piece of life here too.

Collectif

Ⓐ 37 Endell Street WC2H
9EE Ⓣ 020 7836 3805
Ⓦ www.collectif.co.uk
Ⓞ Mon–Wed, Fri–Sat
10am–7pm, Thurs 11am–
8pm, Sun noon–7pm

Rockabilly, psychobilly, and Bettie Page pin-up style repro is what Collectif is all about, both here and in its Spitalfields branch. Fit and flare, curve-accentuating 1950s silhouette dresses in leopard, polkadot, cherry and hibiscus prints, often cut without sleeves (to better show off tattoos) fill the racks. Slinkier wiggle dresses with draped and crossover necklines cater to the more demure, Dita von Teese by way of Vivienne Westwood side of the look. Sizes run from 8–22 in most designs, and some run from 6–24. Feathered fascinators, short crinolines, tattoo necklaces and seamed stockings tie it all together.

Most dresses are priced around £60; while there are bargain gingham Western-style blouses with appliqué swallow tattoos or flamingos at the shoulders (cut tight for cleavage). A sale basement, half the size of the main floor, is full of last season's remains at half price.

The materials are inexpensive, often synthetic blends, and the finish is not fabulous. Interlock stitched hems are visible inside some sleeves, and prints do not always line up – but this is true for most of the high street. For vintage fashion authenticity, this is not the place to go, but it won't kill your wallet either.

The Counter at The Delaunay

Ⓐ 55 Aldwych WC2B 4BB Ⓣ 020 7871 3990 Ⓦ www.thedelaunay.com/counter
Ⓞ Mon–Fri 7am–7.30pm, Sat 11am–7.30pm

This Viennese café brings the spirit of 1930s Mittel-European refinement to life with its rounded Deco dark wood mouldings, and framed lobby cards from German-language films of the day on the walls. For background music, piped-in crooners warble standards over tinkling pianos, and if smoking was allowed, it would be no surprise to see a trouser-suited Marlene Dietrich propping up the bar. For lunch (under £10 with a drink) the cuisine is sausage- and schnitzel-heavy, though vegetarians can always have a pretzel or bowl of hot borscht. The waiting staff are solicitous – not snooty – in their dapper white jackets and ties as they deliver towers stacked with crustless sandwiches, scones and millefeuille tortes for high tea, or salads with lemons wrapped in muslin on the side. (It's fully licensed, so Prosecco and continental lagers are available too.) On Aldwych, it's situated in the district of some of London's most well-known theatres and historic grand hotels, and is a civilized escape from bustling Covent Garden, a ten-minute walk away.

The Counter shares a kitchen with the grander, darker, and much more expensive Delaunay restaurant next door, and the food is of the same high quality (if a bit less fussy – you won't find any hot dogs next door). Sitting at the marble-topped newsstand table to flip through stacks of magazines and hanging newspapers (or even just browsing the Internet) with a strong coffee and a small, rich kipferl biscuit or two is a pleasure that's cheaper than one of the giant coffee chains. Short on time? As a high-end deli, everything on the menu can be ordered to go.

Denmark Street ◉

Ⓐ WC2H 8NJ, nearest tube: Tottenham Court Road

Known as the UK's Tin Pan Alley, music has been performed, recorded and sold on this small street since sheet music suppliers set up shop in Victorian times. The Rolling Stones recorded their first album in **REGENT SOUNDS STUDIO** on the street, while in the 1970s The Clash and other punks hung out at Giaconda snack bar. The studio is now a guitar shop and the Giaconda a snazzy restaurant but while changes occur, Denmark Street remains stubbornly attached to its musical roots, and is still wonderfully evocative of when

Britain's musos ruled the airwaves. It remains the place to come if you're after musical equipment and there is one studio, **TIN PAN ALLEY** at no.22, that is still operating. There are shops crammed with saxophones, pianos, drums and amps, and, in a throwback to its beginnings, you can still buy sheet music. **ROSE MORRIS** (no.10), established in 1920, is probably the oldest store – selling a wide range of instruments, but it's the guitar that provides the true sound of Denmark Street. There are plenty of handsome models for would-be rock stars to deliberate over. **HANKS** at no.27 claims to be London's most famous guitar shop, specializing in acoustic guitars; the entrance to **WUNJO'S GUITARS** (no.20) meanwhile, is plastered with hopeful notices from bands seeking members. Inside teenage boys tentatively strum the strings of the guitars of their dreams, as they've done on this street for decades. Then there's **VINTAGE & GUITARS** (no.6) who sell seriously classy instruments at seriously high prices.

The acquisition of new instruments or band members can be celebrated in the **ALLEY CAT CLUB** (no.4), once the basement of the building which housed Regent Sounds Studio, or the **12 BAR** (no.26), which offers live music every night. Bands play squashed onto a tiny stage, next to an old forge in a space that was a stable back in the 17th century. It's the best spot to seek out the stars of the future playing while paying dutiful homage to a long musical heritage.

Ed's Easy Diner ⫼

▲12 Moor Street, Old Compton Street W1D 5NG (also Mayfair, Euston, Trocadero) ☎020 7434 4439 Ⓦwww.edseasydiner.com Ⓞ Mon–Wed noon–11.30pm, Thurs–Sat noon–midnight, Sun noon–10pm

There's a spot of Soho whose heart, since the 1980s, has belonged to 1950s America. Now a chain with branches all over the UK and four diners in London

alone, the first Ed's Easy Diner started out at this location back in 1987. It seems like very little has changed since then, either in the decor or on the menu (perhaps with the exception of some careful labelling about the provenance of the meat). Ed's is the kind of place that, thanks to popular culture, you feel like you've visited hundreds of times. It's the burgers, hot dogs and fries of movies you've seen, washed down with the shakes and floats of countless TV shows, as you sit on red bar stools at a horseshoe bar looking out onto the street through large windows worthy of a Hopper. While some things don't feel so authentically American – the classic fries are much closer to British-style chips, for example, and the portion sizes don't share the abundance of their American counterparts – it's all forgiven as this place is so unashamedly good-natured. Staff are friendly, and suitably un-British in their levels of service, coke and lemonade are happily kept topped up, and mini reconditioned jukeboxes sit on the counter top with your song pick available for only 20p. Of course the jukeboxes are only filled with the finest rock'n'roll. Ed's Easy Diner offers an unapologetic slice of nostalgia for '50s Americana, albeit filtered through the British imagination.

Forbidden Planet 📖

Ⓐ 179 Shaftesbury Avenue WC2H 8JR Ⓣ 020 7420 3666 Ⓦ www.forbiddenplanet. com Ⓞ Mon–Tue, Fri–Sat 10am–7pm, Wed, 10am–7.30pm, Thurs 10am–8pm, Sun noon–6pm

The cult entertainment chain's flagship megastore might well be your ideal solution for keeping a fashion-unfriendly partner occupied while you explore the Seven Dials and Covent Garden vintage scene alone. Superhero stories, video game franchises and all that is sci-fi, fantasy and fanboy is given free rein here – and then some. The range of model figures alone is astounding with brilliant, if rather pricey, replicas of DC Comics' villains, Marvel heroes and *Dr Who* characters: the level of obscurity is truly satisfying. Among the collectables there are prints, posters, weapon replicas, props and more types of merchandise than you could shake a sonic screwdriver at.

There's also great coverage of anime, manga and comics and graphic novels of every stripe. While it doesn't feel particularly geared to vintage specialists, the jumble of present favourites and past masters is stimulating and will jog memories. Don't miss going downstairs where a staggering, Tardis-like amount of books lies in store for you.

If you are in the area, it's also a short hop to **THE CINEMA STORE** at 4B Upper St Martin's Lane, where there are a limited amount of signed posters and other artefacts for cinephiles, as well as lots of cult movies on DVD, remainder books and new movie titles for those of us who like to explore the world of retro films and classic-era Hollywood.

Førest London 🪑

🅰 115 Clerkenwell Road EC1R 5BY ☎07535 637731 Ⓦwww.forestlondon.com
Ⓞ Mon–Fri 11am–7pm, Sat noon–5pm

Førest is a relative newcomer to Clerkenwell's design scene, a former pop-up shop that's now established more permanent roots. Its owner, Eva Coppens, offers a carefully curated range of mid-century Scandinavian and northern European furniture that fits in perfectly alongside the other contemporary designer furniture stores of the area.

Provenance is key here and the stock includes items that are widely regarded as design classics, such as Verner Panton's FlowerPot light, as well as other designers, like Hvidt and Mølgaard-Nielsen, who are less well-known outside their native Denmark. Either way, the selection of furniture is intended to show off design savvy and any purchases should probably be viewed as investment pieces. The prices certainly reflect this, going into the thousands.

The shop is beautifully presented with decor that would not look out of place in the hippest of eateries. Particularly appealing is the use of a blackboard which is chalked up with the outlines and the prices of Scandinavian ceramics that are on sale. It's a fun touch in what could otherwise become quite an austere shop.

Another pleasing aspect is their Førest Finds section, which features small displays by artists that are sympathetic to the style of the shop and helps create a more engaging atmosphere for both collectors and first-time buyers. After such a promising start, it's interesting to speculate on what the shop might do next but, for the moment, Førest offers a fresh take on both the Clerkenwell and the vintage furniture scene.

The French House 🍸 🍴

🅰 49 Dean Street W1D 5BG ☎020 7437 2477/2799 Ⓦwww.frenchhousesoho.com
Ⓞ Mon–Sat noon–11pm, Sun noon–10.30pm

Run for most of the last century by Belgian Victor Berlemont and his son Gaston, The French House is probably the most famous of Soho's many legendary boozers (rivalled only by The Coach and Horses in Greek Street). A favourite haven of French emigrés during World War II (including General de Gaulle), the pub has changed little since then and its wood-panelled walls are covered with signed photos of French stars of yesteryear. In the 1950s through to the 70s, the pub (then called the York Minster) was frequented by a motley band of artists, actors, writers and other would-be bohos: Dylan Thomas was a regular and Francis Bacon could often be found propping up the bar. Refreshingly free of slot machines, music and football screenings, it has managed to retain its slightly raffish character and still has a genuinely local clientele. Good, unpretentious food is served at the bar until 4pm.

GN Furniture 🪑

ⓐ 31 Exmouth Market EC1R 4QL **ⓣ** 020 7833 0370 **ⓦ** www.gnfurniture.co.uk
ⓞ Daily noon–7pm

Exmouth Market is the kind of street that's especially well suited to browsing. But while it's easy to pick up a cup of coffee or a trinket from one of the nearby shops, you're unlikely to pick up anything from GN Furniture on impulse.

It's not that it's not a fun place to browse, as there's plenty of things in GN Furniture's range of mid-century furniture and ceramics that will appeal to window shoppers. However, this shop is really a place to invest in quality, non-pick-up-able objects like sideboards, tables and chairs. The parameters of their stock are much wider than those in nearby Førest and include British and international designs, as well as Scandinavian classics, so you can expect to see the likes of Ercol and Merrow Associates alongside items by Verner Panton and Hans J. Wegner. The shop also sells a range by modern British designer Vicky Thornton, whose simple ceramics and textiles chime well with the mid-century look. But there are some other oddball pieces thrown into the mix that definitely wouldn't sit so well with period purists: fancy a 1970s fluorescent artwork of Grace Jones, or a mid-19th-century French wine rack?

The staff are friendly and enthusiastic about their products, and will keep their eyes out for you if you're after something specific. In fact, if you've overloaded on goodies from its neighbouring lifestyle stores, GN Furniture is the ideal place to seek out some vintage storage options.

Gosh! London 📖

ⓐ 1 Berwick Street W1F 0DR **ⓣ** 020 7636 1011 **ⓦ** www.goshlondon.com
ⓞ Daily 10.30am–7.30pm

At the upper end of one of Soho's seediest corners is the refreshingly light and airy Gosh!, a haven for cognoscenti comic lovers of all kinds. Gosh's repository

lies in the basement, of course, and sells vintage comics, small press or graphic novel specialities, superhero standards and 1970s vintage items. The staff are young, the vibe dynamic and there are lots of events and book signings taking place and to judge from their website comic book creators from Art Spiegelman to Robert Crumb seem to pop in daily.

A canny bookplate programme of original prints signed by artists and authors also gives the store regular kudos with the knowledge you might have one of only two hundred such of these in the world in your favourite new edition. What most connects Gosh! with the vintage ethic aside from the old comics is the curation of a living indie tradition, with distinctive classic styles connecting the past of comics with the present.

Grays 🎨 💺 🎭

Ⓐ 58 Davies Street & 1–7 Davies Mews W1K 5AB Ⓣ 020 7493 9344 Ⓦ www.graysantiques.com Ⓞ Mon–Fri 10am–6pm, many dealers open Sat 11am–5pm

With the frenzy of Oxford Street only a stone's throw away, the two hundred plus dealers housed in the two buildings that make up Grays antique centre provide a welcome shopping alternative. Between them, the dealers sell a vast range of antiques and cover every kind of speciality, whether that's fine art or teddy bears; militaria or make-up compacts.

Grays claims to sell goods dating as far back as 40BC but the riches drawn from the 20th century alone are more than enough to happily occupy vintage bounty hunters. Elegant pieces of jewellery and handsome wristwatches dominate the Davies Street building, manned by dealers whose knowledge is as dazzling as the items they sell. There's some fantastic pieces for the home available too: **R.G. GRAHAME** (stand 129–130) sells prints, with a particular interest in classic movie memorabilia, such as the kitsch framed Joan Crawford cut-out doll available on a recent visit, while **DIANE HARBY** (stand 148) deals in stunning examples of antique lace.

In the Mews section, it's impossible to miss the stand of **LINDA BEE** (L18–30) whose colourful Bakelite bangles, glittering brooches and fantastical bags are the stuff of little girls', and plenty of grown women's, dreams. **VINTAGE MODES**, a mini-emporium of different vintage fashion dealers, is downstairs. It's almost jumble-like but is overflowing with the kind of names to make any fashionista salivate, including Biba, Ossie Clark, Ungaro and Pierre Balmain. Prices start at about £85 for an unlabelled 1950s dress, and then go much higher. Think of them as the heirlooms of the future.

James Smith & Sons

ⒶHazlewood House, 53 New Oxford Street WC1A 1BL Ⓣ020 7836 4731 Ⓦwww.james-smith.co.uk Ⓞ Mon, Wed–Fri 9.30am–5pm, Tue & Sat 10am–5pm

This isn't hand-me-downs or pale imitations, James Smith & Sons deal with the real thing, the very serious business of umbrellas. Established in 1830 as a whip maker, they now specialize in this great British accessory as well as an impressive range of traditional walking sticks.

While some designs are more workaday, the majority of their products are pieces for the discerning connoisseur. Intended to simultaneously complement and protect a well-tailored suit, the emphasis is on quality materials and finishing details. A brolly with a resin spaniel's head for a handle (parrots, eagles and even dinosaur heads are also available) costs £75, while for the same price you could buy one of the slim rolled "London" umbrellas, designed for gents about town.

While, in that most British of ways, their products don't shout for attention, their shop frontage certainly warrants it. This is something to behold in the midst of grey New Oxford Street, brass panels proudly proclaim the history of the shop, bright red signage announce its wares, and windows showcase brollies lined up for browsing delight. One window contains a photograph showing the shop as it looked at the queen's jubilee – that's Queen Victoria's jubilee. It doesn't look that much different today.

The inside has also managed to bypass the passage of time. Many of the original shop fittings remain including impressive wooden cabinets and mounted stag antlers. Downstairs, tucked out of sight, is the workshop where many of the umbrellas and walking sticks continue to be made. The mixture of woods and resins used in the products gives the shop its own distinctive smell. It's that particular combination of British craftsmanship and heritage that makes the whole shop one of a kind.

Kingly Court 🏛 👤

Ⓐ W1B 5PW, nearest tubes: Oxford Circus, Piccadilly Circus

REVIVAL RETRO BOUTIQUE Ⓐ 2.11 Kingly Court ☎ 020 7287 8709
Ⓦ www.revival–retro.com Ⓞ Mon–Wed, Fri & Sat noon–7pm, Thurs noon–8pm,
Sun noon–6pm

IT'S SOMETHING HELL'S Ⓐ 2.1/2.2 Kingly Court ☎ 07896 153491
Ⓦ www.itssomethinghells.com Ⓞ Mon–Sat 11am–7pm

FUR COAT NO KNICKERS Ⓐ 2.15 Kingly Court ☎ 07814 002295
Ⓦ www.furcoatnoknickers.co.uk Ⓞ Mon, Wed–Sat 11am–7pm, Tues 11am–5.30pm,
Sun 12.30pm–5pm

Carnaby Street, once London's alternative hub, is now overrun by multinational youth brands, but its spirit of independence lives on in Kingly Court, a three-storey courtyard just off the main thoroughfare. While its vintage offerings have slightly reduced over the last few years, it's definitely worth the trek up to the top level for a star trio of vintage stores. The **REVIVAL RETRO BOUTIQUE** came into life when its owner, Rowena, found it hard to track down a pair of period appropriate shoes for swing dancing. The shop is now very proud stockists of Re-Mix, who offer faithful footwear reproductions of shoes from the 1920s through to the 1940s, and Aris Allen's specialist swing dance shoes. These shoes are complemented by a range of other popular repro brands, including fun patterned blouses from Jitterbuggin', glamorous German brand Vecona Vintage and Stop Staring! whose dresses will make you do anything but.

Your ensemble selected, head a few doors down to **IT'S SOMETHING HELL'S** to address tonsorial needs – it's the salon of choice for rockabilly rebels and pin-ups. Miss Betty primps and preens the girls while Mr Ducktail's switchblade haircut separates the men from the boys. The interior is suitably rock'n'roll: think leopard skin and crushed red velvet and, of course, it has its very own jukebox.

Finally, **FUR COAT NO KNICKERS** is an invaluable stop-off for brides-to-be who want a vintage feel to their wedding ensemble. Book an appointment to try on some of their gorgeous dresses: there's a full alteration service to ensure the dress of your dreams fits perfectly, or you can commission a vintage-inspired design to be made for you. If that kind of service is beyond your budget, this pretty, perfumed store also sells vintage hair combs, shrugs and the kind of beaded bags and Lucite purses that would enhance the wardrobe of any woman, engaged or otherwise.

Lucy in Disguise 🎩

Ⓐ 48 Lexington Street W1F 0LR **Ⓣ** 020 7434 4086 **Ⓦ** www.lucyindisguiselondon.com
Ⓞ Mon–Tue 10am–7pm, Wed–Sat 10am–8pm, Sun noon–6pm

As might befit a vintage shop owned by the pop star Lily Allen – who famously accessorized her 1950s prom dresses with high-tops – Lucy in Disguise is the kind of place that's prepared to overlook historical formalities in favour of having a good time. With lots of pretty, sexy and eye-catching dresses dating from the 1920s onwards, it's the right place to visit if you're searching for a party dress – the shop specializes in the kind of clothes that almost demand to be taken out dancing.

The store itself is modern, white and welcoming with much more space allowed for browsing the rails than is offered in many of the pile-them-high vintage shops nearby. The staff are chatty and enthusiastic, and even the labels given to the clothes are flirty: the description on one 1960s fuchsia frock remarks that the pink will "make the boys wink". With an area of the shop dedicated to hairdressing and beauty, the atmosphere in Lucy in Disguise is similar to getting ready at your best friend's house before embarking on a big night out.

Although the shop doesn't appear to take itself too seriously, it does stock some serious vintage pieces. On my last visit, there were several Ossie Clark numbers for sale as well as a jaw-droppingly beautiful 1950s Dior New Look evening dress, with an equally jaw-dropping £650 price tag attached. Those are the exceptions, however, and most items cost the equivalent of the higher end of the high street. There's also the potential for some bargains if you are prepared to rummage through the suitcases filled with clothes discounted to £10 and £20. Although, of course, that might mean you miss out on some precious party time.

On the Beat ⦿

Ⓐ 22 Hanway Street W1T 1UQ ☎ 020 7637 8934 Ⓞ Mon–Sat 11am–7pm

Hanway Street is just the place where you might expect to find a shop like On the Beat. It's a curving back street, worlds away from Oxford Street and Tottenham Court Road despite offering a convenient route between them (avoiding the hectic corner around the tube station, and it would be beloved to Londoners for this reason alone). To call a record shop atmospheric is almost a tautology, but On the Beat genuinely deserves to be singled out for the mood of the place; it's as though some law of donation contributes a selection of things to this tiny place before a particular era is allowed to slip gracefully into the past. The shop is the real treasure to which all of the individual treasures merely contribute.

The collection ranges across rock, soul, jazz... everything seems to be represented somewhere despite the shop's modest proportions. There's a good collection of CDs at the front of the shop, besides the vinyl that's obviously its focus, and the last odds and ends of the space are filled out with old copies of music magazines, and a few pieces of vintage clothing, and a small number of things that belong to no particular classification (a description that needs to fade to a whisper).

Also on Hanway Street you'll find tiny **JB'S RECORDS** (at no.36), a quirky place where the little room seems to waver and fade if the music grabs your attention (until you find yourself staring stupidly at whatever records happen to be at the front of the racks – a colourful parade of unconnected oddities). Any trip to Hanway Street should also involve **BRADLEY'S SPANISH BAR** (nos.42–44), an absolutely unique little place that is particularly glorious given its location within metres of Oxford Street.

Orbital Comics 📖

Ⓐ 8 Great Newport Street WC2H 7JA ☎ 020 7240 0591 Ⓦ www.orbitalcomics.com
Ⓞ Mon–Tue 10.30am–7pm, Wed–Thurs 10.30am–7.30pm, Fri–Sat 10.30am–7pm, Sun 11.30am–5pm

From the outside, Orbital looks like just a small outlet focusing on recent comic releases. But walk to the back of the store and an extensive back catalogue display can be found. Orbital makes a habit of buying collections, so there are rarer items kept under lock and key – it is well worth asking them if you are after a particular classic or rarity. There's a pleasing old-school vibe to the place and it's fair to say that the gender balance of customers isn't 50/50 (notwithstanding some of the knowledgable and helpful female staff). The webstore, blogs and podcasts all suggest the place is trying to reinvent itself but it would be a big mistake not to visit and have a good old rummage. There are plenty of signings and launches, with authors such as Alan Moore or titles like the new *Regeneration Transformers* series being celebrated here. While Gosh! on Berwick Street probably has the edge over Orbital on graphic novels, it's fair to say for old or new comics Orbital is the place to go in central London. It covers the mainstream well enough but it follows all the minor tributaries too with a strong British focus to boot.

Peekaboo Vintage 🎭

....

Ⓐ In store at Topshop Oxford Circus, 36–38 Great Castle Street W1A 1AB Ⓣ Call Peekaboo direct 020 7328 9191 Ⓦ www.peekaboovintage.com Ⓞ Mon–Sat 11am–7pm

Hidden away in a corner of the basement in Topshop's flagship branch is Peekaboo's vintage concession, filled with fabulous clothes that make braving the Oxford Street crowds worthwhile.

Like Topshop's own designs, Peekaboo stocks wearable, trend-influenced women's vintage. If you enjoy the thrill of the rummage, this probably isn't the place to visit; the enticing selection of stock indicates that staff have already trawled through piles of vintage and cherry-picked the best pieces for their customers. They are clearly proud of their work: each item of clothing has a Peekaboo Vintage label sewn into it before it goes on the shop floor.

Expect to pay slightly more for a piece at Peekaboo than you would for its contemporary Topshop counterpart. Dresses start at around £40 but can go much higher, especially for more unusual pieces – a gorgeous fur-trimmed, mint green cape, for example, priced at a cool £350.

Clothes are displayed to grab the eye without too much attention being paid to historical specifics. Rails are organized by colour, rather than era, so shoppers generally need to know their 1950s originals from their 80s tributes to be sure they are getting exactly what they think they are. But that may not matter. If you simply want to find a striking outfit that you can guarantee no one else will be wearing, you're sure to fall in love with something here. And if you really can't cope with Topshop's masses, Peekaboo also has a reassuringly comprehensive online store.

Pop Boutique

Ⓐ 6 Monmouth Street WC2H 9HB **Ⓣ** 020 7497 5262 **Ⓦ** www.popboutique.com **Ⓞ** Mon–Sat 10.30am–7pm, Sun 12.30pm–6pm

The sign on the front window says it best: "Don't follow fashion – buy something already out of date!" Tongue in cheek and a bit of fun, Pop Boutique has never been fashionable or unfashionable, but through the years it has established itself as a place to find vintage "basics" on a budget. With the exception of some mens' brogues and motorcycle boots (£68), almost everything is under £40: Trench coats and coloured macs from the 1960s to the 80s, cutoff Levis for festival goers, ladies' leather skirts and trousers, Farah and Sta-prest trousers for men and plaid flannel shirts for everybody. These are the kinds of vintage gear that can be incorporated into everyday dressing as staples.

Own-line skinny cords, minidresses with Wednesday Addams collars, Breton tops and A-line minidresses made from reworked 1990s oversized washed silk shirts in curry colours update and undercut the revamped versions sold down the road at Urban Outfitters and others. Trendy accessories, like stretch belts or tartan, crocheted or tie-dyed tights, are under £10. Older and more unusual dresses cost a bit more, like a tweedy late 1950s beatnik sack style or a loop-print nylon shirtwaist with a pleated circle skirt from the same era, at £50 each.

Retromania

Ⓐ 6 Upper Tachbrook Street SW1V 1SH **Ⓣ** 020 7630 7406 **Ⓦ** www.retromania.org. uk **Ⓞ** Mon–Sat 10am–6pm, Sun 11am–5pm

While Pimlico is home to some excellent charity shops such as the British Red Cross on Ebury Street or Crusaid on Churton Street, where you can pick up second-hand designer items at a fraction of their original price, its vintage offering is virtually nonexistent, especially after the closure of the longstanding vintage store Cornucopia a few years ago. A happy exception to this rule is Retromania.

Retromania is actually a charity shop as well, for the children's charity FARA, but it is set up like a dedicated vintage shop with only the best pieces making it to the shop floor. In fact, it puts many privately run enterprises in London to shame: it's well organized, thoughtfully displayed and reasonably priced.

The shop mainly stocks womenswear items that are grouped together roughly by period, with a smattering of homewares too. The bulk of the clothes date from the 1970s onwards, though there was a rack of fabulous psychedelically patterned 60s shift dresses selling for £30 each on a recent visit. Impressively, for a small shop, they've even got a section dedicated to wedding dresses – with new stock arriving each Wednesday, it's worth checking back to see if they've got your dream dress in store.

Aside from a spot of mislabelling – a pair of Miss L-Fire repro wedges marked up as genuine 1970s, for example – Retromania is a little treasure. It's also worth combining any visit with a trip to the Regency Café on Regency Street. This traditional English café, and also a backdrop to many period TV programmes and films, was established in 1946 and, like Retromania, provides a rare spot of vintage delight in this London postcode.

Soho's Secret Tea Room 🧁

....

Ⓐ Upstairs at the Coach and Horses, 29 Greek Street W1D 5DH Ⓣ 020 7437 5920 Ⓦ www. sohossecrettearoom.co.uk
Ⓞ Daily noon–6pm

THE COACH AND HORSES is the stuff of Soho legend. This old-school boozer runs weekly old-fashioned piano sing-alongs, is host to *Private Eye*'s legendary lunches, and had a former landlord who claimed the dubious honour of being

the rudest in his profession in London. Its latest, somewhat more refined attraction, is its "secret" tearoom.

Though well hidden (you need to climb up the staircase behind the bar), the tearoom is probably one of Soho's worst kept secrets. In fact, such is the popularity of their afternoon tea, that booking in advance is advised. Once you've successfully navigated your way inside, the clinks of pint glasses downstairs are replaced by the more delicate chink of teacups and a soundtrack of classic 1940s records.

While the room itself is decorated simply and tastefully, it's the food that makes the greatest impression. Lovers of the classic afternoon tea may despair of the introduction of the cupcake into proceedings but apparently the Secret Tea Room disagrees, with an undeniably impressive line-up of cupcakes on display. After that, it may come as a relief to know the rest of the tearoom experience is much more traditional: £17.50 buys afternoon tea which, as well as a cupcake, includes a pot of tea, crust-free sandwiches, huge scones and a slice of cake of your choosing. All of this is served on a vintage cake stand and a pleasing assortment of jumbled chinaware, accompanied by very proper silver cutlery.

While it might seem an obvious venue for birthdays or hen parties, my fellow customers included a large group of blazer-sporting, middle aged men who were tucking into their feast with relish, visibly demonstrating that the delicacies of this tearoom, cupcakes included, can satisfy even the most substantial hungers.

The Vintage Magazine Shop 📖

39–43 Brewer Street, W1F 9UD ☎ 020 7439 8525 🌐 www.vinmag.com 🕐 Mon–Thurs 10am–8pm (basement closes 7pm), Fri & Sat 10am–10pm (basement closes 8pm), Sun noon–8pm

This pop culture temple in the heart of Soho is two shops in one: on the ground floor, memorabilia and gifts relating to music, TV and the movies, and downstairs in the basement, an enormous and authoritative collection of vintage magazines. Progressing from one to the other feels like a journey from nostalgia into the past itself.

In the memorabilia shop there are books, posters, prints, postcards, greetings cards and calendars, just as you'd expect, but there's also wrapping paper covered with the stars of Hollywood's golden age, a bar stool decorated with Sex Pistols iconography and *Confessions of a Driving Instructor* T-shirts. It's a fantastic place to pick up unusual presents at reasonable prices.

The magazine collection in the basement is a sight to behold: it looks like something that ought to attract public funding. From innocent to not-so-innocent pleasures, from housekeeping journals to *Playboy*, everything seems to be here. Are you looking for the TV Times for 24-30 October 1992 (with a vintage Noel Edmonds exploding out of the cover)? Don't worry, it's here. But there's also a huge collection of rare items from the 1930s onwards, overflowing with the energy of these disposable forms, vivid imagery and dynamic typography: still doing everything they can to persuade you to buy them.

The Vintage Showroom

Ⓐ 14 Earlham Street WC2H 9LN **Ⓣ** 020 7836 3964 **Ⓦ** www.thevintageshowroom. com **Ⓞ** Mon–Sat 11am–7.30pm, Sun noon–6pm

This is, hands down, the best source of vintage menswear in central London, if not all of London, especially for admirers of the easy, casual elegance sported by the gentlemen of Scott Schuman's Sartorialist blog, or the 1960s collegiate cool chronicled in any of the recent wave of books on Ivy League style. This is vintage for men who do not want to dress up – either in a formal and mannered style, or to show allegiance to a subcultural tribe – but who want to dress well.

The Showroom was originally exactly that – an industry-only showroom in west London, full of archive clothing and research pieces, that designers would visit for research and inspiration. So many people wanted to buy these clothes that a shop was inevitable.

It's all quality, from plaid campus wool blankets and Harvard sweatshirts to bullet-stoppingly thick Harris Tweed blazers (£135). Plastic horn rim frames from the sixties are £45; saddle shoes £95. GPO Army jackets, perfectly soft bandannas, Letterman jackets, all of the classics from England, the US, and Europe, from roughly the late 1950s–70s. Its buyers look for no particular period when buying their stock, but for quality cuts and finishes, or interesting textures.

Wow Retro 🙂 👨

Ⓐ 10–14 Mercer Street WC2H 9QA (with another branch at 179 Drury Lane WC2B 5QF) Ⓣ 020 7379 5334 Ⓦ www.wowretro.co.uk Ⓞ Mon–Fri 11.30am–6.30pm, Sat 11am–7pm, Sun 12.30pm–5.30pm

There are two shops in one here: one side is the women's shop, and next door is the men's. Neither is particularly fashionable; they're bare-bones warehouses with the odd bit of fake leopard skin tacked to the sales counters. There is little logic to what ends up on the shelves, as 1990s Joseph trousers and 1980s Girl Guides shirts rock up next to rails loosely separated by decade, with a few more rails of modern, mostly high-street, second-hand clothes from the last few years. Men can find Farah trousers here, mod cardigans and rollnecks, and a good selection of biker jackets (including Belstaff), classic Aquascutum and Burberry macs, along with more modern Ben Sherman and Paul Smith.

The typeface on its sign is a nineties hangover, the music playing is dreary dustbin indie, and it feels like the one cool vintage store in a provincial town that has wormholed its way to Covent Garden. But it is cheap, friendly, and can turn up the unexpected gem: a flowered green 1960s silk shift with a nipped-in waist that could have been worn by Jackie Kennedy, for £45, would have fetched double that in the shops off Brick Lane to the east. Both sexes can find the odd bit of Vivienne Westwood here, from time to time, for around £30, which is well under even the eBay resale price. If you want your vintage to be pre-cleaned and sold to you in an aesthetically pleasing environment that compliments your good taste, stay well away. But if you're after a bargain find and just don't care, there are some rewards to be had.

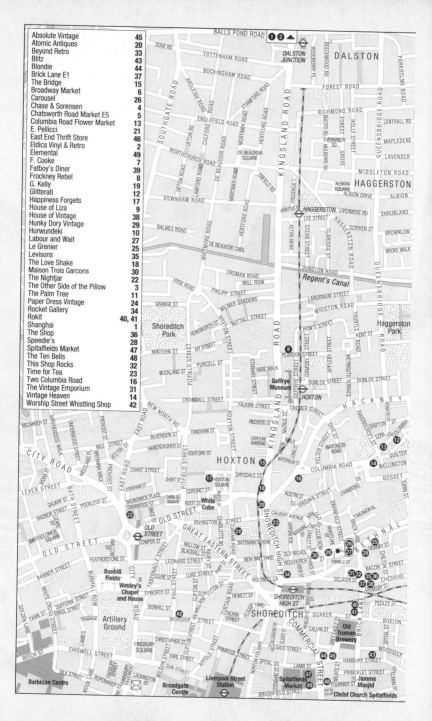

Absolute Vintage 45
Atomic Antiques 20
Beyond Retro 33
Blitz 43
Blondie 44
Brick Lane E1 37
The Bridge 15
Broadway Market 6
Carousel 26
Chase & Sorensen 4
Chatsworth Road Market E5 5
Columbia Road Flower Market 13
E. Pellicci 21
East End Thrift Store 46
Eldica Vinyl & Retro 2
Elemental 49
F. Cooke 7
Fatboy's Diner 39
Frockney Rebel 8
G. Kelly 19
Glitterati 12
Happiness Forgets 17
House of Liza 9
House of Vintage 38
Hunky Dory Vintage 29
Hurwundeki 10
Labour and Wait 27
Le Grenier 25
Levisons 35
The Love Shake 18
Maison Trois Garcons 30
The Nightjar 22
The Other Side of the Pillow 3
The Palm Tree 11
Paper Dress Vintage 24
Rocket Gallery 34
Rokit 40, 41
Shanghai 1
The Shop 36
Speedie's 28
Spitalfields Market 47
The Ten Bells 48
This Shop Rocks 32
Time for Tea 23
Two Columbia Road 16
The Vintage Emporium 31
Vintage Heaven 14
Worship Street Whistling Shop 42

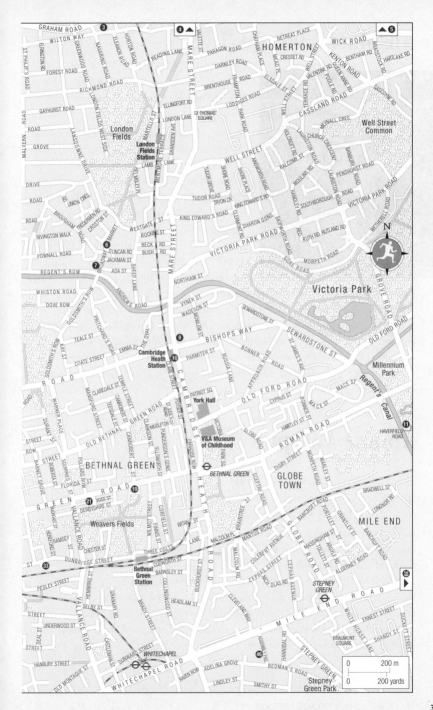

Absolute Vintage 🎭🎭

Ⓐ 15 Hanbury Street E1 6QR Ⓣ 020 7247 3883 Ⓦ www.absolutevintage.co.uk Ⓞ Daily 11am–7pm

Stylists and everyday shoppers alike rate this cavernous store for its vast inventory of mostly 1970s and 80s pieces, especially the range of second-hand ladies' handbags and shoes. These should keep you busy for at least half an hour, then there's the poufy prom dresses, including the occasional antique with a bigger price tag. The substantial men's section offers sports jackets, waistcoats, novelty ties, flight bags and reams of denim, and the back wall is a patchwork of brightly coloured scarves.

Regular sales keep the customers piling in, and the window displays tend to be bang on trend, helping thrifty folk to self-style on a budget and convincing newbies to take the leap into second-hand clothing. You generally won't break the bank here: handbags start at around a fiver and you can get a decent pair of shoes from £18. Their sister store, Blondie (see p.36), is just around the corner on Commercial Street.

Atomic Antiques 🪑💡

Ⓐ 125 Shoreditch High Street E1 6JE Ⓣ 0207 7739 5923 Ⓦ www.atomica.me.uk Ⓞ Tue–Sun 11.30am–5pm

Go in. Go right in. Even on the busiest weekend, it's worth persevering to get through the bottleneck of a doorway. Get past that and, while the rest of the store isn't much more spacious, you'll be rewarded with some great furniture, the kind you can easily imagine fitting into your own home. Rather than being governed by particular eras, the stock is selected on how different pieces work together. There are lots of traditional mid-century items, such as 1960s Danish armchairs selling for about £450, as well as everyday basics like industrial stools and swivel chairs. These classics are enlivened by displays of the occasional *objet d'art* or simple artwork like a framed Frank Lloyd Wright exhibition poster.

A particular strength of the store is its range of lighting with something to please connoisseurs of almost every 20th-century style. There's Sputnik numbers for fans of the space age look, as well as 1960s brass sculptural floor pieces and glittering Art Deco shades. There's a wide selection of heavy-duty ceramic lamp bases available too. Fast turnover of stock means it's worth popping in as often as you get the opportunity; in this store it's the most determined shoppers that capture the best pieces.

Beyond Retro 🧑 👕

Ⓐ 110–112 Cheshire Street E2 6EJ (other stores on Stoke Newington Road N16 7XB and Great Marlborough Street W1F 7JY) Ⓐ 020 7613 3636 Ⓦ www.beyondretro.com Ⓞ Mon–Sat 10am–7pm, Thurs till 8pm, Sun 11.30am–6pm

This retro giant is well-loved for its overflowing rails of used 20th-century clothing, affordable prices and rock'n'roll feel. The Cheshire Street warehouse was the first of three London stores, and its newer and larger cousin is just a short bus trip away at nos.92–100 Stoke Newington Road. The ceiling is cheerfully hung with rows of frou-frou underskirts, and the changing displays cleverly interpret current trends. The vast range of footwear includes masses of heels and chunky cowboy boots, and there's a strong men's section with lots of hats, denim and plaid. Prices are never what you'd call high, but particularly good deals are to be found in the bargain bins near the entrance, where the emphasis on sustainable fashion is evident. You can pick up basic recycled items made from vintage fabrics at a very low cost: perhaps some fetching bloomers for a fiver, or headscarves for even less. A steady stream of shoppers flows through the doors under the sleepy gaze of Tiny the shop cat, and few leave empty-handed.

Blitz 👕 🧑 💿 🧁

Ⓐ 55–59 Hanbury Street E1 5JP Ⓣ 020 7377 0703 Ⓦ www.blitzlondon.co.uk Ⓞ Thurs–Sat 11am–8pm, Sun–Wed 11am–7pm,

Blitz calls itself a vintage department store, and comprises five large, bright rooms set over two floors in a Victorian warehouse. Nine thousand square feet of well-presented stock awaits you, and it's all carefully selected, from the old vinyl, upcycled furniture and 1980s Swatches, to the rare second-hand couture pieces and mid-century Americana.

You enter to a self-consciously cool soundtrack to be greeted by a vast array of quality second-hand clothing, but you can't appreciate the dimensions of the place until you pass through to the back room – a light-flooded space with more packed rails and a selection of homeware. The clothing continues in the large basement, where lots of the cheaper items are to be found. Prices are pretty fair in general; you might pay £5 for a stripy Breton T-shirt or £95 for a Burberry mac, with the majority of items sitting somewhere in between. You could easily spend a good couple of hours in here wandering from section to section just like in a regular department store, stopping for coffee breaks in the stylish café.

Blondie 🙍

Ⓐ Unit 2, 114–118 Commercial Street E1 6 NF Ⓣ 020 7247 0050 Ⓦ www. blondievintage.co.uk Ⓞ Daily 11am–7pm

The sister shop of nearby Absolute Vintage, Blondie sits within the vast spread of the Art Deco Exchange Building just across the road from the corner of Spitalfields Market. Where Absolute sells a wide range of men's and women's clothes, Blondie takes a more selective, high-end approach concentrating exclusively on women's wear – shoes and accessories as well as clothes. The modern shop interior reflects a briskly efficient approach: there are two changing rooms, everything is well organized and clearly laid out, with none of the musty, shabby-chic feel of many vintage outlets.

The first thing that strikes you on entering the store is the array of boots lined up in the centre of the shop. In fact, footwear is something of a Blondie speciality (they've even sold a pair of green ladies' shoes from the early 1800s). But be warned: these are luxury items rather than everyday wear, with prices to match. Four rails of clothes line the shop and although 1950s and 60s dominate there is often material from earlier decades, with plenty of branded items, including Chanel. A small but good selection of bags and scarves (Prada and Hermès frequently appear) round off this quality outfit, which is well worth dropping in on if you need that special something.

Brick Lane 🏛️🧑‍🦰👤🧁🍴💿💡🪑👨

Ⓐ E1, nearest tubes: Aldgate East, Aldgate & Liverpool Street Ⓦ www.visitbricklane. org Ⓞ From 9am on Sun; some markets also open on Sat

Brick Lane is a hive of activity thanks to its innumerable shops and curry houses, but on Sundays it's especially crowded, with keen shoppers browsing along the main street and in the old Truman Brewery buildings. You'll find a variety of markets taking place here; some are fairly ordered operations with a good concentration of high-quality vintage, and others are made up of a disorganized sprawl of pavement pedlars, selling anything from used clothes to electronics of questionable provenance.

Worth a browse are **THE TEA ROOMS** (Sat 11am–6pm, Sun 10am–5pm), a charming indoor warren of stalls with a café, plus good-quality antiques, homeware, records and books. Next door is the **BACKYARD MARKET** (Sat 11am–6pm, Sun 10am–5pm), good for second-hand cameras, and new and used clothing at relatively cheap prices. The **SUNDAY UPMARKET** (Sun 10am–5pm) has a mix of affordable secondhand and new clothing, and it's also good for vinyl and quirky jewellery. Be sure to follow the makeshift signs at street level inviting you upstairs or downstairs to more vintage and craft markets. Brick Lane also has a wealth of first-rate vintage shops (start with the charming **VINTAGE EMPORIUM**, see p.60), and the merchants of second-hand ephemera in the cavernous side-street lock-ups also yield the occasional gem.

Food choices from all corners of the world abound in this area on market days, but you'll find an authentic piece of old East End life at the two rival Jewish bakeries at the northern end of the street, **BEIGEL SHOP** and **BEIGEL BAKE**. Queues form all day long for the cheap and simple food here (under £4 for a salt beef beigel in each). It's up to you to decide which is best.

The Bridge 🧁 🍴

Ⓐ 15 Kingsland Road E2 8AA Ⓣ No phone Ⓞ Daily, roughly noon–midnight

The Bridge is a local favourite for its remarkable interior. The downstairs room has a mock-Dickensian feel – there's a long, dark-wood bar running the length of the room, and all around the walls is a random assortment of old photographs, clocks, posters and other paraphernalia. The copper coffee machines and old-fashioned cash register add to the curiosity-shop effect. Sustenance comes in the form of salads, sandwiches, tea, coffee, cake and bottled beers, but all of this is secondary to the off-beat interior.

If your first impressions are favourable, then climb the stairs to the rear to see the first-floor lounge, a bizarre but attractive Moulin Rouge-style boudoir – a slightly bonkers set-up that really works. Cuts of deep-hued cloth block out the day, and low electric light emanates from Art Deco-style globes held aloft by carved female figures. Ormolu mirrors dot the walls and reproduction furniture with dark pink and red upholstery is set around low coffee tables. There doesn't seem to be much method in the madness, but it's an undoubtedly atmospheric place to meet a friend for a drink – and you can observe the lone paperback readers surreptitiously dropping off on the outré sofas.

Broadway Market 🏪 👤 👤 🍴 🕴 🪑

Ⓐ Broadway Market E8, nearest station: London Fields Ⓦ www.broadwaymarket. co.uk Ⓞ Sat 9am–5pm

This bustling market, dating back to the 1890s and regenerated by locals in 2004 after a period of decline, is now a lively food market, selling everything from fruit and veg to organic meat, as well as hot takeaway meals. There are some good-value vintage clothing stalls too, where you can pick up a jumper for a few quid or a decent handbag for a few more, as well as some general bric-a-brac and jewellery vendors. Among the local shops are a couple of furniture and antique stores (such as **STELLA BLUNT,** no.75), plus the cheap and cheerful **LA VIE** (no.18) for second-hand women's clothing, and, at the opposite end of the price scale, **STRUT** (2b Ada Street), selling high-end men's and women's second-hand designer clothing. It's mostly contemporary stock here, with the odd Ossie Clark dress thrown in – try its sister boutique in Stoke Newington for classic vintage finds. At no.9 there's favourite local café, **F. COOKE**, a must-see for its well-preserved interior (see p.44).

Once you reach the northern end of the street it's worth dropping into tiny **NETIL MARKET**, with its attractive selection of mid-century and older furniture (and its insanely good Lucky Chip burgers). From here you're in prime position to wander into the green space of **LONDON FIELDS**, with its restored 1930s outdoor pool – you're allowed in to have a look even if you don't intend to swim.

Chase & Sorensen

Ⓐ 238B Dalston Lane E8 1LQ Ⓣ 020 8533 5523 Ⓦ www.chaseandsorensen.com
Ⓞ Tues–Fri 8am–5pm, Sat 9am–6pm, Sun 10am–5pm

Specializing in Danish furniture and homewares, Chase & Sorensen comes close to capturing that elusive feeling of *hygge*, a Danish expression meaning something along the lines of contentment and well-being. In any language, this shop is a lovely place to spend time. It's large and light and filled with stock sourced from across Denmark. While pieces aren't always the best or most pristine examples of their kind, they do make the clean lines and craftsmanship of Danish design more attainable to shoppers on a budget. Pricing is very reasonable: a set of six teak dining chairs, for example, costs £400 or a 1960s lounge chair, of the type slavishly copied on the high street, is yours for under £300. The homely feel in the store is enhanced by authentic ceramics and serving ware, also for sale, and supplemented by cushions and bags from contemporary makers. For a real taste of the country, pick up some of the confectionary on sale at the counter or sit back on some of the stock and sample Scandinavian food from the in-store café. Other than hand over the keys, there's not that much more this store could do to feel more welcoming.

Chatsworth Road Market

Ⓐ Chatsworth Road E5, nearest station: Homerton Ⓦ www.chatsworthroade5. co.uk/market Ⓞ Sun 11am–4pm

Following a successful relaunch after a twenty-year hiatus, Chatsworth Road Market is now a popular weekly operation. The street itself is lined with independent businesses, both old and new, and the chic coffee shops and the upmarket **RUSSELL'S B&B** (no.123) are signs of the upwardly moving status of the area.

The market comprises high-quality stalls, with a healthy scattering of vintage articles for sale: women's clothing and accessories from **AURELIA DUPAS**; used paperbacks at **FIREFLY BOOKS**; collectables at **PROPER OLD**; revamped vintage kids' clothing at **BORN AGAIN KIDSWEAR**; and retro cookware and books from **KATHARINE TASKER**. Worth a look among the surrounding shops is **THEA VINTAGE** at no. 65, a laidback affair with 1940s to 80s fashions and furniture, and the rockabilly-styled **CAKEY MUTO** at no.25, a quirky little cake shop complete with retro jukebox, candy-coloured fittings and events such as Rock'n'Roll Bingo.

Columbia Road Flower Market

Ⓐ Columbia Road E2, nearest station: Hoxton Ⓦ www.columbiaroad.info Ⓞ Sun 8am–approx 3pm

On Sundays, this beautifully preserved street is crammed with flower and plant stalls – some of the traders have held pitches here since the late 1940s and 50s, and it's their cheerful bellows, the huge array of foliage and the prices dropping incrementally as market day draws to an end, which pull in the crowds every week.

The commercial premises feature a mix of upmarket and traditional establishments, with beigel and seafood merchants rubbing shoulders with high-end art and design shops, jewellers and delis. The sixty independent shops here include some great vintage, or vintage-style, places, such as **GLITTERATI** (no.148) for costume jewellery, **VINTAGE HEAVEN** (no.82) for homeware and **THE POWDER ROOM** beauty parlour (no.136; see p.161). **JESSIE CHORLEY AND BUDDUG**'s shop (no.158a) sells vintage-style gifts and accessories in a prettily appointed boutique, **OPENHOUSE** (no.152) offers new and antique homeware, **SUCK AND CHEW** (no.130) sells traditional sweets and there's also **TREACLE** (nos.110–112), a cutesy retro bakery and kitchenware shop. Local pearly kings and queens make regular appearances at the market (Ⓦ www.pearlysociety.co.uk/events), fundraising for charity in their many-buttoned finery; it's a traditional touch of the old East End right in the heart of one of its best-loved market streets.

E. Pellicci 🍴 🧁

Ⓐ 332 Bethnal Green Road E2 0AG Ⓣ 020 7739 4873 Ⓞ Mon–Sat 7am–4pm

Behind the pale Vitrolite-decked exterior of this little building lies a wonderful Deco-style interior of marquetry panelling (a 1946 addition responsible for the current Grade II listing), complete with stained-glass features bearing the name of the family who have run this café since 1900. The founding Pelliccis were Tuscan immigrants, and their descendants still run the place today in the jocular and gently chiding fashion now famous to locals. It has an old-school, convivial atmosphere, exaggerated by the proportions of the room which force diners into close proximity, and often impassioned debate. Like many establishments in the area, the café has its own slice of Krays history as the brothers were regulars from childhood; but it's had many a celebrity patron since, including what appears to be most of the cast of *EastEnders*, whose autographed images you'll see on the walls.

But the punters aren't just here for the decor, the atmosphere and the celebrity spots. They're here because they're hungry, and because the food is very good. Meals are expertly cooked by Maria, head of the kitchen since 1961. The menu lists a range of excellent-value Italian and British classics, with most plates sporting a massive heap of hand-cut chips. It's busy at lunchtimes, and pretty much all day on Saturday, when there's often a queue of ravenous folk snaking onto the pavement outside. Fans of classic cafés (and carbs) should make a beeline for Pellicci's at their earliest convenience.

East End Thrift Store

Ⓐ Unit 1A, Assembly Passage E1 4UT ☎ 020 7423 9700 Ⓦ www.
theeastendthriftstore.com Ⓞ Thurs–Sat 11am–7pm, Sun–Wed 11am–6pm

You're guaranteed to get a good deal at this outpost of vintage cool located
down an unassuming little passage off Mile End Road. The bulk of the stock
dates from the 1980s and 90s, with a smaller stash of 1950s, 60s and 70s
dresses, and there are plans to bring in a premium line of rarer earlier pieces.
It's mostly wearable day-to-day stuff, with the occasional show-stopper. The
buyers have an excellent and current eye and you'll always be able to pick up
something reflecting the trends of the moment for a fraction of the price.
If the main section still isn't quite cheap enough for you (jackets or dresses
mostly around £10 or £15), check out the special reduction rails, colour-coded
from £1 to £5. Women will find lots of printed shirts and blouses, dresses of
all sizes and shapes, and plenty of denim, and on the men's side there are tons
of jackets, camouflage-print separates, T-shirts and stylish coats.

It's certainly off the beaten track, but then that's part of the appeal, and word
of mouth does its job as you can see from the turnout at their packed shopping
events. If you're up for the competition, bring some sharp elbows to fight for
your swag, or just admit defeat and come on a calmer day.

Eldica Vinyl & Retro

Ⓐ 8 Bradbury Street N16 8JN ☎ 020 7254 5220 Ⓦ www.eldica.co.uk Ⓞ Tue–Sat
11.30am–6.30pm, and usually Sun noon–5pm

This unpretentious shop, set on a quiet street behind Dalston Kingsland station,
is crammed with second-hand vinyl, sourced and sold by Andy and his family.
There are thousands of records in the frequently updated collection, including a
large selection of soul and funk, plus jazz, calypso, rap, reggae, and more. Eldica
has a good reputation with DJs and collectors, so you'll need to squeeze your way
around the musos snapping up rare new arrivals to get a good look in all the nooks
and crannies. Second to the packed boxes of records lining this miniature cave
of a shop is a seemingly random assortment of retro 1970s and 80s items, from
framed prints to glassware, furniture, collectable magazines and retro electronica.
It's just like second-hand shops used to be, before vintage became big business.

Elemental

(A) 67 Brushfield Street E1 6AA **(T)** 020 7247 7588 **(W)** www.elemental.uk.com **(O)** Tue–Sun 11am–6pm

Elemental's stock comes from shops, schools and factories, rather than big-name designers. The shop's slogan is "found, restored and back again" and for fifteen years they've been demonstrating how industrial goods can be repurposed for a domestic environment with striking effect. Their all-encompassing stock includes the likes of haberdashery cabinets, café chairs, instructional charts, train luggage racks and even colourful, long-empty fuel cans. While the majority of the pieces date from the middle of the 20th century, there are some interesting exceptions such as 19th-century stock mannequins and some fanciful diversions from the industrial look too, like an ornate Chinese cabinet dated to 1800 that was recently in the shop.

Upcycled items are also part of the store's appeal, whether cabinets assembled from mismatched drawers that were once part of other pieces, or side tables made from industrial insulators with added Perspex tops, giving them a ready-made Pop Art look. They're yours for £960 each. Elemental are quite cagey about their prices – while labels on each item give detailed information about its materials, place of origin, date and dimensions, the price is conspicuously absent. Cynics may argue that this is because prices are relatively high and you could find similar for less elsewhere. The persuasive counter to that is, when the choice of stock is as good as it is here, the effort of looking elsewhere becomes pretty worthless.

F. Cooke 🍴

Ⓐ 9 Broadway Market E8 4PH Ⓣ 020 7254 6458 Ⓞ Mon–Thurs 10am–7pm, Fri & Sat 10am–8pm

This classic pie and mash shop opened in 1900, and serves the same filling meals today as it did then. The café thrives on non-market days, when hungry customers aren't distracted by the organic takeaway goods and sizzling pots of international cuisine on offer along Broadway Market every Saturday. The airy canteen-style room is decked in primrose tiles, tables are marble-topped and set between wooden benches, and light pours in from the back through the sun-motif stained glass – all of this helps it retain a sense of history, and has earned this place several TV appearances.

It's a family-friendly place, with a simple menu of plain food: meat pies, fruit pies, and hot or jellied eels, all served with mashed potatoes and liquor – a parsley-flavoured gravy. Prices remain low, making this a good-value alternative to the neighbouring restaurants and upscale Saturday market stalls.

Fatboy's Diner 🍴 🧁

Ⓐ Trinity Buoy Wharf, 64 Orchard Place E14 0JW Ⓣ 020 7987 4334 Ⓦ www.fatboysdiner.co.uk Ⓞ Wed–Sun 10am–5pm

Trinity Buoy Wharf, an industrial complex formerly the site of busy shipyards and buoy manufacturing, is now a quiet and slightly isolated waterside home for

the creative industries. There are studios and workshops, some set in bright stacks of converted shipping crates, and there's even a lighthouse. But unless you work on the wharf, it's unlikely you'd stumble across the rather special Fatboy's Diner.

It's worth making the pilgrimage out here to take in the atmosphere of this well-preserved 1940s dining car, incongruously set at the water's edge. The menu features standard diner grub: eggs any style, hot dogs, deli sandwiches and burgers, from the classic regular at £3.95 to The Hillbilly at £7.35, featuring a double patty with cheese, bacon, barbecue sauce and chilli topping. Calorific beverages, such as the Black and White (coke float) and the Flamingo (cream soda with strawberry ice cream) cost £2.45, and if you need a dessert after all that, choose from the range of pies, sundaes and frozen yoghurt. On a sunny day it's a real pleasure to sit in one of the booths and gaze across at the developing vista of North Greenwich, with the Emirates Air Line cable cars gliding from bank to bank over the water.

Frockney Rebel

Ⓐ 242 Cambridge Heath Road E2 9DA Ⓣ 020 8127 8609 Ⓦ www.frockneyrebel. com Ⓞ Tue–Sun noon–7pm

This bit of Cambridge Heath Road isn't an obvious shopping destination, but with more and more trendy little enterprises setting up in the area, Frockney Rebel is standing its ground. It even has its own online shopping space with retail giant ASOS, which says a lot about the broad appeal of the stock. The small, bright shop is packed with clothing and accessories for women and men, plus the odd carefully selected piece of homeware. Everything is handpicked, mostly from the 1970s and 80s. Chunky jewellery abounds, as do printed frocks, hand-painted brooches and sturdy boots. As the garments aren't particularly old, the prices remain very reasonable – a skirt for £17, a cable-knit men's jumper for £22 – and you'd really struggle to find anything above £50. A good place for a spree on a budget, without the jostling Brick Lane crowds.

G. Kelly 🍴

Ⓐ 414 Bethnal Green Road E2 0DJ
Ⓣ 020 7739 3603 Ⓞ Mon–Thurs & Sat
10am–4.30pm, Fri 10am–7pm

This is one of several traditional old
pie and mash shops still functioning
in the East End, and a smaller,
cosier alternative to the G. Kelly on
Roman Road Market, part of a set
of three that were founded by the
same family generations ago. It's a
compact, white-tiled space, and you
might struggle to get a seat during
the busy lunchtimes, when long-
term regulars file in to take up their
places in their favourite corners.
You dine at cast-iron tables, seated under a row of black and white prizefighter
portraits, a nod to local boxing history. Here you can fill up on freshly baked pie,
mash and liquor for £2.65 – a pretty decent price by anyone's standards. Gourmet
cooking it ain't, but it's tasty and will certainly set you up for the rest of the day.

Glitterati 💂 👤 📖

Ⓐ 148 Columbia Road E2 7RG Ⓞ Sun 9am–4pm

A favourite on Columbia Road since 1999, this teeny Aladdin's cave of a
boutique certainly does sparkle as you enter, packed to bursting as it is with
high-quality vintage jewellery, watches, accessories, and more. The specialism
here is for signed costume jewellery (bearing the maker's mark) from the 1920s
onwards, complemented by the range of pretty antique beaded handbags,
delicately old-fashioned ladies' compacts, a small and selective stash of precious
vintage clothing, some attractive retro homeware, random collectables and a
backroom stuffed full of secondhand books. It's an inspiring haul to browse
through, and the marvellous range of around 600 pairs of vintage cufflinks
makes this place a great favourite on the Christmas shopping trail, with rare
styles to suit even the fussiest of people.

Happiness Forgets ⍦

ⓐ Basement, 8–9 Hoxton Square **ⓣ** 020 7613 0325 **ⓦ** www.happinessforgets.com
ⓞ Mon–Sat 5.30pm–11pm

This bijou subterranean bar in Hoxton Square is a chic, low-lit space taking
its style cue from the New York bar scene. It's stylish without being overdone,
with candles and lamps offering just enough light to give an impression of
the barely adorned brick walls. This is where discerning enthusiasts of spirits
gently sink expertly mixed potions, including the delicious gin-based Earl
Grey Mar-TEA-Ni or the Pernod-laced Dapperman Sour (both £8), served in
old-style champagne saucers. Service comes from stylishly professional staff,
with bartenders in waistcoats, classic shirts and braces. There's no late opening,
so it's a good place for a sophisticated rendezvous with a civilized ending, or
alternatively for kicking off a big night out without having to queue eight
people deep in a crowded pub. Arrive early or book in advance to be sure of a
seat. And brush your hair first.

House of Liza ⍦ ⍦

ⓐ 9 Pearson Street E2 8JD **ⓣ** 020 3487 0782 **ⓦ** www.houseofliza.co.uk **ⓞ** Mon–Sat
11am–6pm

Rather out of place with the surrounding low-key businesses on quiet Pearson
Street, House of Liza is an upscale boutique selling vintage designer clothing,
generally from the 1970s and 80s, with some stock stretching into the 1990s. It's
mostly womenswear, with plenty of lurid Versace and Moschino, a healthy crop
of avant-garde Comme des Garçons, plus pieces from many more powerhouse
names usually only found in ultra-chic quarters of the city. You might snap up
a two-piece Yves Saint Laurent suit for around £350, and it's very unlikely you'd
find much under £100 here. The shop itself is a gleaming white space – you
know the type, with the hangers all spaced exactly two finger-widths apart – and
has a slightly intimidating feel for a second-hand operation. A far cry from your
standard vintage boutique, but with some really excellent pieces in store for
collectors of high fashion.

House of Vintage 🍸 😊

Ⓐ 4 Cheshire Street E2 6EH Ⓣ 020 7739 8142 Ⓦ www.houseofvintagelondon. blogspot.co.uk Ⓞ Mon–Fri noon–7pm, Sat & Sun 10am–7pm

House of Vintage started out in far-off Toronto in 2003, and the London boutique has been spreading the founder's passion for high-quality vintage clothing since 2010. The shop sits in good company, with a fine array of vintage specialists on and around trendy Cheshire Street. It has a high-end boutique feel; from the back of the shop the light filters through the custom-made stained-glass window featuring the House of Vintage logo, and there are framed psychedelic prints dotting the walls. The buying policy is strict and selective,

resulting in two floors of a carefully edited collection of pre-loved 1920s to 80s wares. There's a particular emphasis on American classics from the 1940s, 50s and 60s, plus a selection of rare US military stock and some high-end designer names. You might find a 1950s men's gabardine bowling shirt for £70, or a 1960s raw silk jacket for £65. There's also a good range of well-preserved ladies' leather goods and some stunning vintage headwear.

Hunky Dory Vintage 🍸 😊

Ⓐ 226 Brick Lane E1 6SA Ⓣ 020 7729 7387 Ⓦ www.hunkydoryvintage.com Ⓞ Daily 11.30am–6.30pm

Hunky Dory Vintage is a little gem offering good-quality vintage at accessible prices. Their tagline, "Plundering the past for your pleasure", is exactly what owners Ian Johns and Ian Bodenham have been doing since they started up in the second-hand clothing business in the mid-1980s. Previously trading from a store in Greenwich, the duo's good taste in wearable one-offs and obvious passion for fashion history has established the store as an integral part of the Brick Lane shopping experience. Shoppers are greeted by a rock'n'roll soundtrack, in keeping with its two floors of 20th-century European clothing and accessories. There's a particular focus on pieces from the 1940s to 80s, and it's a great place to source ladies' outfits for special occasions, or a sharp jacket and shirt from the equally well-stocked menswear section. The information boards from the V&A's 1994 Street Style exhibition are a particularly nice touch, providing a bit of social context for your shopping trip.

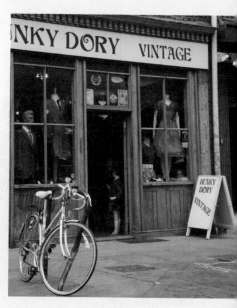

Hurwundeki

A 299 Cambridge Heath Road E2 6QQ
T 020 7749 0638 **O** Daily; hours vary

Hurwundeki started out as a vintage and own-brand clothing shop plus trendy in-store hair salon near Spitalfields Market (now closed), but its most successful venture lives on in the low-key café and restaurant set in the railway arches near Cambridge Heath Station. Known in the area for its excellent coffee (from Nude Espresso), this is an atmospheric place to linger on a lazy morning or afternoon, with its Bardot/Gainsbourg soundtrack sporadically interrupted by the thundery rumble of trains trundling overhead from Liverpool Street into Hackney.

Every time you go in, the place looks a bit different – at the time of writing their hair salon had moved into the second room, leaving a smaller day café morphing into a bring-your-own booze Korean restaurant in the evening. In the daytime, there's often a heaped table of vintage clothing and accessories for sale, where you can pick up something decent for a fiver. A changing arrangement of random ephemera dots the walls and ceiling: taxidermied fowl, some a little worse for wear; stag heads and skulls; antique chandeliers; side-mounted packing crates serving as shelving for antiquated glassware; old top hats and handbags; and even antique ice skates. Food here is good: pastries and muesli for breakfast, sandwiches and salads for lunch and Korean dishes for dinner.

Labour and Wait

ⓐ 85 Redchurch Street E2 7DJ ⓣ 020 7729 6253 ⓦ www.labourandwait.co.uk
ⓞ Tue–Sun 11am–6pm

Located in the former Dolphin pub on the corner of Redchurch and Turville Street, Labour and Wait is a contemporary and stylish take on an old-fashioned hardware store, given an added period charm by its green-tiled exterior. Set up in 2000 by designers Rachel Wythe-Moran and Simon Watkins, the pair's aim was to stock beautifully designed and timeless objects for everyday use. These include things for the home, such as storage jars, balls of string, brushes, and a varied selection of enamel ware (the lampshades are particularly smart), and classic hand-forged gardening equipment from Willem DeWit in Holland.

They also carry a small range of clothes with a similar emphasis on simple elegance, some of which are supplied by the ultimate purveyors of sartorial fogeyishness, Old Town (ⓦ www.old-town.co.uk). Not strictly vintage, since everything is brand new, more an enjoyable wallow in retail nostalgia.

Le Grenier

ⓐ 146 Bethnal Green Road E2 6DG ⓣ 020 7790 7379 ⓦ www.le-grenier.com
ⓞ Mon, Tue & Thurs–Sat noon–7pm, Sun 10am–7pm

Le Grenier sells a range of second-hand 1950s to 70s homeware, furnishings and accessories at mid-range prices from its packed Bethnal Green store. It's a good place to start if you're in the market for a quirky chandelier, lamp, ormolu mirror or vintage tea set, and other one-off pieces for the home. There are some items of clothing, but the selection of accessories is far more interesting: from second-hand shades to chunky clip-on earrings and twinkling brooches. These might set you back £12, whereas a mirror in pristine condition is more likely to cost around £50. For those of a certain age, memories are bound to be stirred by the matching sets of 1970s Hornsea tableware, once so popular in British kitchens and enjoying something of a revival. Also on sale are giant retro European film posters, old-style weighing scales and decorative tins for your sideboard.

Levisons

(A) 1 Cheshire Street E2 6ED (T) 020 3609 2224 (W) www.levisons.co.uk (O) Mon to Fri 11am–6.30pm, Sat 10.30am–6.30pm, Sun 9.30am–6.30pm

Levisons sells clothing from the 1920s to the 80s, and is a particularly excellent outlet for vintage menswear. Those shopping-phobic fellows, who quake at the idea of rummaging for hours in piles of mouldering fabric, will be overjoyed by the classy presentation of wares here, with rails full of high-quality apparel in top condition. Levisons favours classic tailoring, stocking everything from three-piece Savile Row suits and Norfolk tweed jackets, to Guernsey knitwear and 1940s utility shirts. Prices match the quality and condition of the items; you might find a smart pair of brogues for around £80 among the fine collection of men's shoes and boots. The women haven't been entirely forgotten, and there's a decent selection of handpicked vintage pieces for them, from 1950s appliqué skirts to fitted tweed jackets. However, this really should be one of the first stop-offs in the area for chaps who want their second-hand pieces to be both timeless and durable.

The Love Shake

(A) 5 Kingsland Road E2 8AA (W) www.theloveshake.co.uk (O) Tue–Thurs 12.45pm–11.50pm, Fri & Sat 12.45pm–midnight, Sun & Mon 12.45pm–10pm

The Love Shake styles itself as a "media café", and woos the Shoreditch daytime freelancer types with the promise of laptops, free WiFi and wireless printing services. But, as its 1950s-style American diner setting indicates, it takes its inspiration from a less media-savvy age. Designed to a super-kitsch, cutesy blueprint, it boasts upholstered booths in fire-engine red, framed posters, overhead globe lamps and frilly-shaded table lamps, plus an assortment of 1950s collectables on display, some of which are for sale. The menu continues the same theme: burgers, milkshakes, coffees, bourbon and beer, all of which can be enjoyed in the outdoor seating area (weather permitting). In the evenings, the emphasis is on events, from 1970s disco to jive nights, plus monthly late-night speakeasy-style parties.

Maison Trois Garcons

Ⓐ 45 Redchurch Street E2 7DJ Ⓣ 020 3370 7761 Ⓦ www.lestroisgarcons.com/shop
Ⓞ Daily 11am–7pm

This upmarket lifestyle boutique specializes in high-end European furniture and homeware. There's a mix of old and new on display, with more recent arty pieces thrown in alongside reconditioned French antique furniture and mid-century tableware. Even the ultra-modern items, from throw cushions to decorative statement pieces, have a classic feel. Pricewise, it's at the higher end of the spectrum (reflected in the smartly fitted

shop), although you can find the occasional bargain. Quirky rather than snooty, and with lots to choose from, this is an ideal place to search for a really unique gift. Alongside the flamboyant furniture, you'll find clusters of quality vintage handbags, costume jewellery, a few rails of clothing, a decent range of glassware, plus lots of oversized mirrors, both antique and retro-styled.

Nightjar 🍸

Ⓐ 129 City Road EC1V 1JB Ⓣ 020 7253 4101 Ⓦ www.barnightjar.com Ⓞ Fri & Sat 6pm–3am, Sun–Wed 6pm–1am, Thurs 6pm–2am; last Monday of the month is members' night

A stylish late-opening bar in a City Road basement, the Nightjar is one of several Prohibition-themed establishments to appear in London in recent years. Classily fitted out with elegant Deco touches, it has a main room and stage area, which hosts frequent jazz performances, as well as several intimate little booths.

The four separate cocktail lists (pre-Prohibition, Prohibition, Post-War and the wonderfully inventive Nightjar Signatures) ensure that the busy throng of nostalgia-seekers and post-work drinkers have plenty to choose from. The carefully crafted and potent cocktails (from £9) are downright delicious, and there's a choice of good stomach-lining bar snacks to set you up if you're settling in for the night. It's always worth booking a table in advance, particularly on the weekends.

The Other Side of the Pillow 👤 👤 👞

Ⓐ 61 Wilton Way E8 1BG Ⓣ 07988 870508 Ⓦ http://theotherothersideofthepillow. blogspot.co.uk Ⓞ Wed–Mon 11am–6pm

Set on a quiet Hackney street, The Other Side of the Pillow is a small affair. It sells vintage footwear, eyewear and homeware, with a strong emphasis on pre-1994 Vans from the American trainer brand (established in 1966) synonymous with skater style and streetwise cool. Vans-lovers are spoiled for choice, with ladies' and men's styles (from Disney prints to rare two-tone chequerboards) in various sizes, some displayed in the old-fashioned fridge hulking in the corner. And you can even sign up to the mailing list by shoe size to keep up to date with any new additions to the collection.

Also for sale are various pieces of retro paraphernalia, including lamps, decorative tins, plates, glassware and an extensive stock of sunglasses. You can shop online, but it's much more fun to visit this quirky little cave of collectables in person.

The Palm Tree ☿

Ⓐ Haverfield Road E3 5BH ☎ 020 8980 2918 Ⓞ Mon–Thurs noon–midnight, Fri & Sat noon–2am, Sun noon–1am

This old-school East End boozer, with its reliable beer list and revolving guest ales, is a firm favourite in this part of town, bringing in a mixed crowd of locals, cool-hunters and after-work drinkers. It stands firm in the contrasting environs of Mile End's Ecology Park, the two-room interior featuring a nostalgic mix of black and gold wallpaper, bunches of dried hops, creaky benches and large windows hung with heavy red velour curtains. All of this is seen in its best light as the sun goes down and the lamps flicker on. There's an old-fashioned till (cash only) behind the curving bar, which is wood-panelled and fringed with black and white chequerboard floor tiles. Gaze upwards while you wait for your pint to settle and browse the framed photos of jazz musicians; the live jazz sets remain hugely popular and are held every Friday, Saturday and Sunday night. You may well be dragged into a singalong at some point.

Paper Dress Vintage 👤 🧁 ☿

Ⓐ 114–116 Curtain Road EC2A 3AH ☎ 020 7729 4100 Ⓦ www.paperdressvintage.co.uk Ⓞ Mon 10am–7.30pm, Tue–Fri 10am–10.30pm, Sat 11am–10.30pm, Sun noon–6pm

Named after the throwaway fashion phenomenon of the 1960s, Paper Dress Vintage is a multi-purpose beacon of Shoreditch cool. It's not only an excellent

vintage emporium selling clothing and accessories from 1900 to the 1980s (mostly for women), but it also has its own signature collection, plus a café-bar and packed schedule of events.

The cleverly lace-wrapped ceiling tiles can't quite hide the shop's previous incarnation as an office, but the bright displays and well-organized rails of wearable vintage go some way to transforming this into a thriving social space. There are comfortable second-hand sofas on which to enjoy your post-shop Climpson & Sons coffee, or indeed something stronger from the licensed bar. Much fun is to be had at the evening events, featuring anything from classes (jive dancing to fashion illustration), rockabilly nights and live bands, to late-night cocktail and shopping evenings.

Paper Dress's in-house clothing line features ten ladies' pieces based on key retrospective designs. For example, the "Grace", a 1940s-style cropped bolero jacket, or the "Ursula", a 1970s-style kimono. Simply place your order in small, medium or large along with your preferred colour palette, and they'll create it for you from their cache of vintage cloth. The alterations service, especially geared to adapting older clothing to fit modern figures, is a real blessing.

Rocket Gallery

Ⓐ Tea Building, 56 Shoreditch High Street E1 6JJ Ⓣ 020 7729 7594 Ⓦ www. rocketgallery.com Ⓞ Tue–Fri 10am–6pm, Sat noon–6pm

A colourful alternative to other vintage furniture retailers, the influential Rocket Gallery has been through several incarnations in its lifetime: first existing as a publishing imprint and then as a gallery displaying painting, sculpture and furniture. Subsequently its owner, Jonathan Stephenson, has expanded the aesthetic of the gallery into an adjoining shop which offers a permanent space to sell Rocket's specialism: Dutch and Danish design from the likes of Wim Rietveld and Hans J. Wegner.

While those names are likely to whet the appetite of serious collectors, this bright and bold shop also deserves attention from more casual browsers. Multi-coloured Tomado shelves compete for consideration with brilliant 1950s day beds, while primary-coloured contemporary ceramics are strikingly displayed on black tabletops. The dazzling yellow shop floor and the occasional vivid Martin Parr photograph enhance the effect. And there's even a cage with a pair of colourful rare birds in the corner.

As befits the shop's literary background, there are still plenty of art and design books to browse, as well as back issues of *Modernism* magazine to swot up on. Rocket also holds the licence to reissue 1950s and 60s pieces from Danish-born designer Jens Risom, which are made in collaboration with Terence Conran's Benchmark. It's an interesting move that's perhaps indicative of the next direction of this constantly evolving space. Where it leads, others will surely follow.

Rokit

(A) 101 & 107 Brick Lane E1 6SE **(T)** 020 7375 3864/020 7247 3777 **(W)** www.rokit.co.uk **(O)** Mon–Fri 11am–7pm, Sat & Sun 10am–7pm

Rokit is a reliable chain of vintage boutiques, two of which sit a few doors down from each other on busy Brick Lane. Both have a heavy concentration of 1970s and 80s clothing, but the general buying policy is anything from the 1940s to the 80s. Items are at each end of the price scale: you might get a pair of earrings for as little as £3, or a rare vintage 1950s prom dress for £200. There's an online shop and they also do their own Rokit Recycled line, where tired vintage pieces are reworked and given a new lease of life. So a recycled men's tweed jacket could be brightened up with fabric inserts. Definitely worth a look, especially if you have time to rummage.

Shanghai

(A) 41 Kingsland High Street E8 2JS **(T)** 020 7254 2878 **(W)** www.shanghaidalston.co.uk **(O)** Daily noon–11pm

Chinese restaurant Shanghai set up shop in the historic interior of this former pie and mash restaurant in the late 1990s, and is a great example of two worlds colliding. The best views are to be had among the largely Edwardian features in the dining room, with its marble-topped counter, tall mirrors embellished with eel fixtures, padded benches and maritime-themed tiling.

Steaming baskets of dim sum filing in and out against the backdrop of occidental shipping scenes makes for a unique dining experience. There's a large modern extension at the back with extra seating, plus two bookable karaoke rooms. The extensive menu lists all-day dim sum, tasty mains including lobster specials, plus house signatures such as coffee-baked spare ribs and sea bass infused with Oolong tea. Filling food, well priced and with decor to die for.

The Shop

(A) 3 Cheshire Street E2 6ED **(T)** 020 7739 5631 **(O)** Mon–Sat 11am–6pm, Sun 9.30am–5pm

According to Sharon and Michael, the pleasant mother-and-son team who have run this delightful shop since 1994, their store was the first of its kind in an area that now has something calling itself a vintage shop on practically every corner. It's a much-loved resource for textiles, with every item handpicked and in excellent condition.

As you step inside the small space, you'll see colourful old aprons, piles of neatly folded linen, blankets and quilts, and curtain and dress fabric. It's an explosion of colour, with paisley, florals and checks all cheerfully clashing. Of particular interest is the surfeit of multi-coloured scarves – they have a collection of over one thousand, dating from the 1930s onwards. Prices are very reasonable: a hand-knitted children's jumper might set you back £12, and you could pick up a modern scarf from around a fiver, with more precious designer examples priced higher up the scale. In between the stacks of material you can also find handbags, dresses, knitted toys and a selection of hats, as well as lots of lace, upholstery trim, and the like.

Speedie's ⊙ ♖

⒜ 81 Redchurch Street E2 7DJ ☎ 020 7739 4798 ⓦ www.speediesvintage.blogspot. com ⓞ Daily 11am–7pm

Collector and vintage audio specialist Speedie runs this unassuming little grotto of a place. The interior bears no resemblance to the earnest shabby chic of some other neighbourhood establishments, and assaults the eye with a jumbled vista of seventies-era brown (it can be rented as a film location, should you so wish). Making up the slightly chaotic assemblage of items dating up to the mid-1980s are rows of vintage record players, matching kitchenware, school and dining-room furniture stacked up in every corner, and heaps of electronics and other bits of retro kitsch. Among the more eccentric items on offer recently has been an original French dodgem-bumper car from the 1970s –yours for a mere £450.

So come here if you're in the market for a 1960s cocktail bar for your front room, or if you have a special liking for Formica, teak or vinyl upholstery. If you can't stretch to a mega-stylish

swivel armchair, browse the crockery for a few bargains for your kitchen, or alternatively bring your record player in and get it restored by Speedie himself.

Spitalfields Market

Ⓐ 16 Horner Square E1 6EW, nearest tubes: Liverpool Street & Shoreditch High Street Ⓦ www.oldspitalfieldsmarket.com, www.spitalfields.co.uk/markets Ⓞ Traders Market approx: Mon–Wed 9.30am–5.30pm, Thurs 8.30am–5.30pm, Fri 9.30am–5.30pm, Sun 9am–5pm; Saturday Market: rotating guest markets 11am–5pm

A wholesale fruit and veg market until 1991, Spitalfields is now a daily happening, much gentrified by the presence of big corporation offices on Bishopsgate. The Grade II-listed market hall is well preserved, and although the stalls themselves are flanked by chain restaurants, there is still plenty of interest for vintage and reproduction shoppers.

The main market is Spitalfields Traders Market. Vintage items need to be sought out among the new and not-so-special items on sale, but there's always something of decent age and quality on display. You might find a psychedelic 1960s silk kimono, a rare 45 at one of the record stalls, or some long-forgotten 1970s cult paperbacks. There's a record fair on the first and third Fridays of the month (10.30am–4.30pm) and Spitalfields Art Market, which sells contemporary and affordable art, monthly from March to December. Rotating guest markets take the stage on Saturdays, including the excellent Judy's Affordable Vintage Fair (see p.201).

Some of the clothing boutiques installed at the edges of the market offer women's retro styles – such as **COLLECTIF**, with its 1940s and 50s reproduction wear, and **DOLLY DARE**, with its full-skirted florals and sparkling trims. There's a particular focus on antiques and collectables on Thursdays, and fashion on Sundays, when Spitalfields competes with the large concentration of vintage wares at the various Brick Lane markets nearby.

The Ten Bells

Ⓐ 84 Commercial Street E1 6LY Ⓣ 020 7366 1721 Ⓦ www.tenbells.com Ⓞ Mon–Wed & Sun noon–midnight, Thurs–Sat noon–1am

The Ten Bells is famous for two things: its association with the Jack the Ripper killings, and its stunning Grade-II listed interior. And very impressive it is, too. The main bar-room has undergone several remodellings over the years, but the late 19th-century blue and white floral tiles, dado and painted panel ("Spitalfields in Olden Time, Visiting a Weaver's Shop") are still here to enjoy. At the opposite end of the room another panel has been installed: a tableau of "Spitalfields in Modern Times", complete with artists Gilbert and George in the foreground. The centrepiece of the room is the elegant dark-wood bar, and if you can grab a stool here or a seat by one of the windows, you'll be in prime position to observe the comings and goings of the Spitalfields throngs. Be sure to check out the chic first-floor restaurant with its sophisticated British staples. The owners take good care of the pub these days; the basement loos, formerly contenders for the worst toilets in London, are now white-tiled and a comparative joy to behold.

This Shop Rocks 🕴 👤 📖 🧍 🪑

(A) 131 Brick Lane E1 6SE **(T)** 020 7739 7667 **(O)** Daily 11am–6pm

The artistic window displays bring the crowds in off Brick Lane to visit this packed shop, mostly stocked with 20th-century ladies' clothing and homeware. The owners are Sandy and Candy, whose art and antique-dealing past led them to set up their London shop. They fill up the space with things they like, from clothes to painted mirrors, postcards to record players, and toys to books. The earliest garments you'll find here are Victorian, and the latest are from the 1970s, with a larger concentration on the periods in between and a limited selection of menswear. It has a slightly chaotic feel due to the large volume of wares, some of which is more junk than antique. There's a sterling collection of vintage hats, and you could even walk out with a Sandy original, as he makes and sells his own designs here.

Time for Tea 🧁

(A) 110 Shoreditch High Street E1 6JN **(T)** 020 3222 0073 **(O)** Sun 2pm–7pm (sometimes)

It's not always open to the public, but if you can dodge the private parties on a Sunday afternoon, duck into Time for Tea for some crumpets in the cosy 1940s-style tearoom. If it feels like someone's front room, that's because it is.

Johnny Vercoutre, local character, art director and oftentime DJ, blessed with a glorious moustache and a specialist knowledge of all things 1939–59, has lived in the house for years. He books it out as a period location for photo shoots, cinema screenings, birthday parties and other events. He'll be your host if you're lucky enough to find the tearoom open for business. Once you're in, choose from the range of speciality teas coupled with quality cakes or crumpets, then sit back and take in the nostalgic surrounds and bits of bric-a-brac for sale. Share the big table with the other tea-drinkers, or with the charming host himself, before stepping back out onto the busy street and wondering why on earth everything looks so, well, modern.

Two Columbia Road 🪑 🛋

Ⓐ 2 Columbia Road E2 7NN Ⓣ 020 7729 9933 Ⓦ www.twocolumbiaroad.co.uk
Ⓞ Wed–Fri noon–7pm, Sat noon–6pm, Sun 10am–3pm

A particular treat for mid-century interior design enthusiasts, this high-ceilinged, large-windowed space showcases top-quality items for the home, including furniture, artworks and lighting. There's a good general stock of items from Europe and the US, with a special focus on Scandinavian design from the 1950s and 60s. Two Columbia Road has sourced the furnishings for many an exclusive establishment, including Shoreditch House and Milk & Honey, and they have a particular forte for selecting pieces by celebrated designers, such as interiors wizard Joe Columbo and architect and designer Charles Eames. Everything's in mint condition, and that's reflected in the prices: £500 for a 1950s French sofa, £1950 for a 1960s Danish rosewood drinks bar, £1500 for a 1950s American teakwood coffee table. Great for a statement sofa, if you've got the means.

The Vintage Emporium 🎭 🧁

Ⓐ 14 Bacon Street E1 6LF Ⓣ 020 7739 0799 Ⓦ www.vintageemporiumcafe.com
Ⓞ Shop Mon–Fri noon–7pm, Sat & Sun 10am–7pm; café Mon–Fri 11am–10pm, Sat & Sun 10am–10pm

If you're on the Brick Lane trail, then this diamond of a vintage store should on no account be missed. Not only does the Vintage Emporium's basement boutique house an astounding range of ladies' clothing and accessories, but it also has a charmingly nostalgic tearoom, complete with atmospheric soundtrack.

With their respective backgrounds in fashion design and antiques respectively, Oli and Jess, who stock and manage the shop, have created a real treasure trove of desirable goods sourced mostly from the UK and France, ranging from Victoriana to the 1950s. Their speciality is women's fashions from the 1920s, 30s and 40s, and sizes can be correspondingly petite. Many of the garments are delicate antiques, so priced accordingly; but while you might find a precious beaded gown for as much as £1800, you could also pick up a pair of gloves for around £15. Everything is tastefully presented and well cared for, with shoes displayed pair by pair on old packing cases and ancient furs draped over mannequins. It's the first place to come to finish off a vintage outfit with a classy hatpin or shawl.

The Victorian-style tearoom upstairs, lit by flickering candles all day long, is a cosy and relaxed den, where customers sink into armchairs with tea and cake and cast an eye over the clusters of dried roses and jumble of classic wall prints.

Vintage Heaven 🧁 🍴 🛋 🪑

Ⓐ 82 Columbia Road E2 7QB **Ⓣ** 01277 215968 **Ⓦ** www.vintageheaven.co.uk **Ⓞ** Fri by appointment only, Sat noon–6pm, Sun 8.30am–5.30pm

This family-run affair set behind a pale pink shop frontage is a popular Columbia Road spot, particularly on Sundays when the flower market is in full swing. Mum Margaret takes charge of the excellent vintage homeware boutique up front, and daughter Louise heads up the charming Cake Hole Café (**Ⓦ** www. cakeholecafe.co.uk) to the rear.

Vintage Heaven specializes in English kitchenware from the 1920s to 70s, all beautifully arranged by hue either in sets or in clusters of complementary singles. Choose from high-quality tea sets, plates and jugs, all carefully selected by Margaret and her husband in unfailing good taste. You can also pick up old-

fashioned jelly moulds in glass or tin, classy sets of cutlery, embroidered tea towels and vintage curtain fabric and tablecloths.

A delightful extra comes in the form of the undeniably cute Cake Hole Café, a sunken backroom decorated in a traditional but unstuffy style. If you can get a seat in this buzzing little tearoom, it's the ideal place for a post-market tea or coffee, plus a generous slice of home-made cake.

Worship Street Whistling Shop ⟨Y⟩

Ⓐ 63 Worship Street EC2A 2DU Ⓣ 020 7247 0015 Ⓦ www.whistlingshop.com
Ⓞ Tue 5pm–midnight, Wed & Thurs 5pm–1am, Fri & Sat 5pm–2am

This classy alternative to the standard pub and chain-bar offerings in the Liverpool Street area takes a novel approach to cocktail hour. The Worship Street Whistling Shop seeks to create a clandestine, old-fashioned atmosphere in this spacious basement, complete with low lighting and dark furniture. As you descend, your eyes adjust to the snug bar area, behind which is a larger space with comfy sofas and even a small distillery.

Classically attired bar staff serve up the speciality cocktails (from £9 to £13), some of which feature unusual ingredients and a do-it-yourself approach. You could start with the gin-based Langdales Mood Enhancer: the bartender mixes it in a medicine bottle for you to pour yourself, and serves it on a board with a liquorice lolly and pile of grapefruit sherbet preserve. There's an element of fun in the presentation, which is just as mood-enhancing as the drink itself. Also recommended is the Shivering Jemmy Punch (with Hendricks gin, port and olive oil), the Colonial Boilermaker (complete with butterfat-washed rum), the Mandrakes Fix (with coriander, plus peach and elderflower jelly) and the bourbon-based Million Dollar #2 (complete with chip-pan bitters).

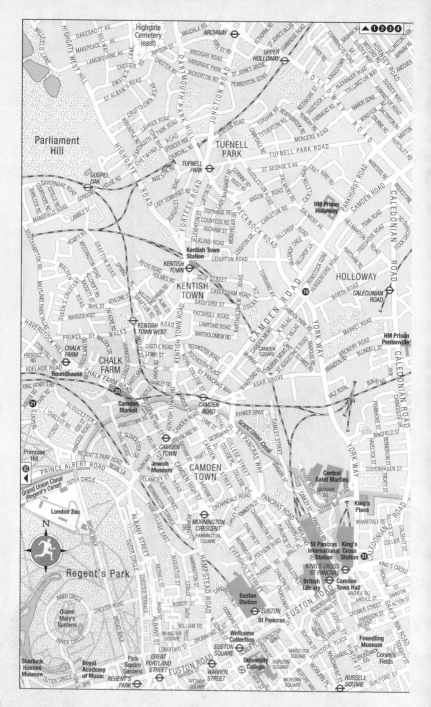

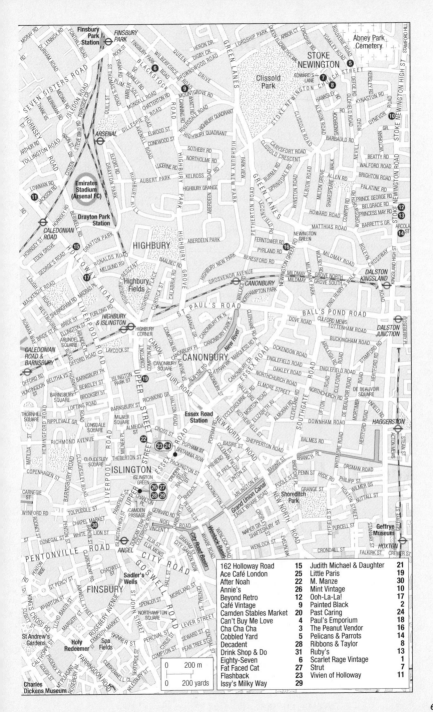

162 Holloway Road		Judith Michael & Daughter	21
Ace Café London		Little Paris	19
After Noah	15	M. Manze	25
Annie's	22	Mint Vintage	30
Beyond Retro	26	Ooh-La-La!	10
Café Vintage	12	Painted Black	17
Camden Stables Market	9	Past Caring	2
Can't Buy Me Love	20	Paul's Emporium	24
Cha Cha Cha	4	The Peanut Vendor	18
Cobbled Yard	3	Pelicans & Parrots	16
Decadent	5	Ribbons & Taylor	14
Drink Shop & Do	28	Ruby's	8
Eighty-Seven	31	Scarlet Rage Vintage	13
Fat Faced Cat	6	Strut	1
Flashback	27	Vivien of Holloway	7
Issy's Milky Way	23		11
	29		

162 Holloway Road 👤 👤

🅐 162 Holloway Road N7 8DQ 📞 020 7700 2354 🅦 www.londonvintagestore.com
🅞 Mon–Sat 10am–6pm, Sun noon–6pm

It would be easy to overlook the vintage shop at 162 Holloway Road. It's not even obvious what the place is called, as a CND symbol takes the place of a shop sign. While your credit card statement will tell you it's Twenty-First Century Vintage and the labels on the clothes refer to the London Vintage Store, to its devoted fans, it's simply known as 162.

Don't get put off by the small, old-fashioned-looking window either – it's not indicative of the vast size of this Tardis-like store. Instead come prepared for an energetic rummage as 162 is crammed full with so many clothes that to leave empty-handed feels like some kind of failure. The clothes range from the wearable to the ridiculous, covering virtually everything in between. For around £35 you can take your pick from a vast range of cotton 1950s day dresses or 60s shifts that could easily be worn to the office, but if your taste veers towards the *Abigail's Party* end of the spectrum, you'll also be spoiled for choice. Men's shirts, likewise ranging from the sublime to the unwearable, are priced from just £3.50. There's tons of just about everything, including shoes and bags to accessorize with, and even a substantial section devoted to virginal cotton nightdresses.

Once past the deceptive frontage, 162 has a straightforward approach to selling vintage that extends to everything from the pricing to the shop staff, who have something of a reputation for dishing out brutally honest advice. Leave your ego behind and you'll enjoy the hunt.

Ace Cafe London 🧁 🍴

🅐 Ace Corner, North Circular Road NW10 7UD 📞 020 8961 1000 🅦 www.ace-cafe-london.com 🅞 Mon–Sat 7am–11pm (2am on live music nights), Sun 7am–10.30pm

Hitch a ride on the back of a motorbike or wangle your way into the passenger seat of a classic car so you don't have to arrive at the Ace Cafe by foot. Though you could easily do so – Stonebridge tube is five minutes away – the Ace Cafe is all about the open road: the point of departure for bikers and drivers leaving London, or a friendly stop-off on the way home.

Built as a transport café in the late 1930s, the Ace Cafe's notoriety was at its peak in the 1950s when it was a meeting point for three post-war growth industries: motorbikes, rock'n'roll and rebellious teens. Impromptu races on the north circular and music from Ace Cafe-grown bands like Johnny Kidd and the Pirates were the order of the day. Today, there's still rock'n'roll, either coming from a juke box or a live band and, with its own community of bike and car fanatics and various meets, including their famous ride to Brighton, it's the closest to rocker perfection you'll find on the north circular.

There are always bikes parked outside, and inside leathers are worn as standard. Under 1950s-style black and white banners, customers sit at wooden communal tables to enjoy huge mugs of tea and bacon sarnies while conversation inevitably turns to that prize set of wheels on the forecourt. Look out of the café's huge windows, past the vehicles if you can, beyond the modern retail units, and the Ace Cafe gives you an unexpectedly romantic view. It's the open road and it looks as if it's yours for the taking.

After Noah

Ⓐ 121 Upper Street N1 1QP **Ⓣ** 020 7359 4281 **Ⓦ** www.afternoah.com **Ⓞ** Mon–Sat 10am–6pm, Sun 11am–5pm

In other hands the distressed display cases, *chanson* soundtrack and retro magpie aesthetic might feel fake, or fey, but After Noah has been ploughing its own quirky furrow since long before vintage became trendy, and the nostalgia here never hits a false note. You could spend 10p (on a wad of old-school bubblegum) or £500 (on an original Bakelite telephone), or pretty much anything in between. You could furnish a lifestyle shoot with aesthetically battered utility chairs or relive your childhood, real or imaginary, in the toy section, piled high with tin kazoos, Ludo boards and Rubik's cubes, along with more recent but invariably beautifully designed toys and games. Good design is the keynote throughout: contemporary stationery, books and gifts on a vintage theme snuggle up comfortably with chipped 1950s table lamps, Commonwealth-era globes and painted plaster flapper-girl heads. Whatever your budget, you'll be beset by

tricky choices. Even a simple candy jar full of wooden chess pieces becomes a thing of beauty in this artfully cluttered treasure trove. And who knew that an old apothecary bottle once filled with "worm disease" remedy would suddenly feel so essential? After Noah's furniture, some of it vintage, other pieces created by modern designers working with an impeccable vintage sensibility, includes streamlined aluminium cabinets, leather Oxford chairs and brass utility bedframes, and they offer a restoration service, too.

Annie's 🎎

Ⓐ 12 Camden Passage N1 8ED Ⓣ 020 7359 0796 Ⓦ www.anniesvintageclothing.co.uk Ⓞ Daily 11am–6pm; opens earlier on Camden Passage market days

Annie's, which has occupied a corner spot on Camden Passage, Islington's antiques alley, since the 1980s, is the grande dame of the local vintage scene. Its location, surrounded by classy antiques shops, feels just right – garments here date back as far as 1890, and to enter is to enter another world. Don't bother with the small selection of everyday clothes – cashmere cardigans, cotton skirts, court shoes; you can get those more cheaply elsewhere. Oozing glamour, Annie's is the place to come when you're after the *crème de la crème*.

It's not cheap, in any respects. Victorian lace jackets, as fragile as cobwebs, could set you back between £150 and £200, while you might find a neat white lawn Edwardian blouse for £95, or a stunning full-length linen day dress from the same era – very *Downton* – for twice that. The 1920s are represented by shimmery flapper dresses, feathery headpieces and decadent satin trousers, and there's a cheeky range of 1930s and 40s silk, crêpe de Chine and lace loungewear. Prices, for this quality, are not outrageous; a hand-embroidered cream silk blouse from the 1960s shouldn't break the bank at around £50, and you'll pay a similar amount for a pair of floaty 1930s silk camis.

The beauty of Annie's clothing is in the detail – delicate stitching, cloth cut on the bias, butter-soft fabrics, exquisite pearl buttons – and everything, displayed lovingly on velvet or satin hangers, is as good as new. Step inside to luxuriate in a time gone by, and to feel history in every garment. Truly, they don't make them like this any more.

Beyond Retro 👤 ✂️

Ⓐ 92–100 Stoke Newington Road N16 7XB Ⓣ 020 7923 2277 Ⓦ www.beyondretro.com Ⓞ Mon–Wed, Fri & Sat 10am–7pm, Thurs 10am–8pm, Sun 11.30am–6pm; café Mon–Wed 7am–7pm, Thurs 7am–8pm, Sat 8.30am–7pm, Sun 9.30am–6pm

You've got to hand it to Beyond Retro, who started out with a Brick Lane shop in 2002 and now have branches throughout London, in Brighton, Stockholm and Gothenburg. This Stoke Newington store is the latest in their small empire, forming a sturdy anchor for the up-and-coming vintage scene blossoming on this scruffy Stokey/Dalston border. Here as in their other outlets, the space is cavernous, the clothes are arranged with a stylist's eye – by colour, fabric and season as well as style and theme – the soundtrack is accessible, the staff are friendly, and the line between vintage and high street is straddled with flair. Check out the cabinet of lace aprons – very Heidi – the static-crackling nylon nighties, or the rack of hand-stitched Mexican felt gilets. You won't find those in Topshop. Their own-brand vintage-style accessories, including felt fedoras, dickie bows, and even tote bags, are cheap and cheerful, while the MADE range – new garments made from old fabrics – is a little more unique. It would be difficult to leave without buying something here – especially given the affordability, with most items hovering around £20 – but even if you don't, you could buy yourself a slice of the Beyond Retro lifestyle in the artfully shabby café, where local hipsters kick back with free wi-fi, espresso drinks and chunky gourmet sandwiches.

Cafe Vintage 👤 🧁

Ⓐ 88 Mountgrove Road N5 2LT Ⓣ 07903 875750 Ⓦ www.cafevintage.co.uk Ⓞ Tue–Fri 8.30am–5.30pm, Sat 9am–5pm, Sun 10am–4pm

The powerful combination of vintage clothing and coffee should not be underestimated. It's something that Cafe Vintage has used to its advantage: a pleasant café in its own right, the addition of vintage stock makes it a perfect stop-off point in the area. The café itself is an enjoyable place to spend some time: its corner location and large shop windows make it an agreeable place to sit and watch north London go about its business while sipping a cup of tea. The

food tends towards well-presented quality basics: think simple sandwiches rather than a deluxe afternoon tea, though there are plenty of options to satisfy a sweet tooth. Small piles of second-hand books on the windowsill and tables, and some eye-catching window displays, provide the vintage feel.

At the back is the shop area, laid out with its own dressing table and a pleasingly large changing room given the limited size of the overall shop. The quality of stock varies visit to visit – trend-influenced 1980s items are staples – but can include men's clothing and homewares alongside the womenswear. Recently they were selling a lovely selection of children's clothes, including patterned cotton tops and sturdy dungarees, perfect buys for local mums and dads without much time to shop.

While the cooking smells can be a little disconcerting as you browse, the fun is popping into Cafe Vintage and knowing that you could easily end up taking away a little black dress along with your black Americano.

Camden Stables Market 🏪

Ⓐ Chalk Farm Road NW1 8AH, nearest tube: Chalk Farm

Visiting Camden, with its strange mix of tacky London souvenirs, badly printed T-shirts, hoards of tourists and overwhelming smell of fried noodles, can be a disconcerting experience for the more rarefied vintage lover. But, if you are feeling brave, it's still worth a visit for more precious vintage too – both clothes and homewares – as the pure volume of stalls means you are bound to unearth some delights.

Head to the Stables Market area where the vintage sellers are clustered. There's lots of choice but the quality on offer varies hugely. For a range of clothing across the decades, your first stop should probably be **VINTAGE PLANET** (Unit D23, no phone). While its stock does include a sizeable segment of 1990s second-hand (and given Camden's key role in nineties Brit Pop, this is well within a local heritage remit), it has some seriously desirable items on sale too, such as the Yves Saint Laurent Rive Gauche coat spotted on a recent visit. Also deserving of a look is **VINTAGE KING** (Unit D04, no phone, Ⓦwww.facebook.com/vintagekingshop), especially for their Tiki shirts for men and corresponding novelty patterned 1950s dresses.

Arguably the more interesting pieces come from the specialist stores that take care of everything from luggage to teacups. Head to **HILARY PROCTOR** (Unit D14, no phone) if you're after an authentic Harris Tweed jacket or your very own alligator purse, though pricewise, be prepared to be spending in the hundreds. **ST CYR'S** (Arch 56, Ⓣ020 8367 1661, Ⓦwww.stcyrvintage.co.uk) selection of ladylike clothing comes as a pleasant oasis amidst the racks of jeans and T-shirts in surrounding stores. Its main draw, however, is a fantastic range of second-hand fashion and textile books. With glossy hardback fashion titles, biographies from designers like Diane Von Furstenberg and Pierre Balmain and old copies of *Vogue*, it has got everything you need for an elegant display on your G-Plan coffee table.

To search for that coffee table, head to **PLANET BAZAAR** (Arch 68, Ⓣ020 7485 6000, Ⓦwww.planetbazaar.co.uk). It specializes in pieces that would fit right into any 1960s or 70s pad, whether that's a Pop Art collectable, a piece of Sarah Moon's artwork for Biba, a 1970s Pirelli calendar or, for a real Swinging Sixties experience, a hanging chair. Their range is far classier than most of the rest of Camden Market might lead you to believe.

Can't Buy Me Love 👤 👕

Ⓐ 16 Avenue Mews N10 3NP Ⓣ 020 8365 4930 Ⓦ www.cant-buy-me-love.com Ⓞ Sat 11am–5pm

Despite its name this shop stocks enough desirable dresses, enviable accessories and covetable homewares to win a place in the heart of even the most hardened vintage shopper.

It's a small but perfectly formed shop: the first of the two rooms is so full of clothes it feels more like a fantastic walk-in wardrobe. There are always plenty of things you'll want to try on in here, with stock ranging from a lace yellow bed coat, perfect for wedding outfits, to a purple pussy bow dress which, when worn with your best vintage spectacles, gives a knowing nod towards that sexy 1970s secretary look. A 1960s bamboo bag, real rockabilly style, can be yours for £30, while £75 will buy you a stunning 1940s dress, which is probably as expensive as things get in this very reasonably priced shop. There's a small rail of menswear

too, while the changing room can be found in the back room, along with a range of items – coffee sets, ornaments and such – for the home.

If you can't make it up to Muswell Hill (which would be a shame with Cha Cha Cha also so close by), Can't Buy Me Love also run a market on the last Saturday of each month at one of London's most rock'n'roll pubs, The Boogaloo in Highgate. The market sells bric-a-brac, cakes, "proper jumble" and, naturally, also some alcohol alongside the clothing, making it an ideal way to pass a Saturday afternoon in vintage style.

Cha Cha Cha

A 20–22 Avenue Mews N10 3NP **T** 07739 517855 **W** www.cha-cha-cha.co.uk
O Thurs–Sat 10.30am–5pm

Cha Cha Cha is the kind of place you wish you lived in, filled with the sort of things you wished you owned – hitting the perfect balance between affordable and desirable. This attractively laid-out shop mainly sells vintage womenswear – unfortunately men are limited to picking from a small rail for their clothing requirements. In terms of things you'd actually want to wear, there are a few things in Cha Cha Cha which lean too far towards the less enviable excesses of the 1970s. But one woman's frou-frou monstrosity is another's party frock and the wide choice available means there is bound to be something that catches your eye. There also some sure-fire hits in store such as an Yves Saint Laurent slinky number found selling for £75. Most dresses are priced around £35 to £45.

It's also worth a visit for its attractive and often substantial selection of mid-century furniture, for example Ercol chairs and Formica tables. Colour and pattern lovers, meanwhile, are bound to fall in love with something from the wide range of vintage fabric lamp shades available. Pleasingly, a number of heavy-duty original ceramic bases to complement the designs are also on sale.

With friendly staff and lots to look at, Cha Cha Cha is the kind of place it's fun just to visit. If they started selling beds alongside their sideboards and skirts, we'd seriously consider moving in.

Cobbled Yard

A I Bouverie Road N16 0AH **T** 020 8809 5286 **W** www.cobbled-yard.co.uk
O Thurs–Sun 11am–6pm

Occupying a 19th-century stable set around – yes – a cobbled yard, just off Stoke Newington's Church Street, this rambling place is a good spot to root around for unusual retro furniture and intriguing home accessories. The stock, displayed attractively in neat, white-painted rooms, changes regularly, and usually features stuff you won't find elsewhere – customized school lockers, old velvet cinema seats, even old Citroën car seats, resplendent in their fading vinyl – along with familiar crowd-pleasers like Tretchikoff paintings and rustic pine trunks. There are even the odd almost-new items – slatted plastic garden chairs, perhaps, though you may well find these for less elsewhere.

Prices depend on desirability rather than age or even quality – a lovely battered vintage suitcase might cost as little as £35, for example, and two 1970s kitchen chairs with original floral fabric are good value at £110 for the pair, but a 1950s standard lamp, at £135, seems a bit steep. They have free parking in the yard and free local delivery, and also offer restoration, repair and upholstery services.

Decadent

A 26 Camden Passage N1 8ED **T** 07762 063318 **W** www.decadentvintage.com
O Daily 11am–6pm

The clue's in the name. You'll find no jumble sale togs or edgy street style in here, no scuffed retro trainers or logo Ts. Whether sourced from the 1950s or the 1980s, or anywhere in between, this is vintage for confident, grown-up women – women who are as happy shrugging on a Chanel bouclé jacket as they are shimmying around in a red silk kimono, and who would think nothing of cinching in a 1940s fur coat with a wide leather belt, accessorizing it with flashy paste jewellery and a jaunty fedora. Batwings and floaty shapes are much in evidence, along with sparkles and feathers, costume jewellery and lace, with everything from satin nightgowns to velvet coats offering a dash of opulent swagger. It's not all flamboyance and flounce, though, and there's plenty for quieter types, too: you might just as easily find a streamlined, colour-blocked woollen dress, a plain shift or a simple Balmain handbag. There's a vaguely 1970s feel to the place – think Faye Dunaway in *Bonnie and Clyde*, or Barbra Streisand in *The Way We Were* – with the gleaming gold-and-black wallpaper on the back wall, very Biba, perfecting the look.

Drink Shop & Do

A 9 Caledonian Road N1 9DX **T** 020 7278 4335 **W** www.drinkshopdo.com **O** Mon–Wed 8am–11pm, Thurs 8am–midnight, Fri & Sat 8am–2am, Sun 10.30am–8pm

Drink Shop & Do states its intention in its title. While it gets big ticks in all three of those categories, vintage also runs through everything this magnificent multi-tasker of a café/shop/craft place/club does, whether it's the simple menu of old-fashioned British grub or the homespun art hanging in the loos. It wears its vintage lightly and fashionably. Upstairs is decorated in retro 1950s-style pastels, a charity shop-like mish-mash of coffee tables, chairs and drinks cabinets under a huge disco ball. Downstairs, the Drink Shop & Dance venue has a more glamorous feel. Within its black and white decor, candles twinkle between rows of vintage decanters and the light reflects off the sides of mounted shiny 80s boom boxes.

There's some substantial drinking to be found behind the style too with a list of classic cocktails and 33 different types of gin available, nearly half of them from London. You can shop as you drink, as the fittings in the upstairs space are for sale, with a classic 1960s-style room divider marked up as £240 and a 50s display cabinet yours for £300. There's also a selection of vintage teacups and bottles available and a charming retro sweets selection. As for the doing, they run a varied list of sociable activity nights, from Lionel Richie-themed clay modelling to rude scrabble. Monday and Thursday evenings are devoted to vintage hair and make-up, where stylists create glamorous new looks for an already immaculately styled crowd. £10 will get your hair or make-up done, or £15 gets you both. The only thing left to do after is to hit their dancefloor.

Eighty-Seven

Ⓐ 87 Blackstock Road N4 2JW **Ⓣ** 07751 906 739 **Ⓞ** Mon & Tue 10am–2pm, Wed–Sat 10am–6pm, Sun 1pm–5.30pm

With erratic opening hours (it's best to phone ahead before making a special trip) and a load of boxes stuffed full of old picture frames sitting on the pavement outside, the initial impression of Eighty-Seven is that it's rather chaotic. But don't let that put you off, as inside the shop is a completely different story, stocking a great range of furniture and collectables that you would kick yourself for walking past.

It would be foolish to snootily overlook the frames outside, though – they're definitely worth a rummage for some bargain art, for example a gorgeous original rose embroidery selling for only £3. There are plenty more posters and artworks inside, where the experience is slightly more ordered. Jazz music helps create a calm atmosphere for browsing the store's covetable homewares, including re-upholstered 1950s chairs that wouldn't look out of place in the most fashionable of living rooms, or a perfectly formed set of tables and chairs from the same period selling for £395. More niche areas are also successfully catered for, whether that's 1960s chrome candleholders or toy vehicles (head for the cupboard at the back of the shop). There's a generous array of 70s ceiling lights and an impressive stack of vintage luggage too.

Considering its lack of pretensions, and the fact that its range and prices are better than at many similar places, perhaps it's no bad thing for those prepared to look beyond its outward appearance that Eighty-Seven remains a delightful secret.

Fat Faced Cat

Ⓐ 22–24 Camden Passage N1 8ED **Ⓣ** 020 7354 0777 **Ⓦ** www.fatfacedcat.com **Ⓞ** Mon, Tue & Thurs 11am–7pm, Wed, Fri & Sat 10am–6pm, Sun 11am–5pm

Fat Faced Cat is a beautifully presented, thoughtful kind of shop. While, on the hanger at least, they don't carry the kind of clothing that bowls you over with its glamour, every item has an excellent pedigree, skilfully made from quality fabrics. So, while it might not be love at first sight, affection for anything bought here is likely to grow through the years.

On the women's side, a few Lurex jackets are about as jazzy as things get. The store imports a lot of its stock from Los Angeles and it really shows – it's full of examples of the luxurious casual style that Americans made their own. The LA link seems more surprising when you look at the men's side (for once about equal in size to the women's section). With tweed hats, blazers and Fair Isle jumpers, it feels quintessentially British. Everything is given its own detailed label, listing its era and materials.

For such a cerebral shop, it's hardly surprising it also carries an impressive selection of books, from the orange Penguin editions of classics like *Billy Liar* to the vividly colourful Pan mass-market paperbacks of the 1950s and 60s. Rupert annuals and a large selection of Ordnance Survey maps complete the bookshelf. Other interesting vintage objects are artfully placed throughout the shop, everything from spectacles to cameras.

With this level of attention to detail, perhaps the higher price tag is to be expected. Books and accessories aside, most items start at just under £100 and many go far higher: an embroidered 1950s dress was priced at over £400. Think of them as pieces to last you a vintage lifetime.

Flashback

Ⓐ 50 Essex Road N1 8LR Ⓣ 020 7354 9356 Ⓦ www.flashback.co.uk Ⓞ Mon–Sat 10am–7pm, Sun noon–6pm

Flashback is true to its name, spinning you back in time to the days when keen-as-mustard music fans would spend their Saturdays flicking through crates of vinyl in funky little stores plastered with lo-fi fliers. The LP crates, the fliers and the musos are all there, certainly, along with racks of used CDs, DVDs and even a few cassettes (from 19p; "back by modest demand") – but Flashback has something more. Here you'll find a classy vintage vinyl collection for people with serious intentions and money to spend.

There are plenty of LPs upstairs, going back as far as the 1970s, and costing anything from 99p, along with new vinyl from as little as £10. Down in the basement, where artwork from covetable rarities lines the walls, you're very much in vintage territory. Pricing is based on accepted international price guides, and they're careful not to lower the tone by filling the racks with anything for which collectors aren't prepared to pay, say, £10 or more. Reggae LPs on the Studio One label, for example, can cost as much as £100 for original pressings. They also have a fabulous selection of 7- and 12-inch soul, hip-hop, disco and reggae singles, sorted into readily accessible sub-categories. They're rather sheepish about the small "World Music" section, apologizing for lumping together so many disparate sounds under a single catch-all label.

You can have a virtual shuffle through the entire stock on their user-friendly website, and if you're thinking of bringing in your own stuff to sell, reckon on getting around forty to fifty percent of their selling price, depending on the condition of your collection.

Issy's Milky Way 🧁

Ⓐ 28 Camden Passage N1 8ED **☎** 020 7354 4415 **Ⓦ** www.facebook.com/issys.milkyway

"Free hi-fi access!" The throwaway pun on their flier speaks volumes about this sugar-candy-cute 50s-style soda fountain – as squeaky fun as bubblegum, with a dry sense of humour to boot. Specializing in ice cream sundaes and shakes, they offer a short list of savouries, too – including a hotdog melt toastie and a pastrami bagel – along with irresistible retro cakes (the red velvet with buttercream is to die for). Such vintage fabulousness doesn't come cheap – basic shakes start at £4, the Elvis flavour (peanut butter, caramel and banana) will set you back a fiver, and bagels go up to £6 or more – and although you could cut costs and take out, it's much more fun to perch at one of the Formica tables or the little counter and soak up the atmosphere.

There's a big hunk o' love in the room for Elvis, naturally, and an impeccable collection of ceramics – long-lashed poodles and sad-eyed vegetables, cowboy wagon salt-and-pepper shakers, classic Homemaker china – along with Gene Vincent posters, light-up Bambis, vintage film footage beamed from a retro TV… you get the picture. The soundtrack comes courtesy of a hulking 50s jukebox, mixed with the clatter and chatter of the busy rockabilly staff. When it's time to leave, watch the next set of customers squeal with glee as they enter the room. It's not just a sugar high that will have you walking away with a big grin on your face.

Judith Michael and Daughter 🏺

Ⓐ 73 Regents Park Road NW1 8UY **☎** 020 7722 9000 **Ⓦ** www.judithmichael.com
Ⓞ Mon–Sat 10am–6pm, Sun noon–6pm

Whether it's a pendent flag from the Festival of Britain or a 1960s Miss Elegance trophy, the selection at Judith Michael and Daughter offers plenty of possible answers to the question of what to get for someone who appears to have everything.

Handy then that the shop is in Primrose Hill, whose affluent residents do appear to have everything. Run by the daughter of the shop's title, Gillian Anderson Price, it's a luxury store that perfectly fits its postcode; selling everything you might need for a dream Primrose Hill lifestyle, or some last-minute gift-buying. They really deliver on the promise of "vintage treasures" stated on their sign, offering some sublime examples of homewares and antiques. Their tapestry chairs, antique dressing tables, or reclaimed pieces of shop lighting would all artily enhance a luxurious home, in the same way their sparkling selection of jewellery would put a just-so finishing touch to an outfit.

The shop offers everything you could possibly want to entertain at home in true style, from Sèvres champagne glasses to silver tea strainers and prize 1930s teacups to novelty Deco ashtrays. And prices are reassuringly high. While that Festival flag may set you back £650 and the statue is priced at £198, at least you'd be guaranteed your neighbour wouldn't have the same piece.

The incredible richness of the stock means that it's a fascinating place to browse for serious collectors and wishful thinkers, as well as local residents: even if the pieces, and the lifestyle it so beautifully enhances, are beyond your budget.

Little Paris 🎭 🪑 🛋

A 262 Upper Street N1 2UQ ☎ 020 7704 9970 W www.littleparis.co.uk O Mon–Fri 11.30am–7.30pm, Sat 11am–7.30pm, Sun noon–6pm

As the name suggests, this shop specializes in things with a French flavour. Its range of contemporary jewellery, stationery and homewares, all sourced from across the Channel, is complemented with a well-judged selection of vintage. In fact, the entire basement of the Islington store – the more recent and spacious of the two Little Paris branches – is devoted to vintage furniture.

The vintage selection contains plenty to tickle your French fancy, whether your taste leans towards the more romantic or the industrial side of Parisian style. For the former, look out for dinky cocktail chairs, pretty crockery and framed fashion plates from Costume de Paris; for the latter, Breton-style lattice seats, an extensive selection of Tolix chairs and even some of the rarer Tolix tables are available. Plenty of lifestyle objects are in store too, with 1950s editions of *Paris Match*, vintage *dame-jeannes* for storing precious imported oil or wine and retro educational school charts (in French naturally). There are even some star pieces, such as Panton chairs, which – *quelle horreur* – come from outside France, although are seemingly allowed over the border due to their unquestionable design status. And, while the pricing in the shop isn't always that cheap, with such a stylish range of vintage for sale, there's no denying this store's chic.

M. Manze ⦀

⦁ 74 Chapel Market N1 9ER ☎ 020 7837 5270 ⏱ Mon 11am–3pm, Tue–Sat 11am–5pm, Sun 10.30am–4pm

Manze is a big name among London's pie and mash shops, the fast-disappearing breed that's been dishing up Cockney comfort food since the early 1900s. This splendid caff, while not part of the same dynasty as the celebrated East End Manzes, is a North London institution. Tucked away in Islington's Chapel Market, a corner of the borough that has, for now, valiantly resisted gentrification – give or take the odd deli stall hidden among the fitted sheets, wheelie luggage and washing-up bowls – Manze's has been feeding a hungry local crowd for more than a century.

The meat pies are flaky, flavoursome and filling, the mash piled high on a sea of liquor (a thick parsley gravy). Eels, when they're available, are stewed or jellied and traditionally served with a splash of vinegar, and drinks are limited to tea (70p!), coffee or a few cold drinks. At less than a fiver for a huge plate, the prices have yet to enter the 21st century, but it's the dining room that's the real knockout – restaurateurs from Soho to Shoreditch would give their right arms for these cool, marble-topped tables and polished dark-wood pews,

gleaming white-tiled walls and original mirrors. Unsurprisingly, it's become a favourite for trendy evening pop-ups who lure in the foodies and the bloggers to eat posh dinners in fab retro surrounds. A couple of things: they only take cash, and there's no loo. Small inconveniences, all in all.

Mint Vintage 👤 👤

Ⓐ 71–73 Stoke Newington High Street N16 8EL Ⓣ 0207 249 4567 Ⓦ www.mintvintage.co.uk Ⓞ Mon–Sat 11am–7pm, Sun noon–6pm

Originally based in Covent Garden, Mint relocated to Stoke Newington High Street in 2012. A wise move it was, placing Mint almost exactly halfway between the cluster of vintage shops closer to Dalston, and the pavement café stroll of Stoke Newington Church Street. Mint offers both quality staples and one-off–50s tan barn jackets with corduroy collars for men at £85, or ladies' 80s calf-length, buttery leather skirts and jumpsuits galore (many around £40).

Everything is hand-selected by people who know their trends--for a nineties-does-fifties look, you can find thick Pendleton shirts and Caterpillar boots; for an edgier, early-nineties club look, silk-scarf bomber jackets span a range of faux-Versace prints to striking motifs of polo players in graphic red and white (£45). The more unusual pieces draw attention: De La Soul-style coloured dungarees and oversized cardigans embellished with flower appliqués, stems wrapping around the sleeves, have held pride of place in their front window, to be snapped up the same day.

Hidden in a basement room is a collection of 70s and 80s handbags, and lightly-worn Ferragamo, Stuart Weitzman and even the odd pair of Yves Saint Laurent heels from the same time, for a bargainous £12–£18 a pair. Mint's owners plan to turn this room into a "denim cave" by 2013, expanding from their solid stock of the "big three" (Levis, Lee and Wrangler) vintage brands into a destination for unusual and collectable washes, cuts and labels.

Ooh-La-La! 🪑 🍴

Ⓐ 147 Holloway Road N7 8LX Ⓣ 020 7609 0455 Ⓦ www.facebook.com/pages/Ooh-La-La-Holloway/304777092942652 Ⓞ Mon–Sat 11am–6pm

Ooh-La-La! is a shop for people who like a bit of a challenge when shopping for vintage. Furniture, homewares and unusual one-off pieces: it's all here, if you're prepared to look for it.

Stock is jammed in and piled high (navigation gets tricky if there's more than five in the shop at a time), covering almost every decade and kind of taste. On a recent visit, highlights included an antique wardrobe, a G Plan chest of drawers and a cheery yellow Formica kitchen table. There's always an outstanding selection of home accessories such as dazzling Deco-style lighting, jostling for wall space with old shop signs and every sort of mirror imaginable, from pretty bevelled numbers to ornate hand-held looking glasses.

Make your way to the back of the shop and it's highly likely you'll unearth some brilliantly quirky pieces, whether that's a grooming kit for the most dapper kind of a man, or a gin or whisky dispenser for those in the need of a ready supply of Dutch courage, selling for just £10 each.

It's almost impossible to predict what you might come away with after a visit and that's its great charm. It's the perfect store for those who have a magpie eye, plenty of imagination and a bit of time to spare, rather than simply deep pockets.

Painted Black 🧑 🧑

Ⓐ 22 Veryan Court, Park Road N8 8JR Ⓣ 020 3417 6161 Ⓦ www.paintedblack.co.uk
Ⓞ Mon & Wed–Fri noon–6pm, Sat 11am–6pm, Sun noon–5pm

Painted Black is a small, busy and sociable shop. It's possible to chat to its staff for quite a while about their dog, Rose, and other pressing matters without even mentioning vintage (as their website states, "bitches and women alike love to shop at Painted Black"). However, talk to them about their stock and they'll prove to be every bit as enthusiastic and knowledgeable.

For its petite size, Painted Black crams in plenty of vintage, its speciality being womenswear from the 1950s onwards, with a small section devoted to menswear. There are some more unusual pieces too, which recently included a mid-century drinks cabinet and an original Paddington Bear begging to be looked after. Constantly changing displays are used to showcase anything and everything from a delectable selection of hats to the coolest vintage cameras.

If anything, the shop is almost too full of interesting things. Digging out the gems requires some dedicated scouring of the rails. Efforts are generally well rewarded though, whether it's with a glamorous 1950s number or a bargain £20 frock. Or just ask the staff, who will happily provide help and an honest opinion.

For more second-hand hunting in this neck of north London, pop into the Junk N8 Disorderly furniture shop just down the road, or visit one of the Crouch End "barboot market" nights in which both shops are involved. Combining vintage stalls with booze and music, a good evening is pretty much guaranteed.

Past Caring

A 54 Essex Road N1 8LT
T No phone **O** Mon–Sat
noon–6pm, Sun noon–5pm

Past Caring, wedged snugly
between a newsagent's
and a trendy little Italian
café on a shabby stretch
of Essex Road, has been
selling second-hand gear
since 1973. With few
concessions to fashion,
themes or lifestyle-shoot
styling, this unpretentious
spot has become a friendly
local landmark with its
ranks of coffee tables, old
trunks and headless mannequins crowded on the pavement outside. Pride of
place among this alfresco miscellany is often taken by an Emmanuelle-style
wicker chair – appropriately enough, given Past Caring's age.

Laid-back and easy-going, quietly buzzing with a steady stream of foraging
customers, this is a treasure trove for serious collectors and casual browsers alike.
Fashion types and vintage buffs often claim the place as their little secret, and old
Islington locals have been shopping here for years, picking up coffee tables and
coffee pots for a song. The window and front shelves are filled with the small pieces
– rare Czech glass alongside cheeky Babycham glasses, ugly plaster clown figurines
and retro dialling phones sitting side by side. Covetable vintage typewriters – from
Olivettis to antique Underwoods – are scattered all around, and there's a fair share
of 1950s G-Plan. You can pick up good furniture at amazingly low prices here – a
classic extendable oak table, for example, seating six, for around £175 – but the
bargains do tend to get snapped up fast by the local cognoscenti, so it's always
worth stopping by to see what they've come up with next.

Paul's Emporium ♪ ⸮

Ⓐ 386 York Way N7 9LW ☎ 020 7607 3000 Ⓞ Tue, Thurs & Fri noon–6pm, Sat 10.30am–5pm

A pair of elephant bookends that you remember from your parents' house, an ornament that looks just like one that your Gran owned and a church banner that reminds you of Scout pack meetings: Paul's Emporium is stuffed full with vaguely familiar-looking goods, the result of home and building clearances. The stock bears the noticeable marks of its previous existence and represents a jumble of different eras and styles. While this apparent lack of filtering means there are some items for sale that you'd be happy to leave to your memories, it also means there's plenty of potential for serendipitous discoveries.

Although there are a few larger items for sale – a solid-looking dark wood wardrobe selling for £220 for example – the majority are more portable pieces. Relatively commonplace second-hand finds – stacks of vinyl and shelves of books – are sold alongside more unusual items, such as a selection of handsome-looking walking sticks. Practical mirrors and pretty prints and photographs compete for wallspace with more esoteric artworks, like that old church banner, waiting to be bought by adventurous decorators. A rummage in a box of *cartes de visite* offers cheap thrills, with each image priced at only £1. In fact, bargain hunters are almost guaranteed to leave happy as everything in this shop, from jewellery to light fittings, is very reasonably priced.

Paul's Emporium is enjoyably free of pretensions. Adopt that attitude when you're visiting, and the combination of determination, elbow grease and some imagination will pay dividends in this particular quest for vintage treasures.

The Peanut Vendor ♪ ⸮

Ⓐ 133 Newington Green Road N1 4RA ☎ 020 7226 5727 Ⓦ www.thepeanutvendor. co.uk Ⓞ Tue–Thurs 10am–7pm (occasionally closed on Tue morning; call to check), Fri & Sat 10am–6pm, Sun noon–6pm

This appealingly crammed little furniture store is a perfect fit in its Stoke Newington neighbourhood. You won't find intimidatingly expensive vintage rarities here, nor a load of old tat at prices that saw you coming, but rather a soothing array of personally selected pieces from the owners' many market-scouring trips. The predominant feel is industrial chic, with more than a whiff of mid-century modern, but there are plenty of quirky anomalies, with snuggly wool blankets and 1950s ceramic rolling pins sharing space with modular Cado units and colossal industrial lamps.

Prices aren't the lowest in town, but neither are they stratospheric, and you're bound to find something that you won't be able to resist. A pristine nest of three Ercol beech and elm pebble tables, for around £390, for example, or four dark bentwood café chairs at £250 – the kind of pre-loved stuff that really does make a house a home.

Pelicans & Parrots

A 40 Stoke Newington Road N16 7XJ **T** 020 3215 2083 **W** www.pelicansandparrots. com **O** Mon–Sat noon–8pm, Sun noon–7pm

Pelicans & Parrots brings its own very particular stamp to the increasingly hip Stoke Newington/Dalston border. Housed in an old travel agents', this tranquil

little shop offers an intriguing mix of vintage fashion, retro furnishings and, well, Just Plain Interesting Stuff – how else to categorize the bison skull in a glass bell jar, the shimmering stuffed peacocks, or the huge feathered Bamileke headdresses recycled as flamboyant wallhangings? There's a laid-back, friendly vibe here, which makes it easy to linger – vinyl plays gently on the vintage hi-fi system, and owners Juliet da Silva and Ochuko Ojiri are always ready to chat.

Da Silva, herself a textile designer, sources most of the clothes from Italy, so whether you want to channel Sophia Loren in a sexy peasant dress or a well-upholstered swimsuit, or get spiffy in a sharp Valentino blazer, this would be the place to start – you could pick up a dress, shirt or pair of beautifully cut trousers for less than £40, and you might just end up deciding that the huge rusty keys, the vintage porn postcards or the spooky marionettes are must-haves, too. Their sister branch, Pelicans & Parrots Black, down the road at no.81, takes a similar approach, though with fewer clothes and more furniture – 1950s school desks for

£150, Parker Knoll wingbacks around £300, scuffed Victorian dining tables at £350 – along with more skulls, stuffed birds and birdcages. They also host events and art shows in the basement.

Ribbons & Taylor 🪗 💂

....

Ⓐ 157 Stoke Newington Church Street N16 0UD Ⓣ 020 7254 4735 Ⓦ www.ribbonsandtaylor.co.uk Ⓞ Tue–Sat 11am–6pm, Sun 11am–5.30pm(ish)

Sitting pretty behind its fuschia facade since the mid-1980s – those long-lost days when Stokey's now chichi Church Street was still a shabby hotbed of radical politics and cheap curry houses – Ribbons & Taylor is a vintage clothes shop that's earned the right to feel comfortable with itself. They know exactly what they're doing here, selling well-priced, well-selected and well-presented clothes for women and men in an inviting atmosphere. Offering easy, wearable gear from denim jeans to three-piece suits, Ribbons & Taylor is a staple stop-off for local shoppers whether they're vintage nuts or not.

It's always worth a root around in here. While you'll find some high street stuff – and if you've got a thing about M&S cashmere cardis, you're in luck – there are more than enough offbeat one-offs to keep the most eccentric sartorialist happy. A rail at the back, next to the wall-to-ceiling mirrors and between the two curtained-off changing areas, is where you'll find fancy dresses and gorgeous glad rags, with satin kimonos, 1950s florals and Lurex maxis making a pretty, very feminine ensemble. Another rail presents an immaculate set of men's woollen suits, still another offers women's suede coats in a variety of colours. The rest of the store is taken up with shirts and tops, boots and shoes, skirts and scarves and jewellery, along with whichever oddments they've laid their hands on this week. There are almost as many men's clothes as women's, with a natty range of waistcoats and a box of bow ties on the counter. Prices are extremely reasonable, with separates from around £10, coats and jackets from £15, and dresses from £20.

Ruby's 🍸

A 76 Stoke Newington Road N16 7XB **W** www.rubysdalston.com **O** Wed & Thurs 7–11pm, Fri & Sat 7pm–midnight

Owned by Castle Gibson, a super-cool props and shabby chic furniture company, Ruby's and its artfully distressed ambience could perhaps feel a bit bogus. Happily, though, this sweet little underground bar actually dishes up deliciously authentic vintage style with a huge dose of heart. Outside, all is simple – just a retro moviehouse sign above a plain black frontage – with a shabby staircase, clad in ancient cruddy lino, leading to the drinking den below. Here a dozen or so small tables and the glowing light give off a speakeasy vibe, while the chipped plaster and tile bricks could have come straight from 1970s New York. But then you notice the 1940s fireplace, topped with a little Deco clock and a dark-wood-framed mirror, and the tasselled standard lamps, and suddenly it feels like granny's parlour – all tea, toasted crumpets and evenings around the wireless. Albeit a wireless that's playing ska and classic soul.

It's an eclectic mix, for sure, but one that works. The crowd is friendly and relaxed – just as well, given the small space – and you'll be greeted warmly by the lovely staff, who direct you to a seat and take your order. The vintage beer mats may recall the glory days of Greene King IPA and Castle Bitter, but most people are here for the cocktails – which, at £8 a pop, include classics like the Sazerac, complete with absinthe rinse, and Mojitos served in retro milk bottles. You could also choose a craft beer or a Breton cider, or perhaps a simple glass of wine. Then just kick back and soak up the atmosphere. Granny, we're sure, would approve.

Scarlet Rage Vintage 💇

A 11 Topsfield Parade N8 8PR **W** www.scarletragevintage.com **O** Mon–Fri 10.30am–6pm, Sat 11am–6pm, Sun noon–6pm

Scarlet Rage Vintage comes as a bit of a surprise nestled within the chain shops of Crouch End's high street. And, despite its giveaway name, from the outside it looks more like a contemporary boutique than a vintage store. On our last visit, there were some puzzled faces from long-standing residents trying to get the measure of this relatively new shop. In fact, they'd probably find the boutique comparison helpful, as you could easily go into Scarlet Rage Vintage looking for a special dress for a wedding or other occasion and be expertly guided into buying something stunning. The shop is presented immaculately, from its whitewashed floorboards to the delicate teacups for sale, and the range of womenswear matches up to appearances, excelling in the pretty and the feminine, whether that's a beaded cardigan or a stunning piece of costume jewellery. Scarlet Rage Vintage holds a plentiful supply of dresses from the 1920s and 30s and goes up through the decades to include the loveliest examples of 1950s and early 60s style. The prices aren't bad either, with £85 being about standard for a dress.

There's also an adorable collection of novelty bags for sale. With embellishments that include golfing scenes and fruit baskets, there's probably a bag for almost every taste, and they'd make perfect presents, or a well-deserved treat for yourself. Much like the whole experience of visiting Scarlet Rage Vintage, in fact – a gorgeous, indulgent treat.

Strut

A 182 Stoke Newington Church Street N16 0JL **T** 020 7254 4387 **W** www. strutvintage.co.uk **O** Mon–Fri 10.30am–6pm, Sat & Sun 11am–7pm

When it joined Church Street, Stoke Newington's vintage stretch, in 2008, Strut immediately hit the spot for the neighbourhood's combination of scruffy hipster teens, money-splashing fashionistas and stylish, *Guardian*-reading mums. Its perfect fit was inevitable, perhaps, given that the stuff on sale comes from locals – Strut is a consignment shop, offering fifty percent of the sale price to the donor. The quality is impeccable: a carefully selected, seasonal range from the 1930s to the 1980s, with lots of designer pieces – from Alexander McQueen to Laura Ashley via Chloé, Dior, Moschino and Mugler – and vehemently no high-street or jumble-sale tat. Designer much of it may be, but the setting is comfortingly low-key – this is Stoke Newington, after all. Laid-back staff are always ready to chat, the soul-funk soundtrack is well judged, and, best of all, the prices are low. You'll pick up tops from around £20 and dresses from £30 – and it's a rare piece indeed that costs more than £125.

The front room, unadorned apart from a giant, multicoloured chandelier, features the key crowd-pleasers: dresses, mostly, from 1930s velvet numbers to 1950s florals. Jeans and casuals fill the anteroom, from where a corridor of classy jackets – and, with Strut's typically light touch, jaunty sun hats balanced on antlers – leads to the clearance shed at the back. This is the B-list room, where the less-in-season, less-in-fashion glad rags – the Lurex jumpsuits and the large-lapelled jackets – are relegated. Rest assured that even Strut's B-list, however, is a pretty starry prospect.

Vivien of Holloway 🎀

....

Ⓐ 294 Holloway Road N7 6NJ Ⓣ 020 7609 8754 Ⓦ www.vivienofholloway.com
Ⓞ Mon–Sat 10am–6pm, Sun 11am–6pm

Renowned for her attention-grabbing dresses, Vivien of Holloway has been bestowing this stretch of north London with some much-needed vintage allure since 2009.

Specializing in glamorous repro womenswear, Vivien is best known for her show stoppers: 1950s-style circle dresses, available in bright colours and bold patterns, and slinky 1940s-influenced designs. Her clothes take their cue from the golden age of Hollywood: the Rio top is inspired by Jane Russell in *The Outlaw*, for example, while another dress boasts of creating curves that would make Jayne Mansfield jealous. With playful nautically patterned shorts and waist-cinching halterneck tops also for sale, the shop offers plenty of choice for aspiring vintage starlets.

However, it's not all red carpet dressing. The Utility-style tea dresses are perfect for everyday wear, as are the high-waisted swing trousers based on an original World War II pattern, and the answer to many vintage fans' prayers comes in the perfect figure-hugging pair of jeans. Although you can shop the range online,

there are several compelling reasons to visit in person. One is the glamorous and attentive staff, always eager to pass on styling advice. The other is the clothing measurements, which are based on vintage sizing instead of current high street standards, thereby adding several dress sizes onto the unsuspecting customer. Thankfully, both the staff and the clothes themselves are extremely flattering and you'll definitely leave with your ego, though perhaps not your wallet, intact.

The shop also stocks a fantastic range of accessories, including brooches, hair accessories and shoes by Miss L Fire, and everything else you might possibly need to help create your desired impact.

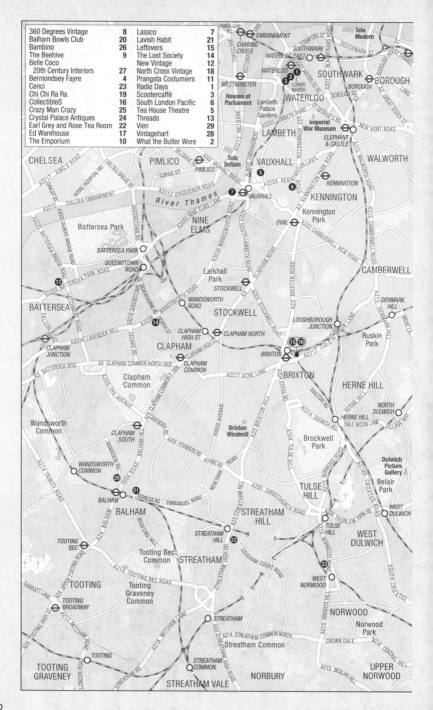

360 Degrees Vintage	8	Lassco	7
Balham Bowls Club	20	Lavish Habit	21
Bambino	26	Leftovers	15
The Beehive	9	The Lost Society	14
Belle Coco		New Vintage	12
20th Century Interiors	27	North Cross Vintage	18
Bermondsey Fayre	4	Prangsta Costumiers	11
Cenci	23	Radio Days	1
Chi Chi Ra Ra	19	Scootercaffè	3
CollectibleS	16	South London Pacific	6
Crazy Man Crazy	25	Tea House Theatre	5
Crystal Palace Antiques	24	Threads	13
Earl Grey and Rose Tea Room	22	Vien	29
Ed Warehouse	17	Vintagehart	28
The Emporium	10	What the Butler Wore	2

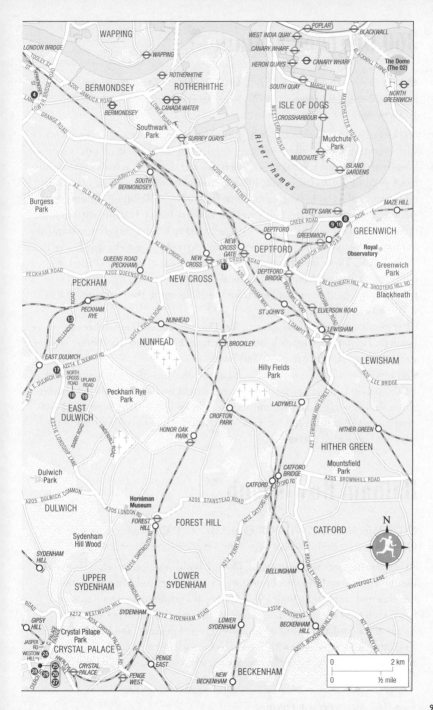

360 Degrees Vintage 👤 👤

Ⓐ 3/3a Greenwich Market SE10 9HZ ☎ 07904 709759 Ⓦ facebook.com/
pages/360–degrees–vintage/191470155232 Ⓞ Thurs–Fri noon–6pm, Sat–Sun
10.30am–6pm

360 Degrees is a mixed bag, evenly split between menswear and womenswear,
with everything from rails of military regalia (precisely labelled to the year and
branch of forces each garment was designed for) to a section featuring second-
hand wedding gowns (including 1950s gowns with full lace sleeves, like the
one worn by the Duchess of Cambridge for the Royal Wedding). The women's
stock varies in quality: the 1970s and 80s rails are full of brightly patterned
one hundred percent silk secretary dresses next to brash synthetics, crimplenes
like steel wool and the kind of nylon so staticky you can get electric shocks by
looking at it. These are all at the same prices as some of the full-skirted 50s
floral day dresses, in hand-stitched floral-printed cotton, on the next rail over. A
few 50s-inspired viscose numbers from the 1980s sneak their way onto the rails,
which may disappoint the purist.

For men's country and casualwear, 360 Degrees shines. It specializes in
Barbour, Belstaff and Lewis Leathers. Heritage brands and sharp overcoats are
well represented, as are foulards and braces to set off the look. A back room has
a homeware section that contains some authentic bolts of modernist printed
1950s curtain fabric, re-covered chairs and bright woollen and knitted blankets.
All in all, it's worth a look in, and a good sight better than the overpriced and
ubiquitous "keep calm and carry on" merchandise and faux-ethnic tat in the
adjacent Greenwich market.

Balham Bowls Club 🍸

Ⓐ 7–9 Ramsden Road SW12 8QX ☎ 020 8673 4700 Ⓦ balhambowlsclub.com
Ⓞ Mon 4pm–11pm, Tue–Thurs 4pm–1am, Sat noon–1am, Sun noon–11pm

This sprawling pub and restaurant, just off Balham's high street, feels like the
best bits of a boarding school refectory and a country pub have been stuck
together and jazzed up a bit by Wes Anderson's set designer. Once an actual
bowls club (and hung with memorabilia), the pub part stretches over three
rooms and a garden. It's full of squashy velvet club chairs and leather sofas to
sink into for an afternoon with friends, colour-supplement-stuffed newspapers
and mugs of real ale. Fires blaze in winter, when local twenty- and thirty-

somethings come here to get cosy. Families are welcome and there are high chairs in the more formal restaurant side.

Food is gastro-British: traditional fare brought into the 21st century. Bangers and mash is "wild boar sausage with garlic mash", and peanut butter ice cream is on offer alongside banoffee pie. Mains are between £9.50 and £12.50, starters around £6. Sundays are exceptionally popular with the brunch crowd. A notice board at the entrance looks like something you might find at a working men's club, tacked with flyers for chess nights, local gigs and events (there is a large function room for hire upstairs). No wonder, then, that The Vintage Event, Balham's monthly retro jumble sale and meet-up, calls the Balham Bowls Club its home.

Bambino

A 18 Church Road SE19 2ET **T** 020 8653 9250 **O** Thurs–Sun 11am–6pm

Unpretentious salvage is the order of the day in this shambolic den of cupboards, cabinets, figurines and props. High-quality pieces, such as a Danish modern vanity dresser, nestle against bargain-priced chipped occasional tables from the 1970s. Anatomical models, porcelain dogs, burnt-orange telephones and framed school photos jostle for space on any available surface. The seasoned ex-Portobello trader who runs Bambino knows the market and everything is priced fairly – though perhaps there are not as many bargains here as you might expect from the layout of the shop floor.

Bambino is spread over two storefronts. One contains mostly larger furniture, while the other presents stacks of naugahyde suitcases, 1970s jigsaws, umbrella stands filled with briar canes and croquet mallets and rails stuffed with combat fatigues and Lewis Leathers. (A biker-themed fashion shoot for *Vogue*, starring Kate Moss, featured Bambino's Lewis stock.) At the front of this side of the shop is a modest coffee bar serving cakes and strong espresso, a helpful pick-me-up for anyone visiting the string of vintage shops along Church Road. Of all the oddities that can be found here, the yellow submarine perched in the front window is the most eye-catching. Rescued from Brighton Pier, it's been lovingly restored, but it is sadly not for sale.

The Beehive 🐝 🐱 ◉

Ⓐ 322 Creek Road SE10 9SW Ⓣ 020 8858 1964 Ⓦ retrobatesvintage.com
Ⓞ Mon–Fri 10.30am–6pm, Sat–Sun 10.30am–6.30pm

It's buzzing, that's for sure. People come to The Beehive to hang out and chat with each other – or to Deborah, the loquacious cat's-eye glasses-wearing manager, who says she "lives in crimplene", and who makes everyone feel welcome. This is entry-level vintage at its most wearable, selected to fit with wardrobes that mix vintage, high street and the odd designer piece. Think 80s prom dresses with ra-ra skirts, 70s cheesecloth blouses, men's terrycloth sportswear, and 90s trousers in primary colours that would work in a TLC video. While few things in here are truly outrageous, neither are the prices, and there are a few sale rails for even better bargains. Stock is equally split between menswear and womenswear, and while there aren't too many shoes here, the glittery disco heels and leopard creepers, at half the price of Topshop's new versions, are ready to party.

The Beehive is half of a two-room shop that also contains Casbah Records, where cratediggers can flick through stacks of vinyl records while their friends or partners try on clothes next door. In a stroke of marketing genius, The Beehive now stocks refurbished plug-and-play turntables with built-in speakers at around £100.

Belle Coco 20ᵗʰ Century Interiors

40 Church Road SE19 2ET 📞 02000 111715/07944 143812 🌐 www.bellecoco. com 🕐 Wed 1.30pm–5pm, Thurs–Fri 10am–5pm, Sat 10am–6pm, Sun 11am–5pm

Do not be deceived by the French barrel planters and wooden benches on the pavement outside: sleek, teak and space-age mid-century modernism is the star of this show, with a sprinkling of Art Deco (there's a birds-eye maple drinks cabinet here that lights up when opened, which would send Noel Coward into raptures). Chairs, side tables, shelves and ornaments fill the shop floor, while larger, more fragile pieces are kept in the basement or in storage offsite. These are best viewed on the store's website, which also boasts a range of props available for hire on film or photoshoots.

Lamps, chandeliers and unusual light fittings – including an anglepoise lamp cluster constructed from a set of hairdressers' dryer pods – dangle from every available inch of ceiling. What's surprising is that they all work. All of the light fittings and plugs are rewired to meet modern power and safety requirements, and are sold with a guarantee. Every piece has been properly researched to restore it to its original glory. A G-plan table has been re-finished to remove any coffee rings left by previous users; the ten-millimetre smoked glass of a Howard Miller chrome trolley has been replaced so well that it's impossible to tell it's a recent fix. For such a highly collectable era, prices are very reasonable, with affordable geometric coloured glass vases at the cheaper end to a flawless Merano hanging lamp at £3000, which looks like it beamed itself down from the set of *Star Trek*. While you won't find any insanely great bargains here, the restorers' skills are such that whatever you find will last another forty or fifty years or more.

Bermondsey Fayre 🙂 😎

Ⓐ 212 Bermondsey Street SE1 3TQ Ⓣ 020 7403 2133 Ⓦ www.bermondseyfayre.
com Ⓞ Tue 11.30am–5.30pm, Wed 11.30am–7pm, Thurs 11.30am–6.30pm, Fri–Sat
11am–6pm, Sun noon–5pm

Bermondsey Fayre sounds like it ought to cater to lute-strumming folkies and
soft-psych fans, or hippies who run barefoot through overgrown lawns while
wearing crowns of daisy chains. This would not be totally inaccurate: incense
and crystals aside, the shop also doubles as a yoga studio (after hours, the rails
are rolled to the sides of the main room, and yoga mats are spread out between
them) and art gallery, and holds empowerment workshops for women.

For vintage lovers, however, the three lines of vintage-styled clothes it produces
are worth a look. Some Like it Holy is a range of dresses cut to 50s shapes from
period fabrics, with shawl collars, three quarter sleeves, and pencil or skater
skirts. Its designer, Malou Mella, ran the original Merchant of Europe vintage
boutique in Portobello Market, and her men's line Spaghetti Western is full of

soft button-down shirts in faded paisleys
and William Morris prints, overblown floppy
silk cravats and reworked tweed vests and
trousers with braces, which would perfectly
suit members of the 60s Canterbury folk/
psych scene. Children's smocks and jumper
dresses, in 1960s and 70s fabrics with the
kinds of prints that inspired Orla Kiely, are
priced at £20–40.

Recycling, especially by local artisans, is
part of the store's ethos. There are craft
kits with materials and instructions to sew a
stuffed owl cushion out of 70s fabrics. Some
of the shop's more crafty offerings may be
a bit *Portlandia* put-a-bird-on-it, but this
shop has its heart in the right place.

Cenci 🙂 😎

Ⓐ 4 Nettlefold Place SE27 0JW Ⓣ 020 8766 8564 Ⓦ cenci.co.uk
Ⓞ Mon–Sat 110am–6pm

It's not the easiest place to find, tucked away in an industrial estate, with the door hidden behind an intimidating steel grille. But buzz through to enter, and you'll be admitted into an instantly welcoming shop smelling of clean, warm wool. While Cenci specializes in all kinds of clothes for men and women (and some childrenswear) from the 1940s to the early 1980s, it is known for supply of bright, quality knits untouched by moths or the ravages of time. Woollens are stacked by type – Breton button-ups, white 1940s gym jumpers, soft angoras for 50s sweater girls – and so are berets and felted hats in a rainbow of colours.

Cenci began as a vintage store in Florence in the early 1970s, and had a previous long life trading from a shop in Covent Garden after that. Higher rents closed the Covent Garden store in the early 2000s, so the current site – the former warehouse – opened to the public. It is both huge and crammed, with air-hostess bags and letterman vests (studded with 50s rhinestone pins and sweater guards) stuffed into every crevice. Often clothes are layered on hangers, styled into looks with cinematic flair, like a 70s sky-blue maxi dress with micro-accordion pleats with a contrasting silk jacket slipped on top and a scarf tied at the neck for good measure. Men's suits – mostly Italian – are around £70, and there are shelves of button-downs from the sedate to the acid-inspired still in their original packages.

Chi Chi Ra Ra 👤👤

Ⓐ 18 Upland Road SE22 9EF **Ⓣ** 07714 961 027 **Ⓦ** www.twitter.com/chichirara1
Ⓞ Tues–Sat 10.00am–5.30pm & some Sundays 11am–4pm (phone first)

Chi Chi Ra Ra has always been ahead of the game, catering to East Dulwich's most fashionable and eccentric dressers for the past fifteen years, long before

the area grew into the village it is now, with its artisanal delis and shops selling educational toys. These early adopters now come in to flick though 1940s lavender and floral shirtwaist day dresses and coo over the cyclamen pink silk chiffon lounging pyjamas with a double row of buttons down the front – very Chanel – with equally well-dressed kids in tow.

It's a small shop, but does not feel crowded or fussy, and locals hang around and chat. Fragile fabrics, including some of the filmiest, creamiest silks and crepe chiffons of the 1930s and 1940s, are well-tended and smooth, with none of the tiny pin holes or stains that plague even the most cared for pieces from that era. Heather, the owner, is a former designer for Vogue, and her eye for proportion and detail is evident in the choice of patterned blouses, rainbow-sequined disco jackets, or geometric printed scarves. (Vintage runs in the family, too – her brother runs Hunky Dory in East London's Brick Lane). She personally chooses everything here, knows the stock inside and out, and can also tell customers whether a piece will suit their shape, suggesting more flattering options with supreme tact and thoughtfulness. It's no wonder they keep coming back.

CollectibleS

Ⓐ 82 5th Avenue, Brixton Village, Coldharbour Lane SW9 8PS **☎** 07946 038430
Ⓦ www.collectible-s.co.uk **Ⓞ** Tue–Sat 10am–5pm, Sun 10am–4pm

A sweet and unpretentious stall in Brixton Market, with its homely checkerboard black and white linoleum floors, CollectibleS sells tea sets, picnic hampers and other vintage crockery with no hard sell or outrageous mark-up (and no teacups filled with candles, either).

Bright colours rule-porcelain jugs with a Clarice Cliff-inspired swirly pattern in sherbet hues sit next to a complete, unchipped goldenrod tea set from the late 1960s with plates and bowls, and an orange 50s fiestaware jug that could set off Geiger counters. Display cases in the centre of the room sparkle with eye-

catching gold bow tie, circle and rhinestone brooches and "button" style earrings made of large faux pearls – all at £10, and a nearby original music box with pirouetting ballerina is £25. A shelf of "orphan" unmatched teacups and saucers is worth a look, with many priced between £5 and £10, in odd but colourful patterns. Like everything else in CollectibleS, they are ladylike and proper, but slightly wonky, and all the more appealing for it.

Crazy Man Crazy

Ⓐ 18a Church Road SE19 2ET **Ⓟ** 020 8653 6548 **Ⓦ** www.crazymancrazylondon.co.uk
Ⓞ Thurs–Sun 10am–6pm

This menswear shop is situated halfway down Crystal Palace's vintage-district Church Road, but it might be easier to find by looking out for hot rods parked outside, or slick-quiffed bikers slouching around the door, having a smoke. The shop is small, but carefully decked-out for fans of the 50s greaser, biker, rockabilly aesthetic. There are a few rows of heritage macs and brogues, flat caps and even the odd Biggles flight hood, but Americana reigns supreme. Denim is straight-cut to a James Dean silhouette while hard-wearing big-E Levis, Edwin and original Japanese Evisu jeans are all stocked. Selvedge fans in search of the perfect turn-up will not

be disappointed. Pristine Italian suits and Hawaiian and tiki shirts hang from the walls, between bongo beat and skiffle albums and local artists' paintings. It's a sad truth that high-quality vintage menswear is always harder to source than womenswear, but repro steps in to fill these gaps, and efforts from German brand Pike Brothers and others offer better than passable flying jackets, plaid woollen capes and workwear in a full range of sizes (that other bugbear of the vintage-chasing man). To top it all off, don't miss the shop's own line of T-shirts, screenprinted with the small ads from 40s and 50s American motorcycle magazines, in all their typographical glory.

Crystal Palace Antiques

Ⓐ Junction of Westow Hill and Jasper Road SE19 1SJ **Ⓣ** 020 8480 7042 **Ⓦ** www.
crystalpalaceantiques.com **Ⓞ** Mon–Sat 10am–6pm, Sun 10am–5pm

This is the anti-IKEA: a former Victorian warehouse converted into four floors of furniture, from the 1850s to the 1970s, with mazes of rooms which are a pleasure to get lost in. (That said, if you have small children in pushchairs, or difficulty with stairs, this may not be such a pleasure.) Quality and prices vary wildly; the grand and the garish are often side by side.

Arts and Crafts dining tables, Art Deco and Art Nouveau chairs, mirrors and dressing tables, and unusual ornaments are sprinkled through the two upper floors. A lumpy velvet-covered Edwardian chaise longue sits around the corner from an egg-shaped space age 1960s white sofa with a tangerine cushion.

The first thing visible on entering is a ground floor laden with heavy and serious Victorian furniture, followed by a room containing industrial planning cabinets, slightly seedy 1970s sofas and framed paintings of children with big eyes and a single falling tear. The basement is full of Scandinavian modern furniture yet couldn't be further from IKEA: these pieces are the real thing, signed and priced accordingly (from £400–£1000 or more).

Earl Grey and Rose Tea Room 🧁

Ⓐ 1 Streatleigh Parade, Leigham Road SW16 1EQ **Ⓣ** 020 8696 0375 **Ⓦ** www.twitter.com/EarlgreyandRose **Ⓞ** Mon–Fri 9.30am–5.30pm, Sat 10.30am–5.30pm, Sun 10.30am–4.30pm

Decorated in a bright, breezy explosion of floral chintz fabrics to put Cath Kidston to shame, Streatham's lively tearoom and café regularly tops lists of bloggers' favourite vintage-themed haunts. It is also the hub of south London's DIY crafting and baking scene. Everything on sale here – from salad dressings, chutneys and the bunting that drapes across the walls and ceiling – is hand-made in store. Crafters are more than welcome: a bank of sewing machines to the side of the dining area can be hired for £3.50 per hour by anyone aged over sixteen who knows how to use one. Sewing and jewellery-making classes offered in store have proved very popular.

You can sip herbal or flavoured boutique tea from delicate, mismatched teacups and saucers while sampling one or more of the lemon, rose or strawberry cupcakes in rainbow pastels. (A window is filled with cake stands heaped with so many flavours of cakes and pastries that it is difficult to choose.) Savoury dishes are available for visitors who just want a deli sandwich in a fresh-baked sourdough baguette or a salad: a good lunch or tea and cake can be had for under a tenner. Get here early for the Guinness and chocolate cupcakes – a local favourite that sells out quickly.

Ed Warehouse 🪑🗼👤🐟

Ⓐ 1 Zenoria Street SE22 8HP Ⓣ 020 8693 3033
Ⓦ www.edwarehouse.co.uk Ⓞ Tue–Fri 10am–5pm, Sat 10am–6pm, Sun 11am–5pm

Five years ago, Ed Hynes transformed this old electrical wholesalers' warehouse into a vintage department store of sorts: individual sellers' wares are displayed in sections devoted to clothing, furniture and homeware. There is also a watch-repair stand, a coffee bar, a stall selling wool and knitting needles and – as befits the family-friendly nature of East Dulwich – a store devoted to childrens' shoes that properly fit.

Upstairs, in the furniture section, the quality of items is hit or miss. A few chairs that look like hotel banqueting surplus share space with a 50s Formica-topped teak dining table and a leather and chrome 1970s sofa. The price asked for a set of four, unsigned, Scandinavian modernist wooden chairs seems a bit steep, though they are quite attractive. This inconsistency is probably due to quirks of particular vendors. Homeware and clothes are downstairs (with the aforementioned concessions). Vintage fabric-covered cushions are comparable in price to IKEA but much more stylish. Antique mirrors, enamel street signs, mannequins and steamer trunks can all be found in a back room. Out front, clothing concession Pure Vintage gathers its stock with an eye to the 1970s style of Yves St Laurent and Guy Bourdin photographs. Look out for magentas, mustards and purples, and slinky long chiffon gowns. A black 1940s crepe skirt with a bustle is £45, and a houndstooth Karl Lagerfeld suit from the 1980s, in a 1940s film noir cut, is £75.

The Emporium 👤 👤

ⓐ 330–332 Creek Road SE10 9SW ⓣ 020 8305 1670 ⓞ Wed–Sun 10am–6pm

The snazzy, jazzy Emporium is the place for lounge lizards or sharp-dressed aspiring Rat Packers, selling deadstock and as-new tweed and wool suits from the 1960s and 70s. Dinner jackets rub shoulders with 70s beige safari jackets and cotton button-down shirts. Racks of mostly narrow silk and knitted ties in dayglo, sunset and baby powder pastels complete the look, as do cases of the kind of thick black plastic specs favoured by Michael Caine in his heyday, and sunglass frames by Dior, Cazal and Ferrari. There are shelves of men's hats for all occasions. (Hats are all new here, so that they can be "worn in" to each customer's head shape, and also for reasons of hygiene, avoiding decades-old dandruff.) Perhaps unsurprisingly, there is a cache of photos near the tills of

Emporium clothes that have been used in films.

The ladies' selection is smaller, but jacquard dresses in cream and cocoa with a chain-link weave and original Italian shop tags and a turquoise straight-cut brushed polyester shift would suit a glamorous suburban Mrs Robinson. For today's wannabe bombshells, there are long evening gowns from the 1930s to the 70s, which are zipped up in garment bags behind the counter to protect delicate satins, feathers and fringing from grabby hands. But the staff are more than happy to pull them out if asked.

Lassco

A 30 Wandsworth Road SW8 2LG **T** 020 7501 7775 **W** www.lassco.co.uk **O** Mon–Fri 9am–5.30pm, Sat 10am–5pm, Sun 11am–5pm; café is open 8.30am–5.30pm; restaurant is open for lunch 1pm–3pm and 6pm–11pm for dinner, Tue–Sun

Lassco bills itself as home to "reclamation, ornament and curiosities", and sells all sorts of interior marvels from the mid-19th to mid-20th centuries. The basement is filled with architectural salvage including Edwardian marble chimney-pieces and on the ground and upper floors, vintage decorators can find French horological prints and rolls of the sturdy red, green and yellow tartan moquette that upholstered the original Routemaster buses. In adjoining rooms, you'll find children's stacking chairs designed by Robin Day and a menagerie of game trophies, including the head of a panther shot in India in 1928. Perhaps best of all is a room devoted to doorknobs, hinges, enamelled letters and numbers to mark addresses, all dated and catalogued to take the guesswork out of home restoration projects.

This flagship branch (there are others in Bermondsey and Oxfordshire) fills Brunswick House, an imposing Georgian mansion standing staunchly against the surrounding new-build glass and concrete of Vauxhall. Most of the showrooms

can be hired for a bit of country house elegance for book launches, dinners, parties, photoshoots or other events – phone for prices and availability. During the day, the bar and café (styled like an old music hall) are filled with design types in architectural glasses, sipping flat whites and soaking up inspiration.

Lavish Habit ╫ 🧁 🪑 🍸

Ⓐ 75 Bedford Hill SW12 9HA Ⓣ 020 8355 1270 Ⓦ www.facebook.com/LavishHabit
Ⓞ Mon–Fri 8.30am–6pm, Sat 9.30am–6pm, Sun 10am–6pm

It's not just Balham's top brunch destination, the location of choice for the local yummy mummies and laptop elite to dawdle over cappucinos. The furniture rooms downstairs are a delight, doing the folksy-quirky, upscale flea-market thing that Anthropologie stores do – but better. Lavish Habit's basement is full of repurposed stage lights, slick Olivetti typewriters in shades of racing orange and bits of French rusticism, with cubes of Savon de Marseille olive oil soap, muslin tea towels and ancient mangles to wring them out.

Everything here has been so well preserved that it could pass for repro; where things have been restored, it's with an eye for each piece's historical context. "Upcycling" can be a dirty word, but here, pinball machines have been rewired for modern plugs, and furniture is painted in the dove greys, petrol blues or kitchen greens of the appropriate period. 1930s blond wooden school desks and carbon-coloured filing cabinets are completely unscratched. A G-plan dining set has been polished to a factory-fresh sheen, with chairs re-covered in period-perfect Marimekko fabrics.

Upstairs, there are a few whimsically printed sundresses and ubiquitous owl pendants that look contemporary with a vintage twist. Still, the coffee is freshly ground, sharp and smooth, and the counter is spread with an inviting array of artisanal walnut and raisin bread, loose-leaf teas, Spanish tortillas and small pancakes with Greek yoghurt, berries and maple syrup. For smokers on sunny days, a secret garden stretches out the back, and there is a changing room for mums and dads, with plenty of space for pushchairs.

Leftovers 🗿

Ⓐ Unit 71, Brixton Village SW9 8PS Ⓣ 020 7011 1918 Ⓦ www.facebook.com/
leftoversbrixton Ⓞ Mon–Wed 11am–5.30pm, Thurs 11am–10pm, Fri–Sat 11am–5.30pm

An oasis of calm amid the Brixton market bustle, Leftovers blends 1930s homespun charm with French chic. While there are a few fisherman's woollen jumpers and overalls for very small children, Leftovers is a shop for the ladies – and specifically the kind of ladies who want to dress like a young Coco Chanel or an editorial from *Lula* magazine. Most of the clothes are sourced from antique markets and estate sales in the south of France, and the attention to detail in some of them is breathtaking: handpicked pleats and pin-tucking on linen and

cotton smocks and nightdresses from the 30s or the individually sewn beads on a black twenties flapper dress. A grey lace tea gown from the 1940s here could compete with catwalk creations for its intricate seaming and solid construction.

The real "leftovers" are found in the charming notions cases near the front of the store. Antique lace collars, ribbons, buttons and epaulettes are stacked on hand-stamped cards. Another rail, of 1960s and 70s apron dresses, printed cotton flares, pinafores and polka-dot blouses and a bin of espadrilles in burgundy and navy stripes and sun-washed, unusual colours, add an extra 70s Mediterranean casual feel.

The Lost Society 🧁 🍸

ⓐ 697 Wandsworth Road SW8 3JF ⓣ 020 7652 6526 ⓦ www.lostsociety.co.uk
ⓞ Thurs 5pm–midnight, Fri–Sat 4pm–2am

Lost Society is the kind of hidden oasis of twinkling decadence where one could imagine a pack of Evelyn Waugh's Bright Young Things spilling out of a Packard after a night of parties and dancing, only to step inside and glide upstairs to party and dance until the next day. This former 16th-century barn has been reworked into rooms resembling a panelled, book-lined library, an enclosed garden terrace, and a chandelier-spangled baroque saloon for gaiety girls and their upper-crust gentlemen callers. (Decorative touches from the 1880s to the 1930s are thrown together for an over-the-top, romantic overload.) There are also formal dining rooms for a civilized meal before taking in Friday

evening entertainments of cocktails, dancing, cabaret and burlesque upstairs.

On Saturdays and Sundays, high tea is served from 2pm to 5pm, in surroundings similar to the hotel dining scenes in *Death in Venice*, all white tablecloths and natural light, (£25 per person with cocktails, £20 per person without). Sundays also feature live acts.

It has a sister pub and restaurant: the Lost Angel and Gaslight Grill (Ⓐ339 Battersea Park Road W11 4LS Ⓣ020 7622 2112 Ⓦwww.lostangel.co.uk ⓄMon–Thurs 5pm–11pm, kitchen closes at 10pm). This shares similar aesthetics, but on a toned-down scale. There are dark wood floors, vermilion walls, ferns and playful nods to English eccentricity, like a phone booth with a birdcage containing a taxidermied owl inside. The Gaslight Grill specializes in seasonal British produce, and prime cuts of rare breed meats, especially steak (though there are vegetarian options available). Both are worth checking out for their speciality gin cocktails, especially the "Aviation", mixed with *créme de violet*.

New Vintage 🪑 🍸

Ⓐ 256 Battersea Park Road SW11 3BP Ⓣ 0203 490 6097 Ⓦ www.newvintage.co.uk

Boudoir furniture on a budget is New Vintage's stock in trade. Sturdy oak chests of drawers, repainted in shabby-chic pastels, share floor space with dressing tables artfully decoupaged with pin-up beauties pasted onto Osborne & Little heritage wallpapers. These vanities and occasional tables are handmade by local artist Sue Trenchard, and are popular with the burlesque set.

Small wall mirrors gleam in gilded frames and prints of Napoleonic and Elizabethan courtesans pout fetchingly from the walls. Vintage curtains, in 1950s–70s prints, are all measured, and all £10. Frilly and tasselled lampshades abound, and several of these have been bought by VV Rouleaux, the ribbons and trimmings shop favoured by top designers and stylists, to decorate their interiors in Marylebone. There are a few truly strange things here – a cabinet painted with a portrait of Bruce Lee in his 70s heyday and a guitar case tribute to Bonnie Raitt stood out against the prevailing aesthetic on a recent visit, but both were labelled with "sold" tags. That said, the rail of 50s dresses at the back of the store can turn up real finds.

North Cross Vintage

Ⓐ 31 North Cross Road SE22 9ET Ⓣ 07984 419373 Ⓞ Fri 11am–6pm, Sat 10am–6pm, Sun 11am–5pm. All bank holiday Mondays, noon–5pm. 1–24 December, 11am–6pm, all week.

If you can't find the place, just look for the sheep on top of the car. The entrance to North Cross Vintage is actually around the corner from North Cross Road, on Felbrigg Road, and there's no sign, but between the sheep and the stream of visitors going in, it's not that hard to locate. Inside is a treasure trove of everyday pre-war and mid-century crockery: 1950s enamelled coffee grinders, bread bins and brass jugs. Books and knicknacks here could re-create a fantasy Enid Blyton domestic landscape, as could picnic hampers and nursery china with scenes from Beatrix Potter and anthropomorphic animals (but thankfully no gollywogs). Most is sourced from estate sales throughout England, especially around Bristol and the West Country, which explains the lower than average (for London) prices. (It's worth knowing that the shop only accepts cash or cheques.)

Shelves of Baedeker guides and Penguin classics jostle with wind-up gramophones and French film magazines from the 1930s; for the would-be adventurer, pith helmets, binoculars, stuffed birds in cases and 1930s wall charts mapping far-flung regions of the former empire hang from the walls. Printer's cases – both empty and filled with thimbles and small figurines – flank tables laid with plates and mugs celebrating the royals through the ages. A patio area is lined with garden furniture, from wrought-iron chairs and tables to planters made from steel hip baths. It's all very British and jolly good fun.

Prangsta Costumiers

A 304 New Cross Road SE14 6AF **T** 020 8694 9869 **W** www.prangsta.co.uk
O Mon–Sat 11am–7pm or by appointment

The gothic tattoo-art fairies on Prangsta's shutters give a punky, chaotic Camden Market vibe. Ignore this. Prangsta is a costume hire shop without a hint of any of the plasticky novelties and ill-fitting, flammable nylon tunics in bags associated with fancy dress. Instead, imagine a visit to Angela Carter's magic toyshop by way of Alice's rabbit hole. What you'll find here are rails of silken, hand-beaded flapper and bias-cut dresses from the twenties and thirties to shame the wardrobe department of *Downton Abbey*. Sumptuous velvet suits with jabots and frills await the would-be dandy or gentleman pirate, and artfully constructed masks of Toad, Rat, Mole and Badger from *Wind in the Willows* hang from the theatre-red walls alongside a chain-mail suit so heavy that it comes with a warning. High end, bohemian, theatrical and louche, it's no wonder singer Florence Welch has come here to find outfits for her videos.

For most ensembles, rental prices start at £100 per day, but masks and hats can be rented for £50 per day. While some costumes can be hired on the spot, it's best to phone ahead. Prangsta prides itself on sourcing garments to flatter each customer's shape and to suit any theme, from masquerade to steampunk Victoriana. An off-site warehouse holds even more costumes than can be shown on the shop floor, and the knowledgable staff will sift through these to find a selection of options to suit the most exotic requests.

Radio Days

A 87 Lower Marsh SE1 7AB **T** 020 7928 0800 **W** www.radiodaysvintage.co.uk
O Mon–Sat 10am–6pm except Fri, 10am–7pm and by appointment

Radio Days is a stone's throw from the National Theatre, which must be a huge relief to harassed costumiers and prop wranglers. This is a one-stop shop for anyone looking for vintage magazines (from 1960s newspaper photo supplements to nineties music papers), glassware or bakelite phones in Eames colours. The 1940s to the 60s are the focus here (with a few outlier pieces from the 1920s, 30s or 70s) and anyone looking to complete a top-to-toe look is in accessory heaven. Cases of brooches, watches and eyeglass frames are surrounded by racks of ties, scarves and braces of all widths and materials, packets of dress patterns, stockings and enamel hairgrips, and pipes and cigarette holders. Hats – from sculpted cloches to flying-saucer net confections, as well as panamas and fedoras – line entire walls. There is a fair selection of ladies' clothing from size 16 and up, which can sometimes be tricky to find when searching for vintage. A discount trunk (everything under £20) is stuffed with wiggle dresses in pristine burgundy wool crepe and floaty floral chiffon

hostess gowns – it's overflowing with gorgeous pieces in all sizes. Men's camel-hair and crombie overcoats and Italian wool jumpers are time-capsule fresh. Radio Days also sells vintage furs, such as plush cocoa chubbies and creamy rabbit car coats. Many London vintage and second-hand stores won't sell them, but a sign on the door explains that all proceeds from these sales go to animal welfare charities. The witty, over-the-top window displays are frequently updated and well worth a look if you're in the Waterloo area, even if the shop itself is closed.

Scootercaffè   Y   🧁

....

Ⓐ 132 Lower Marsh SE1 7AE   ☎ 020 7620 1421   Ⓞ Mon–Thurs 8.30am–11pm, Sat 10am–midnight, Sun 10am–11pm

Formerly known as Scooterworks, this fully licensed, open-until-late café is a favourite for book launches and cast parties, and shoppers taking a break after visiting Radio Days or What the Butler Wore on the same street. The name tells you everything you need to know: Scootercaffè is full of scooter parts, photos and rally memorabilia. A large Vespa sign and scooter lurk in the front window. Coffee is appropriately strong, traditional scones and Victoria sponge are freshly baked and generous, and the atmosphere and mismatched furniture add to the feel of post-war, post-rationing teenage excitement.

Scootercaffè is the spiritual heir to the beatnik hangout themed coffee bars like The Moka (opened by Gina Lollobrigida) and La Macabre (decorated with skulls and coffins) that used to line Soho and Piccadilly in the 1950s and 60s. The basement sometimes hosts small gigs, comedy or performance nights (usually on Tuesday and Wednesday nights, but this changes, so phone for details), and the back garden is a haven for smokers. WiFi is free, and it's not unusual to see quiffed laptop warriors tapping away and nursing espressos – or Italian beers – for hours.

South London Pacific 🍸

Ⓐ 340 Kennington Road SE11 4AD **Ⓣ** 020 7820 9189 **Ⓦ** www.southlondonpacific. com **Ⓞ** Fri 6pm–3am, Sat 7pm–3am; phone or check website for Sunday event details

The interior could not have been better designed: wicker and bamboo furniture, zebra-print cushions, low light and a rush-covered hut of a bar strewn with parrots and tropicalia – with a "tiki jail" and a hula warrior shield suspended over the dance floor. It's tacky but not tasteless and a lot of fun. It's not quite what it was when it opened a decade ago, when swing dance had not yet been eclipsed by tease and cabaret, and the lounge/kitsch scene clung to the last of its late 90s cachet. As the 2000s rolled into the 2010s, the lure of the tiki bar lost its appeal to all but the most determined connoiseurs. It's due a comeback but South London Pacific has had to adapt to survive.

On Friday and Saturday nights DJs play reggae, chart pop and classic rock, and while you can still drink classic tiki cocktails, mojitos and capirinhas beneath scowling carved idols, patrons are happy-hour-chasing locals out for a good time at the end of the week, and not inclined to dress the part. But, for the full-on retro experience, every third Sunday of each month hosts "Hula Boogie", a vintage dance party, with jive lessons on the dance floor. DJs play music from the 1920s to the 50s, surf and swing. Forties-style ushers and usherettes offer popcorn to men in wingtips and saddle shoes and women with hibiscus flowers tucked into perfectly rolled hairdos. It's a place to party, pull and wash that man (or woman) right out of your hair.

Tea House Theatre 🧁 🍴 🍸

Ⓐ 139 Vauxhall Walk SE11 5HL Ⓣ 020 7207 4585 Ⓦ www.teahousetheatre.co.uk
Ⓞ Mon–Sat 8am–7pm, Sun 10am–7pm; phone or check website for evening events

Previously, this Victorian pub overlooking Vauxhall pleasure gardens was the inspiration for Thackeray's *Vanity Fair*. It fell into disrepair before a group of enterprising theatre directors and other creative types restored it, with the intention to build a community hub based around traditional tea-drinking. Over thirty types of tea are available; pots for one are around £5 and hold three to four cups. All pots are covered with insulating knitted cosies: the idea here is for customers to linger over a pot as long as they want to sit and watch the world go by. For business meetings, the Tea House Theatre, with its original wood panelling, classical music playing and roaring fireplaces, is a much more relaxing alternative to Starbucks. WiFi is one concession to the modern age.

The Tea House Theatre serves gentleman's club-style sandwiches, cakes and scones, high and low teas and almost as many types of preserves as teas. All of the fruit, meat and cheeses are produced locally, or bought fresh from the nearby New Covent Garden Market, as are the flowers on each table. For children, there are highchairs, board games, a children's menu and old-fashioned penny sweets, sold in imperial measures. Evenings are filled with events from chess and knitting nights to live music and film screenings. While there is no alcohol licence during the day, you can have a glass of wine during evening events. Though the tea selection may be stiff competition.

Threads

ⓐ 186 Bellenden Road SE15 4BW ☎ 07415 994073 Ⓦ www.vintagethreadspeckham. wordpress.com Ⓞ Wed–Fri 11am–6pm, Sat 11am–7pm, Sun noon–5pm

Threads was set up by an actress with a flair for costume and textiles who grew up locally and found the lack of vintage clothes shops in the area frustrating. Clothes in the shop have a theatrical feel – the pink-painted back room is full of 1950s taffeta-skirted gowns in macaroon colours, to be worn with white kid, or

purple chiffon, gloves found in an overflowing basket by the tills, and silk pyjamas and the kind of satiny slips favoured by the young Elizabeth Taylor.

The clothes in the front room are more rugged and casual, covering the late 1960s to the 1980s. If the back room could have kitted out 50s blonde bombshells, the front room is more tailored to Woody Allen's neurotic 1970s New Yorkers. Think simple, homey, classic, and eclectic. A 70s paisley wrap dress and a 60s black lace cocktail dress could have easily been worn any time between then and now. Men are equally well-catered for, with overalls, quality denim, Western shirts and pinstriped seersucker jackets. Stacks of thick unisex fisherman's jumpers may be among the cheapest in London. There is even a substantial children's section that extends beyond babies and toddlers.

Vien

ⓐ 87 Church Road SE19 2TA ☎ 020 8653 6943 Ⓦ www.vienvintage.co.uk Ⓞ Tue–Fri 10.30am – 5pm, Sat 10.30am–6pm, Sun 11am–4pm

This Crystal Palace shop is a scaled-down department store packed with whimsy, selling vintage clothes, white-painted metal-frame sofas with rococo details, and greetings cards covered in glossy fashion images. A tearoom at the back serves locally produced cakes and tea flowers that unfurl in your teacup, on tables fashioned from train station clock faces. There are painted birdcages and buddhas. The overriding atmosphere is a local take on the Parisian quirk of the film *Amélie*.

Half of Vien is devoted to vintage clothes—there is a section of 1930s–1960s dresses in silks, chiffons and satins, emblazoned with beadwork and sequins. A cream chiffon 50s dress with fitted sleeves, a skater skirt and a grey and orange tropical print dress would suit a Miu Miu Lolita (£55), and a 60s silk sheath printed in acid bursts of greens, blues and purples (also £55) is precursor to contemporary digital prints.

All the vintage here is selected with trends in mind, but not marked up to silly prices as a result. A butter-soft Laurèl cropped leather jacket from the early 1980s – without exaggerated shoulders, and easily wearable today – is £42. A row of *Twin Peaks* schoolgirl kilts and sweaters are around £25. An early nineties D&G floral explosion scarf-print blouse is £28, and will make some Dalston clubber very happy indeed. Vien designs its own line of reworked vintage, to modernize strange proportioned garments or to salvage bits of detailing on dresses otherwise falling to bits. And unlike some original vintage dresses, Vien's own label A-line and flapper shapes are cut to flatter many body types, with no need to resort to corsets or Spanx.

Vintagehart

A 96 Church Road SE19 2EZ **T** 07949 552926 **W** www.facebook.com/Vintagehart **O** Tue–Fri noon–3pm, Sat and Sun noon–6pm

Crystal Palace's smallest vintage shop – it fills a narrow corner room at the front of the White Hart Pub – is the heart of the area's burgeoning vintage scene. While there are only four small rails of stock, and a few corners stacked with briefcase-size vintage suitcases full of busily printed scarves, nothing stays in the store for long. What's here is priced very modestly: a Laura Ashley blue spriggy cotton smock from the very early 1980s is £30; a 70s plaid mohair coat, in hot pink, lime and chartreuse with patch pockets is £45, and silk blouses, including a tan, yellow and magenta chinoiserie stunner are £28. Prices are kept low to encourage people to avoid poorly constructed high street fashions that fall apart after one wash.

Vintage Hart focuses almost entirely on womenswear, due to its small size, but it does sell an in-store range of dresses for babies and young children, made from vintage fabrics. Local hat-maker Dawn Wilson also stocks her creations here: turban and fedora-like creations built from 1940s and 1950s base blocks. She designs on commission, too, meeting with clients for a consultation and fitting in her nearby Gipsy Hill studio.

What the Butler Wore

Ⓐ 131 Lower Marsh SE1 7AE **Ⓣ** 020 7261 1353
Ⓦ www.facebook.com/pages/what–the–butler–wore
Ⓞ Mon–Sat 11am–6pm

Lovers of the liquid-sunshine palette of *Yellow Submarine*, rejoice. This cheery shop serves up scooter dresses, sharp-collared paisley shirts for men and women and mohair cardigans, all in saturated cherry reds, acid greens and egg-yolk yellows. Most stock skews toward the tailored mod end of the 60s; there are few velvets or wispy hippy flounces to be found. Designer pieces pop up frequently. A smart, tailored crepe Nina Ricci dress and Bruno Magli courts were among the star pieces on a recent visit, and British 1960s and 70s boutique designers, including Bus Stop and Miss Mouse, make appearances. Menswear accounts for a third of the store, and this is the place to search for patterned shirts, striped hip-huggers or silk kipper ties.

A back room holds bargain rails of dresses and tops – some may have minor stains or tears, but these are helpfully pointed out on the labels – and a door covered with strings of plastic beads and bangles to complement the kaleidoscopic wonders out front. There is also a tattered claret wool coat that is not for sale, but which protects the rest of the merchandise by serving as a scratching post for the store's affectionate cat.

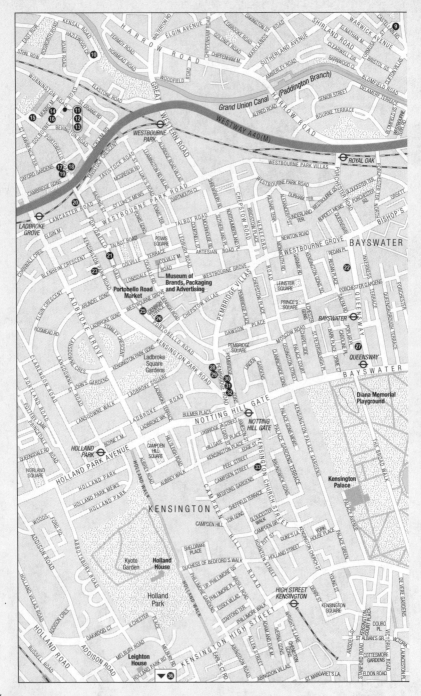

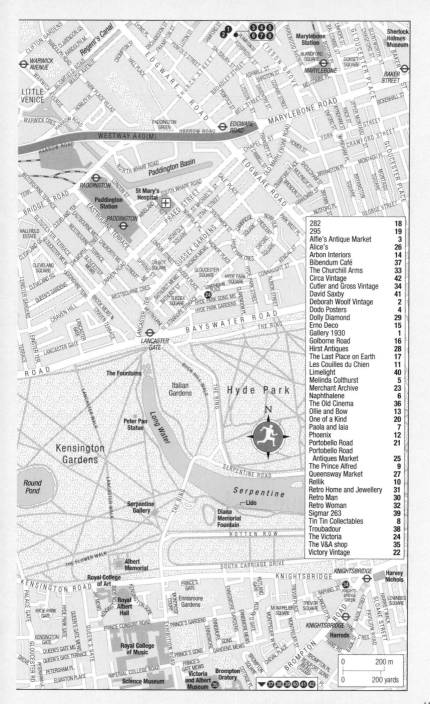

282	18
295	19
Alfie's Antique Market	3
Alice's	26
Arbon Interiors	14
Bibendum Café	37
The Churchill Arms	33
Circa Vintage	42
Cutler and Gross Vintage	34
David Saxby	41
Deborah Woolf Vintage	2
Dodo Posters	4
Dolly Diamond	29
Erno Deco	15
Gallery 1930	1
Golborne Road	16
Hirst Antiques	28
The Last Place on Earth	17
Les Couilles du Chien	11
Limelight	40
Melinda Colthurst	5
Merchant Archive	23
Naphthalene	6
The Old Cinema	36
Ollie and Bow	13
One of a Kind	20
Paola and Iaia	7
Phoenix	12
Portobello Road	21
Portobello Road	
Antiques Market	25
The Prince Alfred	9
Queensway Market	27
Rellik	10
Retro Home and Jewellery	31
Retro Man	30
Retro Woman	32
Sigmar 263	39
Tin Tin Collectables	8
Troubadour	38
The Victoria	24
The V&A shop	35
Victory Vintage	22

282 👤 👕

🅐 282 Portobello Road W10 5TE **☎** 020 8993 4162 **🕐** Fri–Sun 10am–6pm

Like its near-neighbour, 295, this shop knows that a number on Portobello can be enough to establish a brand. This is a paradise for lovers of shoes and boots, with the stock piled up and crammed into the space, unlike the rather timid displays that you often see in vintage stores where the shoes look as if they're lining up for a dance. The emphasis is firmly on quality, and everything is English-sourced giving a certain consistency to the styles.

Besides the footwear, 282 is also strong on jackets and coats, with furs, Barbours and tweeds among the quality stock.

295 👤 👕

🅐 295 Portobello Road W10 5TD **🕐** Fri 8.30am–5pm, Sat 9.30am–5pm

With its pink exterior and intriguing window displays, 295 perhaps seems more eccentric than it actually is – inside you'll find a solid range of vintage and second-hand clothing, most of it at very affordable prices. Racks of dresses going for £15–20 apiece, jackets for £12 upwards, and masses of shirts for under a tenner are just some of the bargains you can hope to encounter.

This is a shop that somehow manages to find space for a bit of everything in its pleasant interior, from shirts and skirts to jackets and hats; and with friendly staff and lai-back music completing the vibe, the enduring popularity of 295 isn't surprising.

Alfie's Antique Market 👤 👕 🗝 📖 🧁

🅐 13–25 Church Street NW8 8DT **☎** 020 7723 6066 **🌐** www.alfiesantiques.com
🕐 Tue–Sat 10am–6pm

Vintage clothing, antique jewellery and watches, posters and prints, vintage fabrics and accessories, silver and ceramics – this list hardly begins to suggest the treasures waiting to bewilder the casual visitor to Alfie's Antique Market in Marylebone. The market has more than sixty dealers lining narrow corridors spread over four floors. With its confined interiors and carpeted floors, at times it can seem like a sprawling house, whose extraordinary contents must have belonged to some obsessive collector who dreamt of possessing an example of every single thing in the world.

At the top of the building there's a popular café, the Roof Top Kitchen, that helps to encourage people to climb the scattered staircases to the remote upper reaches of the honeycomb. The café is a superior spot, recently renovated, with good food and daily specials. Stepping outside onto the café's roof terrace presents views of the surrounding streets that seem like an extension of Alfie's collections – more objects piled up one on top of another, more painted scenes with their details jostling for a space in the composition. At quieter times of the week you can almost have the place to yourself, remarkably, wandering with a mingled sense of surrender and resistance as everything seems to call out for your undivided attention; a happy disorientation seems to be the common experience.

It's worth taking a copy of the market's directory, which you can print from the website, and that attempts to organize the chaos and classify the unclassifiable. Beyond Alfie's – if you can escape – there are other shops along Church Street offering a more manageable and sedate experience of all things design-orientated. It's not easy to select stores and stalls within Alfie's for individual entries, and inevitably many excellent places have been omitted. Listing any more of them now would only repeat the difficulty, but it's a temptation that's hard to resist: one place that you're bound to be attracted to is **TONY DURANTE**, offering a lovely selection in a miniature space (principally bags from the 1940s and costume jewellery from the 1940s and 1950s). Give yourself time to see everything!

Alice's 🍷📖

Ⓐ 86 Portobello Road W11 2QD **Ⓣ** 020 7229 8187 **Ⓞ** Mon–Fri 9am–5pm, Sat 7am–4pm

Tins, crates and jars of every description, watering cans, boxing gloves, old pub signs, vintage footballs and sewing machines – in this place you generalize at your peril, and everything insists on its right to be considered unique. Situated towards the southern end of Portobello – which means close to the beginning for most visitors – Alice's is a wonderful foretaste of the street's riches, and also captures the street's sociable and promiscuous flavour in the cluster of stalls that cling to its sides.

Right in the middle of the front room an old ticket booth from Brighton Pier functions as a miniature office (a sign in the window informs customers that "the owner regrets he is emotionally ill-equipped to haggle"), and invites you to wonder what new purposes might be discovered for all of the things crowding the shop.

Perhaps it's the old globes hanging from the ceiling and sat on shelves that seem most characteristic of the place in the end, and the irresistible thought – as with other places along Portobello – is that as much of the world as possible has been jammed into the room.

Arbon Interiors

Ⓐ 80 Golborne Road W10 5PS Ⓣ 020 8960 9787 Ⓦ www.arboninteriors.com
Ⓞ Mon–Sat 9am–5pm

A lovely rambling place, stuffed with everything from architectural salvage – evocative chunks of marble and stone – and antique fireplaces to crockery and candlesticks. It's the sort of place where there's just enough room left for the customers, and where you find yourself wanting to admire the effect created by

so many appealing things crammed into each of the angles as much as you want to linger over particular objects. It can even take an effort to wrench your attention away from these larger, scenic sensations, and begin to absorb the charms of its diverse collection of oddities and survivors.

Unless you've planned ahead, you're unlikely to walk off with a fireplace, but you might pick up a curious little vase decorated with faded insects somewhat disdainful of the flowers beside them (£15) or a pair of bookends with rather desperate-looking dogs pressing themselves up against the library they're responsible for (£35). Like everywhere else on Golborne Road, the truth about the contents of the shop lies somewhere between carefully-chosen examples and exuberant generalisations.

Bibendum Café 🧁

A Michelin House, 81 Fulham Road, SW3 6RD ☎ 020 7590 1189 Ⓦ www.bibendum.co.uk Ⓞ Mon–Fri 8.30am–5pm, Sat 9am–noon

On the forecourt of this landmark building you'll find a very pleasant café, with a gorgeous array of flowers sharing the space as you sip a coffee or a glass of wine, or enjoy what Bibendum refers to as an "anytime snack". But the building itself – former UK headquarters of the Michelin tyre company – is the centrepiece. It is a wonderful confection of styles dating from the beginning of the 20th century, boasting many unique features – including stained glass windows and mosaics depicting the corpulent Michelin Man, or "Bibendum" as the character was known – beautifully preserved, both inside and out.

It's a striking building to come across in the otherwise rather anonymous Brompton streets, with cars flitting around it as though in a synchronized dance to celebrate this temple to driving.

The Churchill Arms 🍸 🍴

A 119 Kensington Church Street W8 7LN ☎ 020 7727 4242 Ⓦ www.churchillarmskensington.co.uk Ⓞ Mon–Wed 11am–11pm, Thurs–Sat 11am–midnight, Sun noon–10.30pm

Unlike some of London's more famous and historic watering holes, The Churchill Arms still manages to seem like a beloved local. You'll find a varied and lively crowd, with plenty of regulars supporting the bar and a mood of warm contentment, and it's not difficult to see why. The decor doesn't bother itself with narrow consistency – if something feels right then it looks as if a space has been found for it, somehow. The incongruity extends to the menu as well: The Churchill is renowned for its Thai food. If you want to have a drink surrounded by odds and ends of the past, with the cheerful spirits of those vanished eras crowding the room, then The Churchill Arms is as good a place as you could find. Combine your visit with a trip to another fantastic historic pub, **THE WINDSOR CASTLE** on Campden Hill Road, nearby.

Circa Vintage

Ⓐ 64 Fulham High Street SW6 3LQ Ⓣ 020 7736 5038 Ⓦ www.circavintage.com
Ⓞ Mon–Sat 10am–6pm

This is one of London's most famous vintage shops, and understandably so: for lovers of women's vintage clothing it's difficult to imagine a more beautiful selection of things, and as you explore its treasures the care and attention that's paid to the sourcing and restoration of these fantasy garments is easy to see. Circa is a place that takes its business very seriously, and when we visited there was only one non-vintage piece – strictly defined as anything younger than 25 years – in the entire shop (an early 90s Chanel dress). 1950s rose print dresses are their most popular items, but all periods from the 1920s onwards are well represented, with prices starting at around £150 for a 50s dress. There are some very special things here, and some of these garments are almost celebrities in their own right, travelling to photoshoots and fashion campaigns and developing complicated lives with restful breaks in this quiet corner of Fulham, shimmering in the racks of Circa.

There's a similarly discriminating selection of vintage jewellery (with some of the costume jewellery beginning for as little as £10), and a range of other beautiful accessories including bags and scarves.

Cutler and Gross Vintage

Ⓐ 7 Knightsbridge Green SW1X 7QL Ⓣ 020 7590 9995 Ⓦ www.cutlerandgross.com/stores/ Ⓞ Mon–Sat 9.30am–7pm, Sun noon–5.30pm

Stylish spec wearers or sunglasses enthusiasts with an eye for a distinctive look are sure to find something of interest at this fashionable Knightsbridge store. An offshoot of the main Cutler and Gross shop just down the road, Cutler and Gross Vintage was established as a classy way of selling the huge collection of eyewear, from different brands and eras, that founders Graham Cutler and Tony Gross had amassed over the years. While that original collection has been snapped up by eager purchasers, the shop is now kept well-stocked with items from Cutler and Gross's own-brand archives. Since they started hand-crafting frames back in 1969, there's a fair old heritage to be working through. Known for their cool, bold and bright statement pieces that are lovingly made in small numbers, the store partly functions as a "back catalogue" service to long-standing devotees who are heartbroken when their favourite style is discontinued from the main collection. Meanwhile, newer customers can take their pick from a fantastic variety of looks – everything from enormous bug-eyed sunglasses to colourful 80s rims – from a brand that's been worn by the likes of Debbie Harry and Jarvis Cocker and graced the cover of *Vogue*.

The store offers the full optician service of Cutler and Gross, so frames can be made with lenses to your prescription or left as clear frames if it's purely the look that's required. Don't come expecting to pick up a bargain: this is designer style with Knightsbridge prices attached – the frames alone are likely to set you back about £300. However, they're certain to be a vintage style statement that's hard to ignore.

David Saxby 🧑

....

Ⓐ 60–62 Fulham High Street SW6 3LQ **Ⓣ** 020 7610 6558 **Ⓞ** Mon–Sat 10.30am–6.30pm

In this rather remote corner of west London, beyond the end of the Fulham Road and close to the river, two of London's most important vintage shops can be found side by side, comfortable in their certainty that people will make the special journey to buy the special things they won't find anywhere else. For women's clothing and accessories there's **CIRCA VINTAGE** (see opposite), and next door there is David Saxby, one of London's most famous destinations for vintage men's clothing. Trading for many years as Old Hat, the shop is now occupying new premises (leapfrogging Circa along Fulham High Street), with two distinct operations: one for bona fide vintage apparel and the other for their new designs inspired by vintage looks.

Tweed suits are perhaps their signature item, but you'll also find velvet smoking jackets, striped blazers, morning suits, dinner jackets, other formalwear and the hats to finish the look (or to set against ordinary clothes). A quality dinner suit from the 1950s or 60s might cost around £150. If it's becoming more difficult for dealers to find the best vintage men's clothing, then you can expect David Saxby to keep on discovering gems, and this shop will continue to be an indispensable resource for anyone seeking a look with a history.

Deborah Woolf Vintage

Ⓐ 28 Church Street NW8 8EP Ⓣ 07767 437732 Ⓦ www.deborahwoolf.com
Ⓞ Tue–Sat 10.30am–6pm

A fantastic place with a first-rate collection of women's vintage clothing, beautifully organized and presented; the love of these items is palpable and it's easy to imagine a certain regret when treasured items are sold. Detailed written descriptions are attached to every garment, although in some cases the complete biography would occupy many pages as the clothes are regularly borrowed by film and television companies looking for that authentic finish. The eclectic stock ranges from Hardy Amies to Issey Miyake, encompassing important and singular designers from every period of vintage clothing including Ossie Clark from the 1970s and Jean Muir from the 1980s. Prices are very competitive and there are always lots of affordable pieces.

This shop is much more than the sum of its parts; its pleasures lie as much in the organization and combination of things as they do in the quality of individual pieces themselves. Everything is very carefully arranged so that nothing is lost: the objects are set against each other to create harmonious displays with everything singing out for attention. Besides the vintage clothing you'll find bags, sunglasses, scarves and a highly discriminating selection of jewellery.

Dodo Posters

Ⓐ Alfie's Antique Market, 13–25 Church Street NW8 8DT Ⓣ 020 7706 1545 Ⓦ www.dodoposters. com Ⓞ Tue–Sat 10am–6pm

This wonderful collection of vintage advertising posters and packaging occupies a corner on the first floor of Alfie's Antique Market, and is one of the best places in town for the unique intersection of commerce and art that these sort of collectables represent. Whether the posters are promoting Alpine skiing holidays or "Globus High Concentrated Tomato Extract", glamorous drinks or modest household supplies, the images are often extremely beautiful: vivid colours, stylized human figures, striking typography and strong light and shade creating a sense of drama about the business of selling and consuming.

Besides posters you'll find cigarette boxes and tins, tins for biscuits and sweets, and other flotsam and jetsam that has somehow eluded the attrition of time. The posters range in size from smaller items, often promoting store-cupboard essentials like jams and preserves – perfect for a corner of the kitchen – all the way up to giant images of international glamour selling a dream. Prices begin around the £40–50 mark, and continue upwards to whatever you're prepared to spend to secure that unique slice of the past, so much more interesting because it was never meant to be kept.

Dolly Diamond 🕴️ 🕴️

(A) 51 Pembridge Road W11 3HG (T) 020 7792 2479 (W) www.dollydiamond.com
(O) Mon–Fri 10.30am–6.30pm, Sat 9.30am–6.30pm, Sun noon–6pm

One of the smarter places on Pembridge Road – more vintage than retro – this shop offers a very manageable sampling of mid-century styles, with vintage wedding dresses and vintage ball gowns for several hundred pounds at the top of its range. The men's clothes include jackets, shirts and waistcoats, but it's the women's clothes that predominate. Besides the classier items you'll generally find some more affordable buys, and like all of its competitors there's a smattering of accessories tempting the more diffident shopper.

Erno Deco

Ⓐ 328 Portobello Road W10 5RU **☎** 07932 730827 **Ⓞ** Tue–Sat 10am–6pm

Erno Deco is one of the newer shops at Portobello Road's northern extremity, but it already seems as if it's been in this same spot for decades as there's a real sense of settled age in its cluttered and dusty interior. The name itself, Erno, is a tribute to Ernö Goldfinger, architect of the Trellick Tower, looming just to the east, and an appropriate symbol of everything old that refuses to vanish.

This shop has the authentic feel of a lumber room in an old house where all the best things have been thrown, while shiny new stuff fills out the spaces that people see (somewhere out there in the world behind you). Tables, chairs, pictures, mirrors and lighting compete to catch your eye. Perhaps it's the big, battered objects that exert the strongest appeal, with their blank expanses of charismatic decay: cabinets and old chests that look as if they might be the survivors of a disaster. Stories begin to spin themselves without too much effort.

Gallery 1930

Ⓐ 18 Church Street NW8 8EP **☎** 020 7723 1555 **Ⓞ** Tues–Sat 10am–5pm

Church Street in Lisson Grove, just north of Marylebone Station, seems an unlikely place for vintage shopping, and even the locals are sometimes surprised by the scene that's developed; the dealers in Alfie's Antique Market talk about how they meet people who've lived in the area for years without realising

everything that's happening right on their doorstep. Alfie's (see p.118) is at the heart of the action, but along Church Street itself there are lots of appealing shops, some of them very smart, mingling with the cafés and restaurants that remain determinedly local in flavour. Gallery 1930 is one of the most attractive, crammed with ceramics and glassware and furniture – and anything else Nick Jones, the owner, decides that he likes – without becoming chaotic or overwhelming.

You feel that each object in the shop has been carefully chosen, and there's nothing in here that isn't an excellent collectable that could form the centrepiece of a room. The Art Deco ceramics are one of the most striking elements in Gallery 1930's collection, with famous names like Susie Cooper and Clarice Cliff always featuring: Cooper's 1929 Cubist pieces possibly being the star items. This is a great example of the higher end of the local vintage and antique scene, and well worth a trip for a special purchase.

Golborne Road 🏢

🅐 Golborne Road W10, nearest tubes Ladbroke Grove and Westbourne Park

At the top end of Portobello, after you're convinced that everything must be finished and that the ordinary business of London streets – a mixture of houses and familiar shops and whatever else – is about to resume, Golborne Road opens up with a considerable fanfare: broad and straight, and with the Trellick Tower dominating the scene. If anything, Golborne Road feels like an even stronger expression of the vintage spirit than Portobello, perhaps because Portobello is so many other things besides. Along Golborne you'll find a succession of shops dedicated to the weird and antiquated, the beautiful and abandoned – and all the time, there at the head of the street, the Trellick is watching. Was there ever a more appropriate symbol of a street's business? This building is surely the quintessential vintage object: made with great confidence and panache, it has swung in and out of favour since its completion in 1972. It now has a legion of fans but is regarded with a kind of uneasy respect by others who will never find this kind of Brutalist architecture easy to love.

On Friday and Saturday the fascination with everything old and battered spills onto the street, sellers lining the pavement and spreading out everything from bona fide vintage furniture to old toasters. You'll find masses of crockery, glassware, records, pictures, toys and so on, all jumbled together, everything waiting for somebody to recognize its peculiar merits. Perhaps the most striking thing about the street market is the contrast with what's going on in the shops: while the street is jammed with cheap and cheerful stuff that looks as if it's been swept out of somebody's cupboards that morning, the shops are an altogether different affair, distinguished by their quality and quirkiness. The emphasis is on homewares and collectables rather than fashion. We've featured many of these places in separate listings, but here are just a few of the others that deserve a mention:

JANE BOURVIS, at no.89, specializes in vintage bridal couture; walking into the shop is like stumbling into a lady's boudoir, full of dresses and jewels. **KOKON TO ZAI** (no.86) occupies an old butcher's shop and is worth a peek for the interior alone, with its beautifully preserved tiling and comprehensive design in striking colours. The stock itself is a curious mixture of things, with the emphasis on mortality – animals' skulls, shells, jewellery with death's head motifs, and so on. **BAZAR** (no.82) sells antique and vintage continental furniture, principally from the period 1850–1950, with an emphasis on simple, strong, classic styles and pale, subtle colour schemes. These are quality items – cupboards, chests of drawers, cabinets, refurbished armchairs and so forth – with prices to match, but you'll also find smaller collectable items scattered throughout the shop.

Hirst Antiques

Ⓐ 59 Pembridge Road W11 3HG Ⓣ 020 7727 9364 Ⓞ Mon–Fri 11am–6pm, Sat 10am–6pm, closed Sun

This charming shop is a paradise for lovers of vintage costume jewellery. It feels like a deliberate attempt to achieve the maximum visual delight in the minimum space – an exercise in the concentration of visual effects that fits perfectly with the spirit of the beautiful things cramming its shelves. Every conceivable style and material is represented, from silver and gold, intricately worked and woven, through delicate assemblies of sparkling crystal, to outrageous designs in coloured plastics that shout in brazen competition with the shimmering metals beside them.

The general emphasis is on the bold and the bright: this is jewellery that expects to be noticed, and doesn't see any problem in showing off its materials and forms. The stock is organized by designer: Napier, Trifani, Kramer, Askew, Miriam Haskell and Yves Saint Laurent are just some of the names you'll encounter, with many of the pieces dating from the middle of the 20th century. There are items here to suit most budgets, from the very reasonable to the truly luxurious.

The Last Place on Earth 🗣️🗣️ 🕯️ 📖

Ⓐ 305–307 Portobello Road W10 5TD Ⓣ 07958 244609 Ⓞ Mon–Sat 10am–6pm, Sun 11am–6pm

Like many of its competitors, The Last Place on Earth seems to have a secret ambition to encompass the world and fit an example of everything into its four walls. Across two neighbouring stores and the space in front of them, in what amounts to a miniature market, you'll find everything from clothing and sunglasses to pictures and furniture – together with all the things that resist easy classification and would rather be ignored than compared with anything else.

Chaise longues, crockery, mirrors, glassware, lighting and jewellery all manage to battle for space, here at the end of the world. Prices vary wildly, but much of the stock is affordable and, with a good eye and a little patience, you've got a decent chance of unearthing a bargain.

Les Couilles du Chien

Ⓐ 65 Golborne Road W10 5NP Ⓣ 020 8968 0099 Ⓦ www.lescouillesduchien.co.uk
Ⓞ Mon–Sat 9.30am–5.30pm

A beguiling place on a stretch of Golborne Road dense with antiques and collectables. Les Couilles du Chien gathers an eclectic range of curios, with the emphasis front-of-house on lighting and on collectable objects that either preserve or mimic nature (at least at the moment: in common with most vintage shops it doesn't like to stand still). It's a place where the objects seem to circle around you when you step inside, just as interested in your peculiarities as you might be in theirs.

Taxidermy butterflies and other insects are preserved in solitary splendour or in fantastic clusters like a three-dimensional photograph. Mirrors amplify your movements and extravagant lighting presses down from the ceiling. It's impossible to predict what you might emerge with or the justifications that you'd invent after the fact.

Limelight

Ⓐ 313 King's Road SW3 5EP Ⓣ 020 7751 5584 Ⓦ www.limelightmovieart.com
Ⓞ Mon–Sat 11.30am–6pm

Everything in this shop promises excitement, and its images are lodged in our collective imagination. This is the home of original movie posters, with prices beginning under the £100 mark and then continuing upwards into the headier terrain of these glamorous fantasies themselves. The most unusual and interesting pieces are from countries other than the US or UK: Mexican lobby cards for *From Russia with Love*, *Gone with the Wind* in Argentina, Italian Bond, Spanish Sinatra... things both familiar and unfamiliar.

These days Limelight is a bit of an exception on an otherwise vintage-free King's Road. It's a long parade of franchises and chain stores – long enough for the same brands to pop up more than once – sometimes pretending to novelty with shiny makeovers, with just a handful of independents bravely clinging on. Limelight is down at the more interesting western end, opposite the Bluebird restaurant.

Melinda Colthurst 🏴

Ⓐ Alfie's Antique Market, 13–25 Church Street NW8 8DT Ⓣ 020 7723 6066
Ⓦ www.alfiesantiques.com Ⓞ Tue–Sat 10am–6pm

In the directory for Alfie's this shop is listed under "Vintage Fashion, Fabrics and Accessories", which gives no indication of how unique and personal Melinda Colthurst's collection actually is – this is not rack upon rack of garments waiting for impatient bargain-hunters to dismiss them with a clatter of hangers. It's a great example of the unexpected delights hidden in every corner of the market's maze, where most of the shops seem to belong to a category of one defined by the unfettered preferences of their owners. Melinda Colthurst stocks Victorian and Edwardian dresses (and other clothes) in perfect condition, each carefully selected and each giving the strong impression that it's awaiting a particular buyer who will be chosen with exactly the same discrimination. But these aren't the things that will catch your eye first. Bullfighters' jackets, ecclesiastical vestments, enamelled crucifixes and tortoiseshell combs compete for your attention, with the shop's presiding genius sat in the middle of it all in a heavy gothic-revival Victorian chair to complete the unique picture. You may not end up buying a velvet chasuble hand-decorated in oils, but there will certainly be a moment when you'll think it's exactly the thing that you need.

Merchant Archive 🏴🏴🕯

Ⓐ 19 Kensington Park Road W11 2EU Ⓣ 020 7229 9006 Ⓦ www.merchantarchive.com Ⓞ Mon–Sat 10am–6pm, Sun noon–5pm

Very smart Notting Hill boutique which sells a mixture of contemporary and vintage products, divided between clothing and miscellaneous collectables, including expensive items of furniture. The vintage items tend towards the higher end of the market – an early 20th-century film-set light was retailing for £1200 – but the stock is unpredictable, and given its location just to the west of Portobello Road it's an easy place to drop into and investigate.

Naphthalene

Ⓐ Alfie's Antique Market, 13–25 Church Street NW8 8DT ☎ 020 7723 6066
Ⓦ www.alfiesantiques.com Ⓞ Tue–Sat 10am–6pm

You won't find Naphthalene listed in the Alfie's directory, although the names of its owners, June Victor and Carole Collier, are given, along with some minimal information preserving every surprise. This discretion seems entirely appropriate for a shop that is hidden away at the very summit of Alfie's, in the furthest corner of its rambling floors: a concentrated expression of everything which makes Alfie's such a memorable place. Vintage clothes from the Victorian period through to the 1950s are crammed into a series of connected bays, together with costume jewellery and cocktail bags and vintage fabrics and... Even its owners would struggle to finish the list: Jackie, in regular command of this tumbling closet, told us that it was a frequent experience to rediscover long-forgotten items in response to a query (vintage embroidered pillow cases were the most recent example). It's almost as if the wish has caused the desired object to materialize.

Naphthalene feels like the last refuge of obscure, abandoned and peculiar things, and with all the rest of Alfie's to be explored it's not surprising that many people never make it to the building's ragged fringes, where places like Naphthalene bloom in the shade. A fox-fur muff, complete with the unfortunate animal's head, was offered for examination as the perfect illustration of Naphthalene's eccentric riches. As it stared back, a line of christening dresses swung above our heads like little spirits. But there are plenty of things that you can actually imagine walking away with: little cocktail bags, costume jewellery and small pieces of vintage linen are among their biggest sellers and a glittering crystal necklace from the 1950s looked a bargain at its starting price of £28.

The Old Cinema

Ⓐ 160 Chiswick High Road W4 1PR ☎ 020 8995 4166 Ⓦ www.theoldcinema.co.uk
Ⓞ Mon–Sat 10am–6pm, Sun noon–5pm

If it wasn't for the name, and the movie posters scattered about the walls, there might not be any clue to the Old Cinema building's history; but it's easy to imagine that everything in this sprawling shop was featured in the movies before it descended into prosaic reality. Describing itself as "London's only antiques, vintage and retro department store", this instantly appealing place somehow manages to feel both rambling and logical. This may have something to do with the amount of room which is given to each individual thing – an ideal balance between maximizing the use of the space and maximizing each object's separate appeal.

Pay a visit during the week and, if you're lucky, you can almost have the place to yourself. This certainly makes it London's only department store where you might be able to pretend that everything in the place has been assembled for your private appreciation. On our visit we found a polished steel writing table from the 1950s; a ship's lamp from the 1930s; old tennis rackets repurposed as mirrors; a table made from the hubcap of a Boeing 737; a unique wood-and-steel "multi-function work station"; and industrial signage. These singular items may all be gone in the near future, but you can be sure their places will be filled with comparable treasures.

Ollie and Bow

Ⓐ 69 Golborne Road W10 5NP Ⓣ 07768 790725 Ⓞ Tue–Sat 10am–5pm

A giant poster of an obscure Paul Newman movie in the window sets the tone for this unique place. There's something at once familiar and unfamiliar in the image, and inside the shop you'll find yourself surrounded by objects that you can identify easily but seem to be transformed in unsettling ways. It's a fantastic, crowded interior, drenched in age, with battered floorboards and giant historical relics filling the view. It feels like you've stepped into a montage – perhaps something assembled by Terry Gilliam. An odd collision of different perspectives pushes things further away, or draws them closer, or sets them at an angle encouraging you to crane your neck.

Old chemical bottles, mirrors (multiplying the strangeness), battered, tactile furniture, pictures, architectural oddments and fragments, giant commercial signs, tin toys and a whole lot of other stuff are jammed into the corners of Ollie and Bow. A chopper bicycle rides up the wall at the back. Like all the best places, it gets more and more ragged and dusty the further back you go and down in the cellar it feels as if you're invading the memories of a mad life; it's difficult to give any representative examples of the things you might find.

One of a Kind

A 259 Portobello Road W11 1LR
T 020 7792 5284 W www.1kind.co.uk
O Daily 10am–6pm

Walking into One of a Kind is a
memorable experience in itself:
you'll probably need to ring the bell
to enter, increasing the sense of
anticipation, and once you open the
door the impression is that you're
pushing your way inside a luxurious
wardrobe thick with perfume and
memories. Clothes hang from every
available space, instead of sharing
the space with the people who've
come to sigh over them, and sticks of incense burn in hidden corners ensuring
that as many of your senses submit to the experience as possible as you weave a
slow passage between suspended dresses and coats.

One of a Kind is a famous spot, at the top end of the vintage scene, popular
with celebrities and with designers looking for some leftfield inspiration from
their predecessors – or perhaps hoping to spot some surprising collision of
ideas as different styles and periods jostle for space. Besides all the gorgeous
clothes there are bags and accessories, and a room crammed with women's shoes,
leaving just enough space for visitors' feet to pick their way over the floor. The
men's clothes are housed in a separate space. Furthest from the front there is
the smallest room of the lot, devoted to women's coats. Like a network of caves,
everything becomes smaller and tighter the further you go.

Paola and Iaia

A Alfie's Antique Market, 13–25 Church Street NW8 8DT T 020 7723 6066
O Tue–Sat 10am–6pm

It's entirely in keeping with the feel of this place that it tends to be known
by the owners' names and not by its notional brand – "The Originals" – as
this Aladdin's Cave of jewellery and random collectables is as idiosyncratic

and personal as anything you'll find in the vintage scene. It's right at the top of Alfie's Antique Market – close to a seldom-used rooftop terrace – and immediately seduces passers-by with its riotously colourful jewellery. You'll find every style of earring, bracelet, bangle and necklace in this glittering tumble, from delicate, pretty pieces through to more severe, angular, Deco styles; and from abstract geometric motifs through to boldly floral or figurative quotations. Most of the jewellery belongs to the period from the 1910s to the 1960s and most is very reasonably priced. Many of the pieces are in the £10–20 range, and you'll find it easy to pick up something unique.

The shop also stocks a wide range of other collectables, including everything from coronation memorabilia to gardening tools. "Phillips Star Revolving Heels", – attach them to the soles of your shoes before a dance for improved spins – seem eminently practical, and a wooden spinner for stretching washed wool could sit happily in the corner of a room and invite perplexed speculation about its purpose. Best of all is the range of "kitchenalia": a machine for canning your own food, displayed next to an aged tin-opener, was perhaps the best indication of a vanished era.

Phoenix

Ⓐ 67 Golborne Road W10 5NP Ⓣ 020 8964 8123 Ⓦ www.phoenixongolborne.co.uk
Tue–Sat 10am–5pm, Sun 11am–4pm

Phoenix is a light, pleasant, uncluttered shop with a carefully chosen range of vintage furniture and other collectables (mirrors, prints, bottles and so on). The furniture is the focus, and the style is simple and strong: robust, battered shapes; bold colours (reds, greens, blues); and the signature markings of age carefully respected and preserved. The old boxes and chests feel like the clearest expression of these values: six sides, a material which behaves in a particular way that ought to be celebrated, a colour.

Like many vintage shops, the feel of the place is closely aligned to the stock, and because everything here is simple and clean, there isn't a crowding of the space with numerous things, and instead the same virtues of crispness and refinement are expressed in the organization and juxtaposition of these desirable domestic objects.

Portobello Road

Portobello Road W10 🅐 Nearest tubes: Notting Hill Gate (for the southern end), Ladbroke Grove (for the northern end). 🅞 Market: Mon–Thurs 9am–6pm, Fri & Sat 9am–7pm. Usually closed Thurs afternoons except in the summer. Hours can vary, and it's worth checking in advance if you're making a special journey. Shops and specialist markets: different hours apply.

What can't be bought somewhere along the vast, undulating expanse of Portobello? It would be easier to list the omissions than to attempt a comprehensive description of this legendary street. Both shopping parade and spectacle, familiar scene and perpetual surprise, a great storehouse of the past and a promenade of fashions and trends, Portobello is an essential visit (or visits) for anyone interested in any aspect of vintage London. You'll find places that haven't changed for a very long time cheek by jowl with the shiniest new retail experiments, and objects that could have been sold here over and over again – returning through a series of lives – alongside those that didn't exist until yesterday. It's great fun, but it can also be an exhausting experience – particularly on Saturdays, when the crowds are formidable – so either plan to drift along slowly with nothing particular in mind, or be ruthless if there's something you're really hoping to find.

The street divides roughly into different stretches, each with a different focus and personality. Antiques and collectables are at the southern end towards Notting Hill – principally between Colville Terrace and Chepstow Villas – where the attractive old buildings attract photographers by the dozen. Westbourne Grove intersects with Portobello here, and also houses some interesting shops: **MARY'S LIVING AND GIVING SHOP**, which has a good range of quality second-hand clothing, and the **LACY GALLERY**, which is a marvellous specialist shop dealing in antique and vintage picture

frames. If you want the perfect setting for some treasured image (or alternatively if you want to buy a glorious frame and then try to find something worthy of it), then this is the place. The middle portion of Portobello, to the north of Colville Terrace, is a more fluid zone with a mixture of shops, bars, cafés, pubs and food stalls along the street itself.

For vintage fashion, head for the northern reaches of Portobello. Ladbroke Grove is the best approach, bypassing the lower reaches to come in straight to the Portobello Green vintage and second-hand clothing market clustering by the Westway (see p.181). After the Westway the street continues north: carrying on long after you expect it to have run out of steam. There's a shallow ascent which contributes to the sense of an ending, a climax – there's a vintage homewares shop called **THE LAST PLACE ON EARTH** (see p.128), capturing this sensation perfectly. But Portobello continues, and eventually hands over the vintage torch to Golborne Road (see p.127), which runs across it. If you need to escape at any time, the streets to either side are usually very quiet, even on the busiest days, and with a bit of searching you can find cafés and bars off the main drag where you can gather your wits.

Portobello Road Antiques Market

Portobello Road W10 Ⓐ Nearest tube: Notting Hill Gate. Ⓞ Fri & Sat all day, hours vary; some places are open on other days as well. Check specific opening hours if you're making a special journey.

Portobello Road is most famous for its antiques and collectables, concentrated on the southern stretch between Chepstow Villas and Colville Terrace. Outside the hushed spaces of museums, can there be anywhere else in the world where the physical stuff of the past is gathered more thickly and in a greater variety? Cutlery, crockery, silverware, watches and clocks, cameras and other vintage devices, pictures and prints, toys, tools, boxes and jars and tins, musical instruments… the best any list can hope to achieve is to capture something of that sense of a hectic procession that the market and the arcades create. There are some things that you'll find everywhere: bundles of cutlery are ubiquitous; crockery; silver – the sparkle and clink of dinner parties and afternoon teas. But you'll also discover things that are found nowhere else, and if you're not looking for anything in particular then it's this sequence of discoveries that will carry you through the crowds on a secret thread.

Much more extensive than the street market is the sequence of arcades, each with dozens or hundreds of individual sellers. The sensation is of worlds within worlds: Portobello Road encapsulates everything else; each separate arcade with its numerous stalls; each individual stall with its glittering tumble of treasures; each cabinet making its separate display; and the objects themselves: complete, beautifully worked, and disdainful of the chaos surrounding them.

A list of the principal arcades would include (running from south to north): Rogers Antiques; the Chelsea Galleries; the Antique arcade; the Good Fairy – more ramshackle and informal than the others; the Crown; the sprawling Admiral Vernon; the Dolphin arcade; Harris' arcade; and the Portwine Galleries. In each of them you'll find tiny stalls on either side of the passages, most of them with just enough space left for the proprietor to sit surrounded by their treasures. Perhaps the most characteristic stalls are those that seem to stock a little bit of everything, somehow managing to reproduce the entire world of the market in the tiniest space.

The Prince Alfred Y

Ⓐ 5A Formosa Street W9 1EE
Ⓣ 020 7286 3287 Ⓦ www. theprincealfred.com Ⓞ Mon–Sat noon–11pm, Sun noon–10.30pm

As well as a host of Victorian fixtures and fittings, The Prince Alfred's most famous feature is the division of the bar into separate spaces by wooden

screens, encouraging you to stay put and establish a comfortable ownership of your own personal pub. More unusual still are the doors to the street belonging to each of these miniature rooms, further reducing the need for you to acknowledge the existence of anything larger. This arrangement of the space in The Prince Alfred is a more-or-less unique survival from the close of the Victorian period. Snacks (including the requisite burger and chips) are available, and the restaurant menu can also be ordered at the bar.

If you're visiting The Prince Alfred then The Warrington on nearby Warrington Crescent is also a must, with a wealth of period details adorning its imposing spaces, including Art Nouveau friezes and mosaic floors.

Queensway Market

Ⓐ 23 Queensway W2 4QP Ⓞ Mon–Sat 10am–10pm, Sun Noon–10pm [Markets]

Does Queensway Market belong in a guide to vintage London? Many would say not, but there's something about the place that seems to demand a mention. Perhaps it's the contrast with the other quintessential Queensway experience – the Whiteleys shopping arcade – and this mingling of the past and the present in the market's peculiar atmosphere. Or perhaps it's the sense that at any moment something irresistibly strange is about to present itself in one of the cabinets scattered around the corridors of this shabby, rambling, odd, informal collection of cafés and stalls, improbably expanding behind a street frontage that promises nothing much more than some luggage and jewellery.

Rellik

A 8 Golborne Road W10 5NW T 020 8962 0089 W www.relliklondon.co.uk
O Tue–Sat 10am–6pm

You might need to ring the doorbell to get into Rellik, giving you an instant indication of its exclusive nature. This is a well-established destination with a strong reputation at the high end of vintage fashion. Rellik specialises in designer labels such as Vivienne Westwood, but although you're unlikely to pick up any undiscovered bargains, not everything in the shop will cost you the earth.

Right in the shadow of the Trellick Tower, that great symbol of the ebb and flow of taste, Rellik is a great place to come for a one-off look if you've got some money to spend.

Retro Home and Jewellery

A 30 Pembridge Road W11 3HN T 020 7460 6525 O Daily 10am–8pm

One of numerous shops along Pembridge Road stocking every manner of second-hand goods in bewildering profusion, Retro Home feels like it belongs in a story where the chance acquisition of something the hero had never expected to buy – perhaps a "vintage dresser set" or some "vintage shoe-making tools" – has mysterious consequences involving a cast of shadowy strangers. It's a good way to sample the distinctive quality of Pembridge Road: rather shabby and crowded but with a great sense of informality and fun.

Most of the stock is cheap and cheerful, charming not for its great quality or collectability but simply for their straightforward appeal as objects. Glassware, crockery and jewellery form a large proportion of the items washed up onto the shelves, but larger still are the random items that refuse any categorisation: vintage lipsticks, thimbles, bookends, old telephones from the 1970s and the 1980s, vintage bracelet charms for £6 apiece and so on.

You won't need to spend a lot to record your survival of hectic Pembridge Road: jewellery starts around the £5 mark, and you can pick up old cups, teapots, soup tureens and all manner of crockery for as little as £3.

Retro Man

(A) 34 Pembridge Road W11 3HN (T) 020 7598 2233 (O) Daily 10am–8pm

Another branch of the Retro empire that dominates this corner of Notting Hill, this store carries a huge range of men's clothing, with everything from suits to basketball boots. In between these two extremes there are massed ranks of trainers, formal shoes, sunglasses, leather jackets, T-shirts and shirts, other jackets and coats and enervating expanses of second-hand jeans. The range is pretty unbeatable and, as if there wasn't enough to keep you busy until you've lost any sense of what it was that you wanted or needed, downstairs in the "bargain basement" there's everything that's either cheaper or that failed to press its claim to a space in the light.

This is a real mixture of the ordinary and the more unusual, with much of it very new and some of it more genuinely "retro". Making sense of these distinctions seems less important the more you browse; don't be surprised if you find yourself considering the virtues of partnering the basketball boots with the Dolce & Gabbana.

Retro Woman

(A) 20 Pembridge Road W11 3HL (T) 020 7221 2055 (O) Daily 10am-8pm

Retro Woman is at the gateway to one of London's richest areas of vintage shopping – Portobello Road, Golborne Road and the surrounding streets to the north of Notting Hill Gate. Pembridge Road leads north from the tube station and is lined with eccentric emporia of every description, with Retro Woman one of the first places that you'll come across, still fresh and alert, when you exit the tube; or else somewhere you'll wind up after hours of shopping, happy and dazed.

The shop is an appealing place, airy and faded. There are racks of clothes down the centre of the space but it's the shoes that are the real focus, stacked in towering glass cabinets along the side and the back, and with an air of unattainability thanks to their protective display (although the prices contribute to this impression as well). Brands you can expect to find include Marc Jacobs, Dries Van Noten, Miu Miu, Jimmy Choo and Dolce & Gabbana, and although the prices are everything that you might imagine there are bargains to be hunted out. Accessories include belts, sunglasses, clutches and jewellery, but it's the shoes that you'll find yourself agonizing over.

Sigmar 263

A 263 Kings Road SW3 5EL **T** 020 7751 5801 **W** www.sigmarlondon. com **O** Mon–Sat 10am–6pm, Sun noon–5pm

Rather than a specific era or design movement, the owners of Sigmar describe "honesty" as the guide to deciding exactly what pieces make it to the shop floor. For them "honesty" translates as a preference toward natural materials and a design that is respectful of that material. While that judgement call may sound slightly academic, it certainly makes for an engaging selection. In the store, you'll find mid-19th century chairs by Thonet next to pieces by Finn Juhl dating from almost a hundred years later, linked by both designers' inventive ways with wood. As those names might suggest, Scandinavian and Austrian designers are frequently in stock, their design ethos chiming well with the owners' tastes. Every piece has its own particular charm, whether it's a magazine rack designed by Thonet's compatriot Carl Auböck or a small wooden 1930s Estonian suitcase, yours for £350. There are heavy earthenware plates that seem to want to be picked up and fondled while other items, like sculptural metal light fittings, simply demand admiration.

The clean lines and simplicity of the pieces seem slightly incongruous amidst some of the flashier lifestyle stores on the King's Road. But don't be fooled. These pieces are all top quality and have equally high, Chelsea-worthy price tags attached. If money is no problem, you can capture something of the store's style through their interior design service. For the rest of us, it's something rather wonderful to aspire to.

Tin Tin Collectables

A Alfie's Antique Market, 13–25 Church Street NW8 8DT **T** 020 7258 1305
W www.tintincollectables.net **O** Tue–Sat 10am–6pm

This shop subtitles itself "Peculiar Habits", recognising that there may be something eccentric in wanting to dress as though you've stepped out of the pages of *The Great Gatsby*. This is definitely the place for the Gatsby look though, and it's hardly surprising that the film and television industry uses Tin Tin – and other places in Alfie's such as **NAPHTHALENE** (see p.131) – to help assemble their illusions.

The focus is vintage clothing from 1900 to 1950. Shimmering flapper dresses are the most sought-after items. A pale blue dress with sinuous beaded lines seemed gloriously impractical – semi-transparent, and heavy enough to make a languorous attitude pretty much unavoidable. There are also lots of accessories, including robust leather luggage, beaded evening bags and vintage shawls (whether to throw over furniture "or even to wear", as one of the staff expressed it). Prices vary enormously depending on the size and rarity of the piece, but there are many affordable items to be found nestled in Tin Tin's crowded racks and shelves.

Troubadour ▼ ‖‖

Ⓐ 265 Old Brompton Road SW5 9JA **Ⓣ** 020 7370 1434 **Ⓦ** www.troubadour.co.uk **Ⓞ** Daily 9am–midnight

This is a lovely old place, surviving in a precarious historical bubble surrounded by coffee chains and refurbished pubs. It's a coffee house, a bar, a restaurant, a club, a gallery, a wine merchant and even a one-room hotel: "the garret" room is right up among the trees and the chimneys. Its uniqueness is immediately apparent from its long and weather-beaten frontage, and from the door with its painted carvings of musicians. In the windows old coffee pots line sagging shelves. Inside, musical instruments hang from the ceiling – alongside what appear to be farming implements – and old signs, mirrors and pictures ensure that nothing in the view lapses towards the predictable. It's the sort of place where you think carefully about which table to choose in the warren of rooms, as each looks as if it will offer a slightly different experience.

Downstairs there's the little basement club on which the Troubadour's reputation is founded, and where Bob Dylan and Jimi Hendrix, among others, once entertained intimate gatherings. A nice little sunken garden at the back makes an appealing secret spot, although the whole place manages to feel secret despite its glowing reputation and prominent location on the Old Brompton Road.

The Victoria 🍸

ⓐ 10A Strathearn Place W2 2NH **ⓣ** 020 7724 1191 **ⓦ** www.victoriapaddington.co.uk
ⓞ Mon–Sat 11am–11pm, Sun noon–10.30pm

The Victoria is a superb Victorian pub with a beautiful, authentic interior. Rich green-and-gold wallpaper, wooden cornicing, elaborate bar fittings, beautiful decorated mirrors and the ceiling's tessellated mouldings combine to create an appearance that's both impressive and welcoming – exactly the desired effect – and if many of these individual features can seem quite familiar, this is of course because the majority of pubs pay homage to the style perfected in places like The Victoria. It can feel either cosy and confined or rather grand and spacious, depending on where you sit, although given its popularity you're unlikely to have much of a choice in this respect. The stronger bottled beer is the tastiest thing at the bar: try "1845" or (surely not to be missed) the "Vintage Ale".

The V&A shop 📖 🪑 🎭 👤

ⓐ Victoria and Albert Museum, Cromwell Road SW7 2RL **ⓣ** 020 7942 2000 **ⓦ** www. vam.ac.uk **ⓞ** Daily 10am–5.45pm, Fri closes at 10pm

There's a very polite sort of chaos in evidence at the shop in the Victoria and Albert Museum. It's a grand space right in the heart of the museum, and

appears to be a sober and rational assembly of attractive objects, but really it's a freewheeling assortment of eye-catching oddities. Besides the inevitable museum stocks of postcards, tea towels and mugs, you'll find quirky vintage toys, obscure 20th-century posters and prints, kitsch souvenirs of Britain (royal playing cards – "Crowns and Corgis"), stitching kits and brush-on glitter tattoos, an "Ouch" deluxe first-aid kit ("Big Girls Don't Cry"), and innumerable other unpredictable things, many of them loosely connected to the museum's temporary exhibitions, and many of them not. Much of the time it seems as if the object is just an excuse for the style, the colour, the fun.

The centre of the shop is given over to jewellery, mostly by contemporary designers influenced by historical styles in one way or another, and much of it re-creating styles from the second half of the 20th century. Costume jewellery by the Cilea workshop caught the eye: outsized acetate and cellulose flowers and fruits, produced in vivid colours to create statement pieces that are just waiting to be pinned to somebody who isn't ashamed to be noticed.

Victory Vintage 👤 👤

....

Ⓐ Whiteleys, Queensway W2 4YN Ⓣ 020 7792 9549 Ⓞ Mon–Sat 11am–8pm, Sun 11am–6pm

Whiteleys is an attractive building with grand interiors, but most of the shops are the usual chains – which makes Victory Vintage's handsome collection a bit of a surprise. The focus is on the 40s and 50s, although you'll find plenty of items from other periods as well.

The collection revolves with the seasons, shadowing a perpetual past that never advances: dresses from the 1940s and the 50s in the summer, formal evening dresses and classic tailoring from the same period in the autumn, and then furs in the winter – coats and jackets and stoles. Day dresses are available for about £50–100, with evening dresses tending to cost more. Exotic handbags – crocodile

or snakeskin for example – are the core of the accessories.

Unlike many vintage stores, there's as much space given to menswear as to the women's collection. Jackets and suits, coats and formal eveningwear are at the heart of the range – a vintage morning suit might cost around £150. In the winter the collection shifts to sheepskins, aviator jackets, overcoats and other forms of protection against the legendary winters of yesteryear. In the racks of vintage jackets you'll find items beginning at around £50. There's also a range of less formal clothing, including old T-shirts and denim jackets.

LIFE STYLE

1920s Specialists

ANNIE'S ⓐ12 Camden Passage N1 8ED ☎020 7359 0796 ⓦwww.anniesvintageclothing.co.uk Annie frequently visits Paris, returning with her arms full of beautiful lace, feather capes and embroidered shawls. *[See North London]*

BETTY BLYTHE ⓐ73 Blythe Road W14 OHP ☎020 7602 1177 ⓦwww.bettyblythe.co.uk Vintage tearoom with a 1920s slant. Burlesque and Charleston dancing are on offer plus lots of dressing up. Betty Blythe was an exotic movie actress not afraid to flash the flesh in films like *Queen of Sheba* (1921).

HOUSE OF VINTAGE ⓐ4 Cheshire Street E2 6EH ☎020 7739 8142 ⓦwww.houseofvintageuk.com Jewellery and 1920s items are among a collection that spans the decades. This store (and others) is recommended by the 1920s pop-up events group The Candlelight Club. *[See East London]*

REVIVAL RETRO BOUTIQUE ⓐSecond Floor, Kingly Court W1B 5PW ☎020 7287 8709 ⓦwww.revival-retro.com Revival offer several options for flapper dresses online and if you venture to the vintage enclave of Kingly Court there's more 1920s-inspired style to peruse. Swing dance clothing is another speciality. *[See Central London]*

THE VINTAGE EMPORIUM ⓐ14 Bacon Street E1 6LF ☎020 7739 0799 ⓦwww.vintageemporiumcafe.com A wonderfully romantic shop ranging from late-Victorian to the 1950s, with a good selection 20s attire. You can find yourself spending hours in the basement, while the upstairs tearoom offers a mouth-watering array of cakes and teas. *[See East London]*

VIRGINIA ⓐ98 Portland Road W11 4LQ 020 ☎020 7727 9908 ⓦvogue.co.uk/person/virginia-bates *Vogue* blogger Virginia Bates has a whole stream of A-list celebs lining up to wear her handpicked vintage pieces. Situated in affluent Holland Park, this – and the quality of the goods – means that prices tend to be high.

1930s & 40s Specialists

1940s SOCIETY Ⓦ www.1940.co.uk Though not really a London institution it would be remiss not to mention this fascinating site. Lots of useful information and a selection of books, posters and ephemera for sale. World War II material is predominant, but there's lots to engage those more interested in fashion than fascism.

THE BLITZ PARTY *[See Lifestyle: Events]*

HORNETS *[See Lifestyle: Accessories]*

THE LONDON SOUND SURVEY Ⓦ www.soundsurvey.org.uk A fascinating archive of London sounds which includes a selection of BBC location recordings of markets and other public places. The strongest selection is from the 1930s and is definitely more *Eastenders* than *Downton Abbey*.

RADIO DAYS Ⓐ 87 Lower Marsh SE1 7AB Ⓣ 020 7928 0800 Ⓦ www. radiodaysvintage.co.uk Opening in 1993, the shop has a gigantic collection of memorabilia, collectables and clothing dating from 1920. Items are available for hire and to buy. *[See South London]*

TIN TIN COLLECTABLES Ⓐ Alfie's Antiques Hall, Unit G38–42, 13–25 Church Street NW8 8DT Ⓣ 020 7258 1305 Ⓦ www.tintincollectables.net Lace trims, flapper dresses and beautiful accessories dating back to the 1900s adorn this Edwardian Aladdin's cave. The shop attracts costume and fashion designers searching for that perfect prop for film and TV. *[See West London]*

THE VINTAGE SHOWROOM Ⓐ 14 Earlham Street WC2H 9LN Ⓣ 020 7836 3964 Ⓦ www.thevintageshowroom.com Plenty of early- to mid-20th-century vintage menswear, including military uniforms, work clothes, sports and country wear, and classic English tailoring. Even the shop, a former hardware store, is a treat for the eyes.

1950s Specialists

50s VINTAGE Ⓦ www.50svintage.co.uk Online store selling reproductions and originals of 1950s era clothing operating from northeast London.

IT'S SOMETHING HELL'S *[See Lifestyle: Beauty & Grooming]*

JUKEBOX LONDON ☎020
7713 7668 Ⓦ www.jukeboxlondon.
co.uk Islington-based showroom has
models to inspect from 1946 to 1962.
Visits by appointment only, Sundays
recommended.

JUKEBOX JIVE SHOW
Ⓦ www.jukeboxjiveshow.co.uk
Jukebox held a big 1950s exhibition
near London Heathrow in 2011 featuring
jukeboxes, records, clothing and
memorabilia. For 50s fans (especially fans
of 50s music) this show is worth keeping
an eye out for.

LEVI'S VINTAGE CLOTHING STORE Ⓐ5 Newburgh Street W1F
7RG ☎020 7287 4941 The classic jean company providing reproductions from
the 1950s and other eras.

MODERN SHOWS Ⓦwww.modernshows.com Organizers of mid-century
furniture and modern design get-togethers at venues like Dulwich College and
Lord's Cricket Ground. If you can't make a show and are interested in design,
their excellent website has a huge directory of vintage and modern shops you
can dive right into.

VELVET ATELIER Ⓐ13–25 Church Street NW8 8DT ☎07903 147263
Ⓦ www.velvetatelier.com Inside Alfie's Antique Market you will find a treasure
trove of divine 1950s ball gowns, shoes, hats and bags. Remember to take a peek
at their designer stock – you'll discover Westwood, McQueen and Dior pieces.

VINTAGE KING Ⓐ Unit D04, Camden Stables Market, Chalk Farm Road
NW1 8AH A pretty wide vintage range, but the speciality is European and
American casual and formal wear (with the occasional military uniform) from
the 1930s to the 90s. *[See North London]*

WHAT KATIE DID Ⓐ26 Portobello Green, 281 Portobello Road W10
5TZ ☎08454 308943 Ⓦ www.whatkatiedid.com Vintage- and retro-inspired
underwear. Corsets, lingerie, hosiery and cosmetics all with a 1940s and 50s
twist. WKD is a big operation with an excellent website.

1960s & 70s Specialists

LONDON 60s WEEK  www.london60sweek.co.uk Annual festival celebrating the 60s. Lots of music and photography with different events every year. Held at the end of July.

OLDE DOG Ⓦ www.oldedog.co.uk Catering "for Blaggards, Vandals, Vagabonds & Rogues", this online store is where punks young and old can purchase posters, memorabilia and clothes. Not a huge range but will bring back fond memories for some.

POP BOUTIQUE Ⓐ 6 Monmouth Street WC2H 9HB Ⓣ 020 7497 5262 Ⓦ www.pop-boutique.com Established in 1996, selling everything from clothing, homeware and vintage vinyl. Pop have also created their own 60s-style bags, vintage dresses and much more, all made entirely from recycled fabrics. *[See Central London]*

RELLIK Ⓐ 8 Golborne Road W10 5NW Ⓣ 020 8962 0089 Ⓦ www. relliklondon.co.uk Situated at the foot of the iconic Trellick Tower, Rellik hosts an array of vintage pieces from the 1920s through to the 1980s, with an impressive collection of all things punk. *[See West London]*

WHAT THE BUTLER WORE Ⓐ 131 Lower Marsh SE1 7AE Ⓣ 020 7261 1353 Ⓦ www.whatthebutlerwore.co.uk Specializing in 1960s and 1970s men's and women's vintage fashion. You'll find high-quality pieces, extremely helpful staff and a resident cat called Binky! *[See South London]*

WILLIAMVINTAGE Ⓐ 2 Marylebone Street W1G 8JQ Ⓣ 020 7487 4322 Ⓦ www.williamvintage.com *Vogue* calls him "The Vintage King" and Rihanna and Lana del Ray flock to his collection of designer vintage, which includes Ossie Clark, Dior and Courrèges. Remember to book before you visit as it's by appointment only.

1980s & 90s Specialists

ABSOLUTE VINTAGE Ⓐ 15 Hanbury Street E1 6QR Ⓣ 020 7247 3883 Ⓦ www.absolutevintage.co.uk/home2 Voted as one of the top one hundred vintage stores in the world. Everything is handpicked and the store boasts the largest vintage shoe and bag selection in the UK. *[See East London]*

BANG BANG Ⓐ21 Goodge Street WIT 2PJ ☎020 7631 4191 Ⓦwww.
bangbangclothingexchange.co.uk Widely regarded as London's finest and
fairest clothing exchange. Offers cash to take your old clothes off your hands;
alternatively, exchange your clothes for a credit note. *[See Central London]*

BETTY AND GERTY Ⓐ69 & 90 The West Yard, Camden Lock Market,
NWI 8AF Ⓦwww.bertyandgerty.co.uk Market stall transformed to Camden
Lock Market shop, Betty & Gerty also have a website. With a particular leaning
towards women's 1980s clothing especially blouses and jumpers.

BEYOND RETRO Ⓐ110–112 Cheshire Street E2 6EJ ☎020 7613 3636
Ⓦwww.beyondretro.com Situated in an former East End dairy factory down the
far end of Cheshire Street, Beyond Retro showcases a floor to ceiling selection
of vintage clothing and accessories. There's an even larger branch of the store in
Dalston. *[See East & North London]*

MINT VINTAGE Ⓐ71–73 Stoke Newington High Street N16 8EL ☎020
7249 4567 Ⓦwww.mintvintage.co.uk In collaboration with ASOS Marketplace,
Mint Vintage now has a shop selling carefully handpicked garments. With a
substantial selection of vintage clothing and accessories assembled from all over
the world, Mint have grabbed the attention of celebrities and magazine editors
alike. *[See North London]*

ACCESSORIES

THE ANTIQUE JEWELLERY COMPANY ⒶShop 158 Grays, 58
Davies Street WIK 5LP ☎020 7629 4769 Ⓦwww.antiquejewellerycompany.
com Based at Grays Antique Markets (see p.20), the company offers a wide range
of quality pieces with prices mostly at the top end.

BORDELLO LONDON Ⓐ2 Pritchards Road E2 9AP ☎08455 195721
Ⓦwww.bordello-london.com Bordello's saucy showroom can be visited
by appointment only. Online store offers vintage-style lingerie and boudoir
collectables for the budding *femme fatale* or burlesque artiste.

THE BUTTON QUEEN Ⓐ76 Marylebone Lane WIU 2PR ☎020 7935 1505
Ⓦwww.thebuttonqueen.co.uk The place to go for buttons (surprise, surprise).
Utter dedication to the world of buttons, old and new and an online store too.

DREAMTIME VINTAGE Ⓐ13 Pierrepont Row NI 8EE ☎07804 261082
Second-hand shop with vintage accessories, costume jewellery and clothing. The
store has exhibited at London Antique Textile Fair.

THE EYE COMPANY ❹ 159 Wardour Street
W1F 8WH ☎ 020 7434 0988 ⓦ www.eye-company.
co.uk Soho opticians with a prominent vintage eyewear
collection from the 1920s to the 80s.

GILLIAN HORSUP ❹ Grays Antique Market,
Grays Mews, 1–7 Davies Mews W1K 5AB ☎ 0207
499 8121 ⓦ www.gillianhorsup.com Brilliant range of
accessories, particularly strong on jewellery but with
some stylish bags, bangles and other assorteds. Art
Deco items of all descriptions a speciality.

HORNETS ❹ 2 & 4 and 36b Kensington
Church Walk W8 4NB ☎ 020 7938 4949 ⓦ www.
hornetskensington.co.uk "Style. Not fashion" is the
half haughty, half tongue-in-cheek slogan of this
gents outfitters, which is spread over three shops
in the same street. There's a good range of period
clothing, including classic hats and shoes, as well as a
small but discriminating hire service.

ITSY BITSY VINTAGE ⓦ www.
itsybitsyvintage.com Risqué lingerie created with
vintage fabrics by London-based online company.
Burlesque is a big influence, making this the go-to
site for vintage-inspired underwear (rather than
granny's antique originals).

**KLASIK.ORG TWENTIETH CENTURY
EYEWEAR** ⓦ www.klasik.org A wide range of
frames and sunglasses, including classic styles such
as Rayban and Christian Dior, from the 1920s to the
present. You can also check out some of this online
retailer's wares at Old Spitalfields Market.

LAIRD LONDON ❹ 23 New Row WC2N 4LA & 18 Sherwood Street W1F
7ED ☎ 020 7240 4240 ⓦ www.lairdlondon.co.uk No pre-loved headwear, but for
those chaps and ladies who favour an old-style gentlemanly look Lairds have a
tempting array of caps and hats – from Baker Boy caps to toppers and trilbys.

LONDON VINTAGE LUGGAGE ❹ Unit D37, Stables Market NW1 8AH
☎ 07850 936469 ⓦ www.londonvintageluggage.com The place to go for the
classiest luggage including steamer trunks, attaché cases as well as reproduction
leather sports gear, such as old-style boxing gloves. Operates mostly online.

LOVELY AND BRITISH Ⓐ132A Bermondsey Street SE1 3TX Ⓣ020 7378 6570 Ⓦ www.lovelyandbritishlondon.co.uk Eclectic curiosities – mostly mid-century British – are to be found in this Bermondsey store, including furniture, handbags, scarves, mittens and even vintage sherry glasses.

LUNETIER VINTAGE EYEWEAR Ⓐ18 Portobello Green, 281 Portobello Road W10 5TZ Ⓣ020 8969 1541 Ⓦ www.lunetiervintage.com Large international collection of sunglasses and frames, from the 1950s to the 90s. As well as the classy vintage stuff, there's a smattering of contemporary eyewear.

MARYLINE FAVRELIERE AT ERNO DECO Ⓐ328 Portobello Road W10 5RU Ⓣ020 8964 5561 Ⓦ www.marylinefavreliere.com Handmade cushions using vintage fabrics and trimmings. Many of the vintage items have appliquéd motifs, especially letters, which can be customized on request.

OLIVER GOLDSMITH STORE & VINTAGE ARCHIVE Ⓐ15 All Saints Road W11 1HA Ⓣ020 7460 0844 Ⓦ www.olivergoldsmith.com Maker of sunglasses to the stars, Goldsmith's has a store and vintage archive where decades of OG eyewear is kept for inspection and admiration and –if you have the means – inspire you to order a bespoke re-creation of a classic original.

PEEKABOO VINTAGE Ⓐ2 Ganton Street W1F 7QL Ⓣ020 7434 4142 Ⓦ www.peekaboovintage.com Clothing of course, vintage-inspired designer ware certainly, but there's a pleasing depth of choice in the accessories department not to mention jewellery. *[See Central London]*

PENFRIEND Ⓐ34 Burlington Arcade W1J 0QA Ⓣ020 7499 6337 Ⓦ www. penfriend.co.uk Situated in Piccadilly's swanky Burlington Arcade, this long-running outfit has over a thousand vintage pens and pencils to choose from, including Parker, Waterman and Shaeffer, and offers an excellent repair service.

PENNY DREADFUL VINTAGE Ⓦ www.pennydreadfulvintage.com This online boutique offers a range of excellent, moderately priced accessories alongside an extensive online clothes store (for women only). There's also a styling service available by appointment at their Hampstead studio.

ROSIE WEISENCRANTZ Ⓣ020 7263 7655 Ⓦ www.rosieweisencrantz. com Vintage aesthetics and a commitment to recycling are two of the features of this fashionably exclusive jewellery outfit. Every piece is a unique, handcrafted creation, using antique jewellery and trinkets.

SECRET SIREN Ⓦ www.secretsiren.com Secret Siren specializes in clothes and accessories, mostly from the 1940s to the 60s. The stylish and witty website is arranged thematically with categories including Cocktail Hour, Sunday Best, Red Carpet and Bridal. Prices aren't cheap but the quality is consistently high.

STARDUST ONLINE VINTAGE BOUTIQUE ☎020 8368 6884
Ⓦ www.stardustvintage.co.uk Stardust can sell you jewellery, bags and hats but
its range stretches deeper and wider than that. Find aprons, hat pins, scarves,
stoles, bottle openers, cigarette cases and even clothes brushes.

TAYLOR BUTTONS Ⓐ22 Cleveland Street W1T 4JB ☎020 7436 9988
Ⓦ www.taylorsbuttons.co.uk One hundred years in business and housed in
one of writer Charles Dickens's former residences, Taylor Buttons has vintage
buttons including Art Deco designs and some intriguing-sounding glass buttons
from 1940s Austria.

THE THRIFT SHOP Ⓦwww.thethriftshop.co.uk Online store based in
London's Surrey suburbs with wide selection of clothes, scarves, "delicate indie
belts" and shoes. Inspired by the original thrift shops established by charities.

TIN TIN COLLECTABLES ⒶAlfie's Antiques Hall, Unit G38–42, 13–25
Church Street NW8 8DT ☎020 7258 1305 Ⓦwww.tintincollectables.net As well
as clothing from the 1940s, Tin Tin often has a good selection of vintage luggage
and travel accessories.*[See Central London]*

VINTAGE SUNGLASSES LONDON ☎07527 482811 Ⓦwww.
vintagesunglasseslondon.co.uk Frames and glasses from the 1960s to the 90s are
available direct from this site, or stockists across London. There are dozens of
European brands and if vintage sunglasses are your thing, mightily tempting.

THE VINTAGE WATCH COMPANY Ⓐ24 Burlington Arcade W1J
0PS ☎020 7499 2032 Ⓦwww.vintagewatchcompany.com Rolex watches from
yesteryear at futuristically inflationary (or exclusive) prices. The website arranges the
watches by date, so you can buy one from the year of your, or a loved one's, birth.

VIOLET VINTAGE ☎020 7624 9822 Ⓦwww.violetvintagejewellery.com
This online treasure trove aims to take the legwork out of finding the perfect
vintage piece by having their expert buyers look for things for you at vintage fairs,
shops and markets. The collections are clearly divided into originals, reworked
and "new vintage" (i.e. vintage-inspired) and grouped by period and price.

AUCTIONS

BONHAMS Ⓐ101 New Bond Street W1S 1SR ☎020 7447 7447 Ⓦwww.
bonhams.com A longstanding firm with viewings and auctions taking place
throughout the year, Bonhams caters for the top end of the market and prices
can be extremely high, though not as high as Christie's.

BONINGTONS ⒶI Ambrose House, Old Station Road, Loughton IG10 4PE
Ⓣ020 8508 4800 Ⓦwww.boningtons.com Situated just beyond London's outer edge in Essex, Boningtons holds fortnightly sales every other Monday and less regular specialist sales.

CHRISTIE'S Ⓐ8 King Street SW1Y 6QT Ⓣ020 7839 9060 Ⓦwww.christies.com The world's oldest fine art auctioneer is where the well-heeled international collectors buy their baubles. Check the website for upcoming specialist sales where you can go and view even if you don't intend to buy.

CRITERION Ⓐ53 Essex Road N1 2SF Ⓣ020 7359 5707 Ⓦwww.criterionauctioneers.com There's an auction every Monday here at 3pm with viewing taking place on Friday afternoons and over the weekend. Twentieth-century collectables crop up regularly both here and at Criterion's other branch in Wandsworth.

HIGH ROAD AUCTIONS Ⓐ30–34 Chiswick High Road W4 1TE Ⓣ020 8400 5225 Ⓦwww.highroadauctions.co.uk Sales of antiques and collectables take place every Tuesday (with occasional specialist sales) and it's possible to pick up some bargain 20th-century material. This west London outfit also offers online bidding and a repair and restoration service.

KERRY TAYLOR AUCTIONS Ⓐ249–253 Long Lane SE1 4PR Ⓣ020 8676 4600 Ⓦwww.kerrytaylorauctions.com Kerry Taylor, who used to run the costume and textile sales for Sotheby, now has her own London-based auction house specializing in antique, vintage fashion, and textiles. It has handled the collections of style icons including the fashion luminary Daphne Guinness, supermodels Jerry Hall and Marie Helvin, and actresses Leslie Caron and Joanna Lumley. At a 2012 sale Ava Gardner's Balenciaga evening gown sold for £11,000.

LOTS ROAD AUCTIONS Ⓐ71 Lots Road SW10 0RN Ⓣ020 7376 6800 Ⓦwww.lotsroad.com Auctions are held every Sunday afternoon with contemporary furniture and decorative items selling at 1pm, antiques at 4pm. Viewing takes place in the preceding days (except Monday and Tuesday) and there are occasional specialist sales. Though this is largely a general auction house, vintage items crop up pretty regularly.

AUTOMOBILES

ABOUT TOWN ⒶUnit 4, Ferrier Street SW11 1SW Ⓣ020 8871 1112 Ⓦwww.abouttownbikehire.co.uk Though not set up specifically for vintage enthusiasts, About Town has a wide selection of classic motorbikes and scooters and has a film and media hire facility.

ACE CLASSICS  **Ⓐ**101–103 St Mildreds Road SE12 0RL **Ⓣ** 020 8698 4273 **Ⓦ** www.aceclassics.co.uk Sales, hire and restoration, and even a few gift ideas like the Ace Classics Calendar. Wide range of two wheelers plus two vintage Vauxhalls (1951 and 1961) for weddings.

AUSTIN VINTAGE TAXI HIRE
Ⓐ 296 Balham High Road SW17 7AA **Ⓣ** 020 8767 0817 **Ⓦ** www. vintagetaxi.com This unpretentious family-run business can ferry you about in some truly classic vehicles, including 1930s Austin Taxis and a 1973 Rolls Royce Silver Shadow. A red Routemaster London bus is also available for larger groups.

BESPOKES **Ⓐ** 62–66 York Way N1 9AG **Ⓣ** 020 7833 8000 **Ⓦ** www. bespokes.co.uk One-off hiring of Aston Martins, Healeys and Jaguars can be arranged here, as well as top end hires for modern sports vehicles. Activity days give you the chance to drive as many as four classic sports cars to compare rides.

BUTTERCUP BUS **Ⓣ** 07899 965903 **Ⓦ** www.buttercupbus.com A small outfit based in Croydon that hires out three classic BMW campervans from the 1970s, either for holiday trips or events like weddings or even pop festivals.

CAMDEN CAMPERS **Ⓣ** 07776 060344 **Ⓦ** camdencampers.co.uk Vintage caravanning is becoming ever more popular but is more of a country thing than a London tone. Camden Campers buck the trend, selling quality second-hand VW Campervans and Eriba Touring Caravans.

THE CLASSIC CAR CLUB **Ⓐ** 250 Old Street EC1V 9DD **Ⓣ** 020 7490 9090 **Ⓦ** www.classiccarclub.co.uk A membership club where subscription points give you access to a dazzling array of wheels. The classics of the 1960s and 70s are particularly tempting even to non-petrolheads. Even if the basic membership of £1550 a year is not for you, the showrooms are well worth a visit.

CLASSIC CHROME LTD **Ⓐ** 12 Sheen Lane SW14 8LN **Ⓣ** 020 8876 8171 **Ⓦ** www.classic-chrome.co.uk These classic car showrooms in the southwest are the place to go if you are thinking of owning – or parting company from – a vintage MG, Triumph or Porsche.

COYS **Ⓐ** Manor Court, Lower Mortlake Road TW9 2LL **Ⓣ** 020 8614 7888 **Ⓦ** www.coys.co.uk Unique auction house founded in 1919 that specializes in, as they put it, "fine historic automobiles". They also deal in rock memorabilia, old posters and antique sporting guns.

GREAT ESCAPE CLASSIC CAR HIRE ☎01527 893733 Ⓦwww. greatescapecars.co.uk The Islington-based fleet of this classic car hire firm includes a Bentley T1, a Bristol 411 coupe and, the pick of the bunch, an aqua blue Aston Martin DB6.

HI STAR CLASSICS Ⓦwww.hi-starclassics.co.uk Good luck navigating this website, but if you're a vintage motorbike nut then you're certain to find something of interest, be it Lewis Leathers, helmets or just some evocative photos.

JAMES RETRO MOTORCYCLES Ⓐ369 Staines Road West TW15 1RP ☎01784 421700 Ⓦwww.james-retro.com Harley-Davidson specialists based in outer west London near Sunbury. They do restoration and repairs as well as straight selling.

BEAUTY & GROOMING

CANDY POUT ☎07939 722079 Ⓦwww.candypout.co.uk Regulars at vintage fairs and events, Candy Pout are a collective of professional vintage hair, make-up and makeover specialists. All the usual bases are covered.

CLAIRE HAIR ☎07963 057210 Ⓦ Twitter@ClairehairE17 Based in Walthamstow, Claire Cross is a vintage specialist who comes with numerous personal recommendations. Mobile service available by arrangement.

DECO DOLLS ⒶSE24 9DG ☎07980 727746 Ⓦwww.decodolls.co.uk Mobile vintage make-up and styling from Sarah who is based in Herne Hill but able to visit clients. Services include make-up lessons, hen parties and styling for weddings.

GEO F. TRUMPER Ⓐ9 Curzon Street W1J 5HQ & 1 Duke of York Street SW1Y 6JP ☎020 7499 1850 & 020 7734 6553 Ⓦwww.trumpers.com For the genuine posh boy experience head over to Mayfair where Trumpers have specialized in traditional male grooming for well over a hundred years – the Curzon Street shop still retains its original mahogany panelled cubicles. As well as haircutting, both shops offer moustache trimming and tinting, shaving, facials and, for the follically-challenged, hairpiece fitting (in private, of course).

IT'S SOMETHING HELL'S Ⓐ2.1/2.2 Kingly Court W1 9PY ☎07896 153491 Ⓦwww.itssomethinghells.com If you want a rockabilly barnet, here's the place for you. It's a 1950s beauty parlour too. First come first severed for men but get there early if it's a Saturday. *[See Central London]*

KITTY'S VINTAGE LTD Ⓦ www.kittysvintage.co.uk Pop-up salon and mobile beauty services offered in London and surrounding counties. It's an online accessories, clothing and textiles store too.

★ LA BELLE JOLIE ★

Ⓐ 35 Anerley Road SE19 2AS Ⓣ 020 7018 1209 Ⓦ www.labellejolie.com
Ⓞ Wed–Thurs 11am–9pm, Fri 11am–7pm, Sat–Sun 10am–6pm

This is London's first full-on retro spa experience. While the city boasts no shortage of stylists prepared to transform customers into perfect post-war pinups in victory rolls, La Belle Jolie looks further back, to the glamorous world of the fern-filled spas of the twenties and thirties, and to the treatment rooms of Elizabeth Arden and Helena Rubenstein. Treatment days can include retro hair and make-up masterclasses, marine body wraps and sugar scrubs, specialist facials, luxury manicures and pedicures, deep tissue and therapeutic massage, waxing and electrolysis. All treatments use natural ingredients, and the spa has its own line of non-synthetic cold creams and skin care. Between treatments,

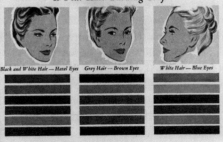

visitors can relax with a cocktail or a glass of fizz in the covered garden, or take high tea, draped in towel turbans and robes like Joan Crawford in *The Women*.

Having spent twenty years as a freelance hair and make-up artist, owner Ruby Rose is a beauty historian with an eye for detail and accuracy. One of the rooms here is modelled on the light greys of the Savoy treatment rooms of 1926, and the other takes its inspiration from Claridges' green and black vitriolite room of the late 1930s. Treatments are comparably priced or cheaper than those in the centre of town – so after a day at La Belle Jolie, you can feel like a silver screen goddess without having spent like one.

LIPSTICK & CURLS ☎ 020 8690 6416 ⓦ www.lipstickandcurls.net A big player in the world of vintage styling, Amanda Moorhouse's impressive operation covers all vintage eras, styles and disciplines. Pretty much every kind of vintage styling requirement is served by her fifteen-strong team, including parties, weddings and pop-up parlours. Clients have included the Scissor Sisters and Amy Winehouse. They also run a hair academy with the Vintage Patisserie.

★ MURDOCK ★

Ⓐ 46 Redchurch Street E2 7DJ ☎ 020 3393 7946 ⓦ www.murdocklondon.com
Ⓞ Mon–Fri 9am–8pm, Sat 9am–5pm, Sun 11am–5pm

From the overabundance of facial hair, ironic and otherwise, bobbing up and down the streets of east London, it's clear why a modern men's barber and grooming store might flourish here. Brendan Murdock set up shop on Old Street in 2006, and has since opened three more branches in central London, including one inside the Liberty department store. Murdock may lack the history of its long-established Mayfair equivalents, but its dapper barbers and classic shaving products lined up in the window provide a real heritage feel. Moustache or no moustache, you can head to Murdock for a sharp haircut or an old-fashioned wet shave, and emerge smooth-faced and smelling of the signature range of reassuringly manly products. Other services include anything from a simple moustache trim for a tenner, up to the relaxing luxury service, that comes with the full works plus head massage and shoeshine.

NINA'S HAIR PARLOUR ⓦ www.ninashairparlour.com Nina Butkovich-Budden ran the UK's "original" vintage make-up and hair salon at Alfie's Market until August 2011. She and her colleague Issidora now operate a private, appointment-only concern. Offering cuts from all bygone eras, including Egyptian and Elizabethan, this is no ordinary business and the celebrity clientele has included Pamela Anderson, Peaches Geldof and Boris Johnson. The diva-ish duo offer lessons too and, one suspects, some intriguing chair-side chat.

THE PAINTED LADY Ⓐ 65 Redchurch Street E2 7DJ ☎ 020 7729 2154 ⓦ www.thepaintedladylondon.com This elegant little hair salon on artsy Redchurch Street has a quiet, intimate atmosphere. It's fitted out in chic vintage style, complete with antique furnishings and a cute taxidermied fox "snoozing" in an Art Deco armchair. The beautifully groomed stylists are walking adverts for what's on offer which is old-fashioned hairdressing techniques and styles for both women and men. The range of classic hairstyles cost from £40 to £50, but there are other services available including make-up and manicure, vintage styling classes and group sessions for special celebrations.

PIMPS AND PINUPS Ⓐ14 Lamb Street E16 EA Ⓣ020 7426 2121
Ⓦwww.pimpsandpinups.com With some of its stylists adept at period styles,
Pimps and Pinups' ambience is 1950s writ large, with Hollywood dressing
room (or rockabilly chic) as the salon decor and a generally relaxed and relaxing
atmosphere. Situated in the heart of throbbing Spitalfields.

★ THE POWDER ROOM ★

Ⓐ136 Columbia Road E2 7RG Ⓣ020 7729 1365 Ⓦwww.boutique.
thepowderpuffgirls.com Ⓞ Sat noon–6pm, Sun 10am–4pm

The Powderpuff Girls was founded in 2005 as a travelling service to satisfy an
increasing demand for vintage styling. The Powder Room boutique then made
a welcome candy-coloured addition to Columbia Road's vintage shopping scene
in 2009, and is now a prime weekend destination for discerning folk in search
of a particular retro image. The boudoir-style salon specializes in classic make-

up, manicures and hair styles, cheerfully applied in a Parisian-style confection
of 1950s kitsch, complete with bulb-studded mirrors, chequerboard floor and
stylists in cutesy baby-pink uniforms. Despite all the super-girly fittings and
matching uniforms, it's an unpretentious, friendly and creative place, helping
you to get a beehive worthy of Bardot or a glamorous makeover à la Monroe.

ROCKALILY CUTS Ⓐ205A Kingsland Road E2 8AN Ⓣ020 3632 3113
Ⓦwww.rockalily.com This friendly Hoxton salon, run by the flame-haired

ReeRee Rockette, specializes in his and hers rockabilly and retro hairdressing. The shop has bags of vintage style, with beautiful antique dressers and mirrors, and you may well get welcomed in by charming Yorkshire terrier Ellington. Customers aren't obliged to get a flamboyant style, but if you want one this is the place to do it; victory rolls in neon blue or red, if you fancy it.

ROCKET BARBER SHOP Ⓐ 401 Hackney Road E2 8PP Ⓣ 020 7613 1604 Ⓦ www.rocketbarbershop.co.uk Bespoke cuts provided at vary competitive prices within a charmingly eccentric period interior (a Morris Minor seems to have driven through a wall in the shop). It does beards too.

BIKES

BOBBIN BICYCLES Ⓐ PO Box 70734 EC1P 1QU Ⓣ 020 3286 8580 Ⓦ www.bobbinbicycles.co.uk Bobbin make old-school cycles with a "university campus" vibe to them – they're similar to Pashley although a little more streamlined and less heavy.

BRICK LANE BIKES Ⓐ 118 Bethnal Green Road E2 6DG Ⓣ 020 7033 9053 Ⓦ www.bricklanebikes.co.uk/vintage Over the last five years this eastend bike shop has been sourcing "golden age" 1970s racing and touring bikes from Europe: frames, components and complete bikes from the likes of Colnago, Rossin and Pegoretti. Guaranteed to satisfy the most hardcore of cycle fetishists.

CAMDEN CYCLES Ⓐ 251 Eversholt Street NW1 1BA Ⓣ 020 7388 7899 This isn't a specialist vintage place, but it does have a very good selection of second-hand bikes, with Raleighs and Peugeots from bygone decades available for cheap prices. It's open seven days a week and is well worth a rummage.

DUTCHIE SUITE Ⓐ 11 Penhurst House SW11 3BY Ⓣ 020 7193 3813 Ⓦ www.dutchie.co.uk Another bicycle manufacturer in the classic-looking Pashley mould, Dutchie specialize in retro bikes modelled on vintage two-wheelers from the Netherlands.

DRUID CYCLES Ⓐ 18 Druid Street SE1 2EY Ⓣ 07760 694061 Ⓦ www.druidcycles.co.uk Druid Cycles is more of a repairs workshop than a retailer. However, they do put together their bikes that adhere to classic models. All are custom painted with flower power and 1970s folk motifs: perfect for the cyclist who drinks real ale and likes Fairport Convention.

HEAVENS CYCLES Ⓐ Broadway Market E8 4PH Ⓣ 07949 309664/07929 660197 Every Saturday you can visit Johnny and Ben's market stall to peruse their vintage continental road and racing bikes, and chic Dutch town and touring bikes. Alternatively, phone for an appointment to view their entire stock.

LUV HANDLES Ⓐ 124 Bolingbroke Grove SW11 1DA Ⓣ 020 7228 5300 Ⓦ www.luvhandlesthebikeboutique.blogspot.co.uk You'll find a decent second-hand selection here, alongside a comprehensive stock of 1950s and 60s re-creations from Velorbis, Ticino and Pashley. Their Clapham HQ also organizes cycling-related socials, outings, night-rides and fashion events.

PEDAL PEDLAR Ⓐ 133 Newington Green Road N1 4RA Ⓣ 020 7226 5727 Ⓦ www.pedalpedlar.co.uk Pedal Pedlar sell covetable vintage European bikes, along with frames, wheels and all manner of parts – all from a small room at the back of The Peanut Vendor furniture shop.

RETROSPECTIVE CYCLES Ⓐ 1c Park Ridings N8 0LB Ⓣ 020 8888 5424 Ⓦ www.retrospectivecycles.com Online-only but with a "showroom" page proudly displaying their latest stock of lean, mean Italian racing bikes. Plenty of advice offered, and they encourage customers to call to discuss wants prior to purchase.

YOUR CLASSIC BICYCLE Ⓦ www.yourclassicbicycle.co.uk If you are in London and simply want to hire a good, old-fashioned-looking bike for the day, then check out this outfit. £20 will give you the choice of either a Pashley or a Raleigh, with the price including delivery and collection, plus helmet and lock.

BURLESQUE

THE BRICKHOUSE Ⓐ 152c Brick Lane E1 6RU Ⓣ 020 7247 0005 Ⓦ www.thebrickhouse.co.uk A nightly dinner cabaret aims to capture the spirit of the "supper clubs" of the 1930s. Entertainments vary but host Lady Beau Peep's Jungle Fever evening offers such marvels as the sacrifice of an Aztec maiden and a witchdoctor of fire. Options for hire and socials, with hen nights a speciality.

BURLESQUE BABY Ⓣ 020 3287 5164 Ⓦ www.burlesquebaby.com Vintage entertainment, particularly varied options for hen events, and England's "premier burlesque academy" not to mention such shopping options as ostrich feather fans and wedding garters. Classes for women such as the Femme Fatale grad pack are offered at various levels at central locations.

CAFÉ DE PARIS Ⓐ 3–4 Coventry Street W1D 6BL Ⓣ 020 7734 7700 Ⓦ www.cafedeparis.com Very much a West End fixture aimed at tourists, the main burlesque evenings (on Friday and Saturday nights) are La Réve and the Wam Bam Club.

LONDON BURLESQUE WEEK Ⓦ www.londonburlesquefest.com
Impresario Chaz Royal has led the way since 2002 with an annual London
burlesque festival, restyled in 2012 as the World Burlesque games. The events,
featuring hundreds of acts, normally take place in early May. In 2013 it takes
place under the heading of the International London Burlesque Festival.

MADAME JOJO'S Ⓐ 8–10 Brewer Street W1F 0SE Ⓣ 020 7734 3040
Ⓦ www.madamejojos.com Justly famous West End institution which houses
the long-established Kitsch Cabaret, club nights (often with a retro slant)
and other burlesque events. JoJo's boasts of its "saucy 50s glamour and
vintage art deco styling" but despite its long history it's always kept abreast
of the times.

MCQUEEN Ⓐ 55–60 Tabernacle Street EC2A 4AA Ⓣ 020 7036 9229 Ⓦ www.
mcqueen-shoreditch.co.uk Thursday evening's "Secret Rendezvous" features
burlesque, circus and cabaret at this elaborate bar/restaurant/club homage to
Hollywood's King of Cool, Steve McQueen, and his life and times.

PROUD CABARET CITY Ⓐ 1 Mark Lane EC3R 7AH Ⓣ 020 7283 1940
Ⓦ www.proudcabaretcity.com Evoking the ambience of a retro Hollywood
supper club and with regular 1920s speakeasy evenings, there's a strong emphasis
on exotic "tease", illicit glamour and delights of the peepshow. Aimed squarely at
the office crowd.

THE TASSEL CLUB Ⓦ www.thetasselclub.com Mobile burlesque and
cabaret show with previous appearances at the Pigalle Club, the South Bank and
Hoxton Hall. Also appears at some vintage fairs and hires out performers.

VOLUPTÉ Ⓐ 9 Norwich Street London EC4A 1EJ Ⓣ 020 7831 1622 Ⓦ www.
volupte-lounge.com Decadence is the keynote here with the dress code liberal
but mostly interpreted as 1920s to 40s. Splendidly rounded offerings ranging
from decadent afternoon teas to burlesque classes and vintage balls. You can see
artists such as the Supreme Fabulettes and shows such as Gin House Burlesque,
and the James Bond-inspired Pussy Galore evening.

CHARITY SHOP HIGHLIGHTS

BRITISH RED CROSS Ⓐ 69–71 Old Church Street SW3 5BS Ⓣ 020
7376 7300 A top-end charity shop with vintage and designer items. The quality
of second-hand produce is probably explained by the upmarket Chelsea
location.

CANCER RESEARCH UK Ⓐ 24 Marylebone High Street W1U 4PQ
☎ 020 7487 4986 Located in villagey Marylebone, this is a cut above the dowdy norm with a reputation for fast-moving designer clothes.

OXFAM SHOP Ⓐ 514–518 Kingsland Road E8 4AR ☎ 020 7254 5318
Ⓦ www.oxfamdalston.wordpress.com Situated in cool, slightly grungy Dalston, this Oxfam provides plenty of creative bargains. Books start at 99p.

RETROMANIA Ⓐ 6 Upper Tachbrook Street SW1V 1SH ☎ 020 7630 7406 Ⓦ www.
faracharityshops.org/site/shopsspecial.html Retromania's thoughtfully curated store – Edwardian to the 1990s in coverage – is well worth a visit, and sufficiently distinctive to provide stock for film and TV. The proceeds all go to FARA, a charity supporting orphaned and abandoned Romanian children. *[See Central London]*

SUE RYDER Ⓐ 46–50 Parkway NW1 7AH Undeterred by the quantity of nearby competition in Camden Town, this branch of the care charity has a special vintage and reference section. Also sells vinyl LPs.

TRAID ☎ 020 8733 2580 Ⓦ www.traid.org.uk Ethical vintage and designer clothes chain with stores in such vintage hotspots as Brixton, Camden and Dalston. Several stock the Traidremade up-cycled fashion label. The name stands for Textile Recycling for Aid and International Development.

CRAFT CLASSES

ART YARD Ⓐ 318 Upper Richmond Road West SW14 7JN ☎ 020 8878 1336 Ⓦ www.artyard.co.uk Distinguishes itself from other craft-workshops-and-parties brigade by having a few more intriguing projects on offer (such as "fabulous fascinators"). It's also very child- and baby-friendly.

CARGO CULT CRAFT Ⓦ www.cargocultcraft.com This blog is invaluable for its "Lonely Crafter's Guide to London" page, which features a fabulous directory of fabric shops and haberdashery suppliers: all the addresses you need, if you are more a maker than a consumer.

CRAFT GUERRILLA Ⓦ www.craftguerrilla.com A collective of designers and makers who put on regular workshops, tuition sessions, craft sales and "crafternoons" in skills such as knitting, crochet, sewing and needle felting.

CREATIVE SEWING STUDIO Ⓐ Unit K103, The Biscuit Factory, 100 Clements Road SE16 4DG ☎ 070 4090 4016 Ⓦ www.creativesewingstudio.co.uk Of the many sewing courses the CSS provides, the vintage dressmaking intro course is particularly intriguing: you can learn how to make your own capelet.

FABRICATIONS Ⓐ 7 Broadway Market E8 4PH Ⓣ 020 7275 8043 Ⓦ www.
fabrications1.co.uk Book a course here to make a creative cushion, or browse the
racks to refresh your wardrobe at this independent gallery, shop and studio.

A GLAMOROUS AFFAIR Ⓐ 235 Upper Street N1 1RU Ⓣ 020 7704 6977
Ⓦ www.thegreatbakeadventure.com/glam_affair A monthly craft fair at the
Library Bar in Islington where everything is either handmade or vintage. A date
for the diary if you're after unique jewellery or one-of-a-kind clothes.

HANDMADE BY YOU
Ⓣ 020 8392 0614 Ⓦ www.
handmade-by-you.co.uk Hosts
craft parties with a "vintage
twist", using pre-selected
vintage and old-fashioned
materials and supplies. Also has
a regular craft club on Tuesday
evenings at the Hampshire Hog
in Hammersmith.

I KNIT Ⓐ 106 Lower Marsh
SE1 7AB Ⓣ 020 7261 1338
Ⓦ www.iknit.org.uk This
self-styled "club, shop and
sanctuary for knitters" provides
all you'll ever need to enter the
world of home-made woollens.
It's not specifically aimed at
vintagistas, but it will offer
advice if you bring along your
grandmother's patterns and
offers several classes for beginners.

LONDON SEWING WORKSHOPS Ⓐ 4th Floor, 138–142 Cambridge
Heath Road E1 5QJ Ⓣ 07967 457679 Ⓦ www.london-sewing.com LSW have
workshops aplenty on offer, such as making a 1950s bolero-style top, or an
Audrey Hepburn swing dress. Wednesdays are open sessions, where anyone can
make use of the many sewing machines.

THE MAKE LOUNGE Ⓐ 49–51 Barnsbury Street N1 1TP Ⓣ 020 7609
0275 Ⓦ www.themakelounge.com Often credited as kick-starting London's
vibrant craft scene, this Islington townhouse hosts workshops in embroidery,
sewing, cupcake decorating and jewellery making and a bi-monthly craft night.

THE MIGHTY STITCH ⒶLaura Lees Studio, 53 Vicars Road NW5 4NN Ⓦwww.themightystitch.blogspot.co.uk Hosting a succession of creative sewing workshops, the Stitch teach all the basics via demonstrations and can take the more experienced sewers on to learn new skills.

THE PAPERED PARLOUR Ⓐ7 Prescott Place SW4 6BS Ⓣ020 7627 8703 Ⓦwww.thepaperedparlour.co.uk The emphasis is on dressmaking but workshops in silversmithery, cloak-making, ring-making, hand-printing a book also take place here: this compact gallery-style space in Clapham provides a lot more than just tea and knitting.

THE SEW GOOD STUDIO Ⓐ70–72 Kilburn High Road NW6 4HS Ⓣ020 8733 2591 Try your hand at sewing or rework some of the old clothes provided. Either way you'll end up wearing something no one else has.

SEW OVER IT Ⓐ78 Landor Road SW9 9PH Ⓣ020 7326 0376 Ⓦwww. sewoverit.co.uk One of many refreshingly quirky shops on Landor Road in not-quite-Clapham, SOI offers dressmaking and furnishings courses, overseen by a bright bunch of expert fashion, textiles and design graduates. Want to make your own Betty Draper-style *Mad Men* dress? Look no further.

DANCING

6TS Ⓦwww.6ts.info This lot have been putting on Northern Soul nights in London for almost thirty years and are still going strong: they organize around ten all-nighters per year at London's historic 100 Club.

BLUES BABY BLUES Ⓦwww.bluesbabyblues.com This annual blues dancing festival, organized by Swing Patrol, was launched in late 2012. The site has useful links and info: a friendly entrée to London's blues dancing scene.

THE CAT'S MEOW Ⓦwww.londonswingcats.com This monthly club night, which meets regularly at Guy's Bar, Southwark, boasts "sensational swing, jumpin' jive, rockin' rhythms, boogie and blues".

CECIL SHARP HOUSE Ⓦwww.efdss.org/events For positively antiquarian dancing, check out the home of the English Folk Dance & Song Society, where waistcoated steampunks can trip the light fantastic baroque style, or pretend to be Vaughan Williams at an English country dancing session.

DIAMOND JIVE Ⓦwww.facebook.com/diamondjive As the name suggests, this crew specialize in jive dancing: rock'n'roll, rhythm'n'blues and rockabilly. They organize dances – usually preceded with a lesson for beginners – in many South

London haunts and at Paper Dress Vintage in the Eastend.

HULA BOOGIE Ⓐ 340 Kennington Road SE11 4LD Ⓣ 020 7820 9189 Ⓦ www.hulaboogie.co.uk Rock'n'roll, jive and 1950s-related dancin' is the order of the day in Kennington's South Pacific Bar, the main headquarters of Hula Boogie for many years now.

LADY LUCK CLUB Ⓦ www.ladyluckclub. co.uk DJs Lady Kamikaze and El Nino organize various different retro-themed dances across London, from lindy hop and swing classes to 1950s and 60s rock'n'roll shindigs. They're also the pair behind the Black Cotton Club, "London's original speakeasy".

THE RIVOLI BALLROOM *[See Lifestyle: Venues]*

SOULNITES Ⓦ www.soulnites.com A seriously ugly website, but Soulnites keep the Northern Soul faith via their sweaty all-dayers at the Dome in Tufnell Park. The site also provides info about other London-based Northern Soul nights.

SWINGLAND Ⓦ www.swingland.co.uk London is saturated with swing classes, but Swingland distinguish themselves by organizing some large-scale parties, grand balls and regularly book the capital's hottest swing combos.

SWING PATROL Ⓦ www.swingpatrol.co.uk Of the many swing dance promoters in London dedicated to the sounds of the 1930s and 40s, Swing Patrol are the busiest, covering all parts of London – every night of the week.

LAS ESTRELLAS Ⓐ 2–3 Inverness Mews W2 3JQ Ⓣ 020 7221 5038 Ⓦ www.tangoinlondon.com A dance studio with a very old-school ballroom kind of atmosphere, devoted strictly to teaching authentic Argentine tango.

VINTAGE DANCING Ⓦ www.vintagedancing.blogspot.co.uk This enthusiastic blogger runs the Mouthful O' Jam dance night, bringing you hot jazz, swing, jump blues and R&B with as much 78rpm vinyl played as possible.

THE QUICK QUICK CLUB Ⓦ www.thequickquickclub.co.uk Their flagship night, the Quick Quick Club, sticks to music of the 1930s, but they also host The Home Front (40s) and Bop City (50s).

X-RAY SOUL CLUB Ⓦ www.xraysoulclub.com The passionate soulboys (and girls) behind this website run a monthly Northern and Motown night called Don't Drop Out. Their site also has some great fanzine-style articles and mixes.

DRESSMAKING, TAILORING & ALTERATIONS

I LOVE VINTAGE MANNEQUINS (LONDON)

Ⓦ www.londonmannequins.co.uk You may not have realized that you wanted a shabby-chic vintage-inspired mannequin. Professionals and eccentrics however may be tempted by this online store.

MRS BEE Ⓣ 07941 942010 Ⓦ www.mrsbeevintagedressmaker.co.uk Mrs Bee
(aka Jax Black) sells her own creations and runs dressmaking workshops. All her work is based on classic patterns from the 1940s to the 60s.

PAPER DRESS VINTAGE 114–116 Curtain Road EC2A 3AH

Ⓣ 020 7729 4100 Ⓦ www.paperdressvintage.co.uk This well-regarded vintage clothing boutique also offers bespoke tailoring/alterations with a view, as they put it, "to help the clothes of the past fit the modern figure".

RESURRECTION BOUTIQUE Ⓐ 3A Archway Close N19 3TD

Ⓣ 020 7263 2600 Ⓦ www.resurrectionboutique.co.uk As well as being a family run clothing exchange business, a bespoke alteration service is also available; everything from repairing missing buttons to designing wedding dresses.

ROCACHA TAILORING Ⓐ 21 Roland Gardens SW7 3PF Ⓣ 020 7373 9910

Ⓦ www.rocacha.com Retro lines with 1940s, 50s and 60s themes and bespoke tailored items. By appointment only. Rocacha have a particular eye for swing, jive and lindy hop attire.

SPLENDID STITCHES Ⓣ 07766 801108 Ⓦ www.splendidstiches.co.uk Splendid

Stitches is London's leading specialist vintage clothes alterations and repairs service, with a specific focus on clothing from the 1940s to the 1970s. Splendid Stitches can do everything from changing a broken zip to resizing a dress or adding a new lining.

THREADNEEDLEMAN TAILORS

Ⓐ 187a Walworth Road SE17 1RW Ⓣ 020 7701 9181 Ⓦ www.threadneedlemantailors. co.uk "Nulli Secundus" (second to none) is the boast of George Dyer, a Jamaica-born south Londoner who's been tailoring for 35 years. His traditional hand cutting techniques and sense of style have appealed to several celebrity clients including Suggs from Madness and broadcaster Robert Elms (author of *The Way We Wore*).

UK TAILORS 38 Mount Pleasant, High Holborn WC1X 0AN ☎ 020 7837 9888 Ⓦ www.uktailors.co.uk A central London tailor that specializes in altering any clothes, vintage or otherwise, that you throw at them.

DRY-CLEANING

BLOSSOM AND BROWNE'S SYCAMORE Ⓐ 73a Clarendon Road W11 4JF ☎ 020 8552 1231 Ⓦ www.blossomandbrowne.com As well as the Holland Park branch listed above, this long-established dry-cleaner has outlets at Clapham, Primrose Hill and Canada Wharf. Vintage and couture clothing has its own specialist service within the company.

CONNOISSEUR DRY CLEANERS Ⓐ 3–5 Fairhazel Gardens NW6 3QE ☎ 020 7328 8111 Ⓦ www.connoisseurdrycleaners.co.uk Dating back to 1955, this family business offers repairs, alterations and specialist dry-cleaning. Proudly emphasizes its eco-friendly approach.

THE MASTER CLEANERS Ⓐ 189 Haverstock Hill NW3 4QG ☎ 020 7431 3725 Ⓦ www.themastercleaners.com Well-established dry-cleaners within the worlds of film, TV and the theatre, The Master Cleaners have a lot of experience of dealing with quality vintage items.

MAYFLOWER CLEANERS Ⓐ 83 Goldhawk Road W12 8EG ☎ 020 8743 0216 Ⓦ www.mayflowercleaners.co.uk Concentrating on vintage clothing, theatrical costumes and hand-finished delicates, MayFlower's client list includes the Royal Opera House and Kensington Palace.

EVENTS & FESTIVALS

40 WINKS *[See Lifestyle: Hotels]*

BACK IN THE DAY WALKS Ⓦ www.backinthedaywalks.co.uk
Barrie Greene runs historic walks around London. His 2012 programme took in
Brixton and Soho's music scenes.

★ THE BLITZ PARTY ★

Ⓣ 020 7724 1617 Ⓦ www.theblitzparty.com

The Blitz Party is an evening of glamorous 1940s-themed fun celebrating the
community spirit of Londoners during World War II. The event is usually held
in one of several suitably atmospheric Shoreditch locations, carefully done out
to resemble an East End air-raid shelter complete with sandbags, 1940s posters
and low lamps. The blackout curtains heighten the clandestine feel, and the bar
menus, reproduced in ration books, add a nice time-travel touch.

There's a strict dress code and everyone makes a big effort. Men tend to go for
military outfits or smart three-piece numbers, with most ladies in 1940s-style
tea dresses with drawn-on stocking seams, victory rolls and poppy-red lips. Live
swing bands provide up-tempo tunes to get you dancing, and themed cocktails
plus Spitfire Kentish ale should keep you going all night. Tickets are available
through the website and cost £20; sign up to the mailing list to be the first to
know about the next event. This is just one of several regular throwback parties
hosted by Bourne & Hollingsworth.

★ THE CHAP OLYMPIAD ★

Ⓐ Bedford Square Gardens WC1B 3ES Ⓣ 020 7724 1617 Ⓦ www.
thechapolympiad.com Ⓞ Annual during July

Every July, something downright silly happens on the approach to Bedford
Square as clusters of finely dressed ladies and gents gather for their own special
sports day – an occasion for cheerful non-athleticism in full period get-up.

Staged by *The Chap* magazine and nostalgia party organizers Bourne &
Hollingsworth, this quirky event encourages vintage-style dressing up, from
Victoriana up to the 1940s. Live music, dancing, food and classic cocktails round
off this spiffing day out – which has proved so popular it was extended to a two-
day event in 2012 (£20 for one day, £30 for two).

Not everyone can compete, so get there early if you want a shot at winning
a gold cravat. Competitors take part in a series of tongue-in-cheek events

celebrating old-fashioned Britishness. Favourites include Umbrella Jousting, Ironing Board Surfing and the Cucumber Sandwich Discus, or how about some nerve-jangling Swooning, or a tense round of Shouting at Foreigners? The lack of traditional sportsmanship is the most entertaining part of the proceedings – to break a sweat is poor show, whereas posing, smoking, drinking gin and cheating your way to the prize are the marks of a true sporting cha(m)p.

LONDON VINTAGE KITCHEN Ⓦ www. londonvintagekitchen.com London Vintage Kitchen have organized two vintage foodie events, the latest being "Eat for Victory 1940s Harvest Festival" with period grub followed by 1940s music and dancing at a central London pub. The kitchen is the brainchild of two graduates of King's College London.

OPEN HOUSE LONDON Ⓦ www.londonopenhouse.org On one weekend every year (usually in September), over 750 London buildings open their doors to visitors free of charge. This is a must for 20th-century architecture nets, since many classic buildings – such as the fabulous *Daily Express* building in Fleet Street or the Granada Cinema at Tooting – are not usually open to the viewing public. There are also neighbourhood walks and talks by experts.

★ TWEED RUN ★

Ⓐ Central London Ⓦ www.tweedrun.com Ⓞ Every April

Round the corner they come, hundreds of bikes ridden by impressive-looking types. One man is wearing plus fours, accessorized with watch and chain, and a fine moustache, another appears to be sporting aviation goggles. Into sight comes a woman in a floral tea dress with scarlet lipstick and hair in a victory roll. This is the annual Tweed Run – a celebration of British style on two wheels, and the opportunity to spot some of the finest vintage dressers the capital has to offer.

The Tweed Run takes place around central London every April. Since the first in 2009, it's become a hugely anticipated event for vintage and cycle enthusiasts alike, and competition for the six hundred or so places (allocated by ballot) is fierce. Spectatorship is open to all, however, and subject to less sartorial scrutiny. The pace is leisurely with plenty of opportunity to see the sights and to pause for refreshments. Prizes are awarded to the most dapper gent and dashing dame as well as the intensely debated category of best moustache. Although it seems a particularly British kind of event, it's spawned spin-offs around the world, from New York to St Petersburg where, for one happy day each year, tweed takes over from Lycra as the cyclist's fabric of choice.

VETERAN CAR RUN ☎ 01483 524433 Ⓦ www.veterancarrun.com
Ⓞ Every November Every November dozens of intrepid drivers in extremely ancient cars (nothing later than 1904) make the sixty-mile journey from Hyde Park in central London to Brighton on the Sussex coast. This is the legendary annual veteran car run organized by the Royal Automobile Club of Pall Mall (and the subject of the classic 1953 movie *Genevieve*). If you can't participate, you can always watch the spectacle along the way (see website for route details).

★ THE VINTAGE FESTIVAL ★

☎ 020 8903 1074 Ⓦ www.vintagefestival.co.uk

Wayne and Gerardine Hemingway's Vintage Festival is a weekend of quintessentially British music, fashion, food and film and art. It celebrates seven decades of British cool: the music, dance, fashion, food, art, design and film from the 1920s to the 90s. The event includes catwalk performances, DJ sets, live bands, dance lessons, vintage retailers, hair and beauty makeovers and arts and crafts experiences. The festival works equally well for the occasional vintage visitor and the serious vintage obsessive. The venue has moved around in the past – the Southbank has featured Hemingway events for example – but wherever and whenever it may emerge in years to come, it is always certain to be one of the biggest dates in the vintage year. Worth checking this site too for other one-off music nights and celebrations which have taken in "Vintage on Ice" at Somerset House, a New Year's Eve event and a Diamond Jubilee bash in Battersea Park.

FILM

THE BARBICAN (A)Silk Street EC2Y 8DS (T)020 7638 8891 (W)www.barbican.org.uk/film The self-styled "home of silent cinema in London" regularly showcases classics with live musical accompaniment (not always just a piano). As well as perennial favourites like *Nosferatu* and *The Cabinet of Dr Caligari*, less well-known silents frequently get an airing.

THE BFI SOUTHBANK (A)Belvedere Road SE1 8XT (T)020 7928 3232 (W)www.whatson.bfi.org.uk The granddaddy of retro movie venues with three cinemas, archive screenings, cult seasons and all manner of classic films. Serious buffs can also while time away at the mediatheque and library now also housed here, and there are frequent exhibitions of classic movie posters.

CIGARETTE BURNS (W)www.cigaretteburnscinema.wordpress.com A blog turned movie programmer that organizes screenings of retro and cult classics at London cinemas such as the Prince Charles off Leicester Square and the Rio in Dalston. Heavily horror in orientation (think Dario Argento's *Suspiria*) and mostly from the 1960s onwards.

THE CINEMA MUSEUM (A)2 Dugard Way SE11 4TH (T)020 7840 2200 (W)www.cinemamuseum.org.uk Artefacts, memorabilia and cine equipment are the stars here, with uniforms and rare publicity material in their collection.

Guided tours need to be booked in advance but it is the prevailing old-school ethos that charms. Regular event screenings include the "Vintage Film Circle".

CORONET CINEMA Ⓐ 103 Notting Hill Gate W11 3LB Ⓣ 020 7727 6705 Ⓦ www.coronet.org One of London's most appealing cinema environments, the Coronet was originally a theatre built in 1898 by the doyen of theatre architects, Frank Matcham. This late-Victorian masterpiece can also be hired for events.

DOCKLANDS CINEMA CLUB Ⓐ Museum of London Docklands, West India Quay, Canary Wharf E14 4AL Ⓣ 020 7001 9844 Ⓦ www.museumoflondon.org.uk/Docklands Part of the Museum of London, the cinema club regularly screens films with a London theme, from familiar oldies, like the Ealing comedies, to recent films by up-and-coming types.

DUKE MITCHELL FILM CLUB Ⓐ King's Cross Social Club, 2 Britannia Street WC1X 9JE Ⓣ 020 7278 4252 Ⓦ www.facebook.com/thedukemitchell Seriously obscure films with a vintage feel shown for free once a month on Wednesdays. Nights have included heist films, 16mm evening and even Turkish grindhouse.

ELECTRIC CINEMA Ⓐ 91 Portobello Road W11 2ED Ⓣ 020 7908 9696 Ⓦ www.electriccinema.co.uk Over a hundred years old and a much-loved icon of west London, the Electric suffered a fire in June 2012. At the time of writing its followers expect that it will have lost none of its atmospheric charm when it reopens – restored and re-upholstered – in late 2012.

FILMBAR70 Ⓐ Roxy Bar and Screen, 128 Borough High Street SE1 Ⓣ 020 7407 4057 Ⓦ www.filmbar70.com Cheap monthly screenings at the Roxy Bar and Screen on Borough High Street of rare grindhouse and exploitation movies, along with retro ads and trailers.

THE FLICKER CLUB Ⓦ theflickerclub.com Rediscovering cinema classics with literary speakers and a new home in the art deco council chambers of Stoke Newington Town Hall. Varied fare with a nostalgic and classics tilt – aimed at those who tire of the multiplex and crave a more exciting setting.

THE PHOENIX CINEMA Ⓐ 52 High Road N2 9PJ Ⓣ 020 8444 6789
Ⓦ www.phoenixcinema.co.uk London's oldest continuously running cinema
opened in 1912 as the Picturedrome. This little gem, with its freshly restored
ceiling and Art Deco panels, is now run as a community trust programming
arthouse films. Conveniently located close to East Finchley tube station.

PRINCE CHARLES CINEMA Ⓐ 7 Leicester Street Ⓣ 020 7494 3654
Ⓦ www.princecharlescinema.com A West End cinema which seems to like its
customers! There's a loyalty scheme for club members and some enterprising
and imaginative programming. Events include silent movie screenings, a regular
classic film season and a *Big Lebowski* Quote Along!

★ RIO CINEMA ★

Ⓐ 107 Kingsland High Street E8 2PB Ⓣ 020 7241 9410 Ⓦ www.riocinema.org.uk

A cinema first opened on this site in 1909 but was rebuilt six years later as
the grandiose Kingsland Empire with an original capacity of around one
thousand (now reduced by almost half). As you'll see from the website's
pictorial history, the building has been the subject of several dramatic
facelifts. From the outside it's not that much to look at these days, and it's
F.E. Bromige's 1937 reworking of the interior, with its Art Deco auditorium,
that is the real draw, complete with a Grade-II listing status. Note the globe
lamps in the foyer before heading into the curvaceous auditorium, decked
out in a kitsch array of blue, red and pink. It's a single-screen cinema, with
a correspondingly selective programme; film festivals, domestic and foreign,
are held here, as well as screenings of new releases, classic oldies and a few
externally curated cult film nights.

SILENT LONDON Ⓦ www.silentlondon.co.uk Great listings site for
all silent cinema screenings in London, maintained by journalist and movie
enthusiast Pamela Hutchinson. Also carries reviews of several classic silents.

HOTELS

★ 40 WINKS ★

Ⓐ 109 Mile End Road E1 4UJ Ⓣ 020 7790 0259 Ⓦ www.40winks.org

Lovers of old-fashioned glamour should seek out the eccentric 40 Winks,
unexpectedly sited in a Georgian townhouse in Stepney. Its current owner

(interior designer David Carter) has refashioned the inside into an opulent, yet comfortable space. You can either visit for one of the acclaimed Victorian-style storytelling events, or for an overnight stay in this very special guesthouse.

Guests at a Bedtime Story Night are first obliged to don their nightwear, after which they are transported back in time within the deep-green ambience of the drawing room. Storytellers, actors and musicians re-create this old-fashioned form of entertainment by candlelight, while guests soak up the magical atmosphere (and the house cocktails) until it really is bedtime and time to leave. The experience costs £30 a head including drinks and nibbles. Alternatively, you book into one of the luxuriously appointed and extremely popular guest rooms (single £105 per night, double £175). Both rooms share a decadent bathroom, and in the morning you can round off the experience by taking your coffee in the pretty little back garden.

HAZLITT'S Ⓐ 6 Frith Street W1D 3JA Ⓣ 020 7434 1771 Ⓦ www. hazlittshotel.com Situated just off Soho Square, this sister enterprise to the Rookery (see below) is made up of three Georgian townhouses and is stuffed with old paintings, prints and more than its fair share of four-poster beds. It is named after the radical romantic essayist and critic William Hazlitt (1778–1830) who spent his last years in one of the houses.

THE RITZ Ⓐ 150 Piccadilly W1J 9BR Ⓣ 020 7493 8181 Ⓦ www. theritzlondon.com Perhaps not an obvious vintage attraction apart from the fact that this Edwardian hotel is one of the grandest and most opulent in London. Pride of place goes to the famous Palm Court, a favourite London location for afternoon tea – though this particular treat will set you back in excess of £40.

THE ROOKERY Ⓐ 12 Peter's Lane, Cowcross Street EC1M 6DS Ⓣ 020 7336 0931 Ⓦ www.rookeryhotel.com Panelled walls, faded glamour, bags of character – this set of converted Georgian houses in Clerkenwell has more than a hint of a friendly gentleman's club, complete with library and conservatory. More antique than vintage but with all the charm you associate with the latter.

THE SAVOY Ⓐ Strand WC2R 0EU Ⓣ 020 7836 4343 Ⓦ www.fairmont.com/savoy-london London's most famous hotel, the Savoy's Art Deco flourishes and unsurpassed history ensure that it is well worth a visit (even if you can't afford to stay). Recently restored, a meal in the legendary Savoy Grill, a cocktail in the American Bar or afternoon tea in the Upper Thames Foyer still provide a genuine "time was" experience, albeit an expensive one.

TOWN HALL HOTEL Ⓐ Patriotic Square E2 9NF Ⓣ 020 7871 0460 Ⓦ www.townhallhotel.com A truly gracious Edwardian interior and stylish art deco features are the reason to check out this 1910 architectural gem in Bethnal

Green, lavishly built and splendidly restored. The Viajante Restaurant offers pricy modernist fusion cuisine within this iconic setting.

LIDOS & SWIMMING BATHS

BROCKWELL LIDO Ⓐ Brockwell Park, Dulwich Road SE24 0PA Ⓣ 020 7274 3088 Ⓦ www.fusion-lifestyle.com/centres/Brockwell_Lido Built in 1937, Brockwell Lido is a Grade II listed building rescued from closure in 2001. Since then the whole place, including the fifty-metre pool, has been refurbished and a gym added.

CHARLTON LIDO Ⓐ Hornfair Park, Shooters Hill Road SE18 4LX Ⓣ 020 8856 7389 Ⓦ www.better.org.uk/leisure/charlton-lido Another lido from the 1930s (its golden age) which has had a chequered history in recent years. Now one of several leisure facilities run by Greenwich Leisure Limited (GLL), the heated outdoor pool has been refurbished and further developments are underway.

IRONMONGER ROW BATHS Ⓐ 1 Norman Street ECV 3QF Ⓦ www.better.org.uk/leisure/ironmonger-row-baths Much nostalgia surrounds this 1930s pool and Turkish baths (which featured in David Cronenberg's 2007 film *Eastern Promises*). The fully restored facility is due to open at the end of 2012 preserving many features, including the rather gloomy exterior.

LONDON FIELDS LIDO Ⓐ London Fields West Side E8 3EU Ⓣ 020 7254 9038 Ⓦ www.better.org.uk/leisure/london-fields-lido Yet another 1930s lido happily rescued by community volunteers. It's now restored and run by GLL. Red brick buildings around the pool give it an intimate feel.

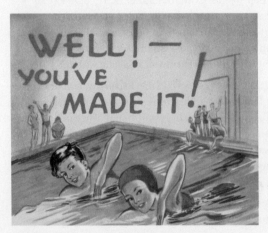

MARSHALL STREET BATHS Ⓐ Marshall Street Leisure Centre, 15 Marshall Street W1F 7EL Ⓣ 020 7871 7222 Ⓦ www.better.org.uk/leisure/marshall-street-leisure-centre There has been a pool at this Soho site since 1852, with the current one dating from 1931. Recently restored by Westminster City Council, Marshall Street is an Art Deco gem with beautiful marble detailing and an impressive arched roof.

PARLIAMENT HILL LIDO Ⓐ Gordon House Road NW5 1LP Ⓣ 020 7485 3873 Ⓦ www.cityoflondon.gov.uk/things-to-do/green-spaces/hampstead-heath/swimming Sixty metres of unheated swimming pool situated on the edge of Hampstead Heath. Very popular in the occasional heat waves that hit London. The lido is close to the legendary men's and women's pools where regulars brave the cold waters at all times of the year.

PORCHESTER CENTRE Ⓐ Porchester Road W2 5HS Ⓣ 020 7792 2919 Ⓦ www.better.org.uk/leisure/porchester-centre Part of an ambitious 1929 complex, that includes a grand hall and public library, the baths are another period wonder that has somehow managed to survive. Turkish baths and a 33-metre swimming pool are on offer, the latter very similar to Marshall Street.

TOOTING BEC LIDO Ⓐ Tooting Bec Road SW16 1RU Ⓣ 020 8871 7198 Some ninety metres long, Tooting is the largest of London lidos and the largest freshwater open-air swimming pool in England. It's also one of the oldest, having opened in 1906. Available for public use between May and September, the rest of the year it is home to the South London Swimming Club (SLSC).

WILLES POOL Ⓐ Prince of Wales Road NW5 3LE Ⓣ 020 7267 9341 Ⓦ www.better.org.uk A splendid late-Victorian building houses the beautiful 33-metre pool, recently restored by Camden Council. The only shame is that the wooden seats of the original viewing gallery are no longer available for use.

MARKETS & CAR BOOT SALES

ALFIE'S ANTIQUE MARKET *[See West London]*

BERMONDSEY SQUARE ANTIQUE MARKET Ⓐ Bermondsey Square SE1 3UN Ⓦ www.bermondseysquare.co.uk/antiques.html The market is open every Friday from 4am to 1pm with the best bargains said to be had at the crack of dawn. Antiques dominate but vintage stuff, especially material from the Edwardian era and the 1920s, can also be found.

BRICK LANE *[See East London]*

BRIXTON VILLAGE MARKET Ⓐ Brixton SW9 8PR Ⓣ 020 7274 2990 Ⓦ brixtonmarket.net/info/brixton-village What used to be the old Graville arcade is now a thriving refurbished market area with numerous shops including

Leftovers (clothes), 2'6 (homeware) and Rejuvenate (homeware and bric-a-brac). When you also throw into the mix the rising buzz about the numerous market cafés here, then it's true to say Brixton is definitely on the up as a budget vintage hub and as a generally good place to spend time and rummage.

BRIXTON RETRO AND VINTAGE MARKET Ⓐ Brixton Station Road SW9 8PE Ⓦ www.brixtonmarket.net Every third Saturday of the month is vintage-themed day with thirty stalls of mixed vintagery. Lively and fun with several food stalls featuring all kinds of cuisine nearby. If you are interested in a pitch, call John Gordon on 07944 787336.

BROADWAY MARKET *[See East London]*

CAMDEN STABLES MARKET *[See North London]*

CAPITAL CARBOOT SALE Ⓐ Pimlico Academy, Lupus Street SW1V 3AT Ⓣ 0845 0943871 Ⓦ www.capitalcarboot.com This takes place every Sunday (except Christmas, Easter and New Year) with public entry from 11.30am to 3.30pm. Entrance is £1, even if it's raining but this is a cut above the car boot norm with bargains to be had amidst the usual clutter.

CAR BOOT JUNCTION Ⓦ www.carbootjunction.com Disorientated by the quantity and unpredictability of car boot sales in London? This site covers the whole of the UK but just look up London in the listings and it can tell you what's normally occurring in your neighbourhood and further afield. Look also at Ⓦ www.boot-fairs.co.uk and Ⓦ www.carboot.com which offer similar listings. For *Time Out* magazine's take on the best London car boot sales visit Ⓦ www.timeout.com and search for "best car-boot sales".

CHATSWORTH ROAD MARKET *[See East London]*

COLUMBIA ROAD MARKET *[See East London]*

DEPTFORD MARKET Ⓐ Deptford High Street, Douglas Way & Giffin Square SE8 3PR Ⓣ 020 8314 2050 A vibrant and colourful southeast London market that operates on three days of the week. Saturday is the best for collectables and vintage, though you'll find second-hand clothes on Douglas Square on Fridays and other market stalls on Deptford High Street and Giffin Square on all three days. There are plans to develop the southern end of the High Street in 2013 to enable better access and traffic flow.

GREENWICH MARKET Ⓐ College Approach SE10 9HZ Ⓦ www. shopgreenwich.co.uk/greenwich-market The covered market in the heart of historic Greenwich has long been a popular destination for antiques, clothes, homeware and crafts, operating on Tuesdays, Thursdays or Fridays from 10am to 5.30pm. In the festive season the Christmas market is still one of the best for varied Christmas fare, with around 150 stalls open every day in the run-up to Christmas. Cutty Sark DLR is the nearest train station.

PORTOBELLO ANTIQUES MARKET *[See West London]*

★ PORTOBELLO GREEN MARKET ★

Ⓐ Portobello Road W10 5QZ Ⓦ www.portobellofashionmarket.com/ Ⓞ Fri–Sun, hours vary: from early morning to late afternoon.

This sprawling fashion market operates in the long shadow of the Westway, the flyover that crosses Portobello Road at its northern end, and the rush of cars over your head certainly contributes to the hectic atmosphere of the place. Within a canopied area, this self-styled "leading vintage and fashion market in London" also sends its tentacles up and down Portobello Road itself in both directions. Every conceivable item and style of clothing seems to be represented somewhere within this tangle of stalls, with the cheapest stuff going for standard prices beginning at virtually nothing (racks of T-shirts or skirts for £2 a piece) all the way up to more expensive vintage items such as beaded tops, iridescent tunics and sumptuous ball gowns.

In the summer the market is particularly strong on vintage dresses: delicate and light, elaborately detailed and beautifully finished, these dresses seem to gather under the canopy of the market like a colony of butterflies, incongruous beside the roar of the traffic. In complete contrast to the market itself, Portobello Green arcade – right underneath the Westway – is a collection of smart little shops, with the emphasis on expensive boutiques: a nice cool antidote to the unmatched vitality of the market. The nearest tube station is Ladbroke Grove.

PORTOBELLO ROAD *[See West London]*

RAG AND BOW Ⓐ The Print House, 18 Ashwin Street E8 3DL Ⓣ 020 3051 8611 Ⓦ www.ragandbow.com "The Roaming Vintage Store" tours widely but pitches up quite frequently in Dalston, Bethnal Green, Kensal Flea (boutique flea market) and other London venues. The excellent website tells all.

★ ROMAN ROAD MARKET ★

Ⓐ Roman Road E3 5ES Ⓣ 07949 010231 Ⓦ www.londoncarboot.com Ⓞ Sat 9am–3pm, Sun 9am–2pm

While Roman Road Market might not offer a lot in the way of vintage shopping, it's certainly got an old-time feel to it. Just before you pass under the market arch, take a look at **GEORGE'S PLAICE**, a long-standing seafood shop more like an old-fashioned beachside shack than a modern fishmonger. Among the market stalls, you'll find cheap clothing, jewellery and second-hand furniture, whereas the shops include halal butchers, bakeries and a decent charity shop. But the most interesting element for vintage-lovers (or pie-fanciers) is **G. KELLY** (Ⓦ www.gkellypieandmash.co.uk) at no.526. Established in 1937, it's a beautifully preserved pie and mash canteen, complete with globe lamps, white tiling and long benches. Black and white photos of the café in earlier days line the wall, and the white-uniformed staff dish out meat pies, sausage and mash, hot or jellied eels and tasty fruit crumbles – you'll eat well for just a few quid here.

SPITALFIELDS MARKET *[See East London]*

★ THE STOKE NEWINGTON CAR BOOT SALE ★

Ⓐ Princess May School, Princess May Road N16 8DF Ⓣ 020 7364 1717 Ⓞ Tue & Thurs 10am–3pm, Sat 9am–4pm

Organized by the London Car Boot Co – who also run sales in schools in Kilburn, West Hampstead and Queen's Park – the Stoke Newington Car Boot Sale has become a weekly ritual for local vintagistas. Turn up early, pay your 50p and get stuck in – you'll find anything from utter tat to unexpected treasures, and many things that could pass as both.

While it's not exclusively vintage, as such – unless boxes of old electrical cables and grubby teddy bears count – the delight here is in the variety, with a lively mix of sellers and shoppers from all strands of Dalston and Stoke Newington's diverse communities. Here you might come across a Hasidic Jewish family picking out a guitar, skinny hipsters scooping up retro Ts from Afro-Caribbean matriarchs, or Turkish couples selling outgrown baby clothes to Stokey's yummy mummies in waiting. The genuinely "vintage" stuff tends to be near the entrance, in the prime pitches snaffled up early by the most serious sellers – rare-issue vinyl, perhaps, or old coins; tables laid with Hornsea pottery; quirky displays of old photographic equipment – but that's not invariably the case. There are two selling areas; one at the front, which gets all of the sunshine and most of the foot traffic, and another at the back, where those stallholders who aren't at the front of the queue when it comes to staking pitches must shiver in the shade. Simple food – tea, coffee, bacon butties and occasional BBQs in summer – is available, and there are toilets on site.

VINTAGE MARKET Ⓐ F Block, Old Truman Brewery, 85 Brick Lane E1 6QL Ⓣ 020 7770 6020 Ⓦ www.vintage-market.co.uk & www.trumanbrewery. com Clothing and accessories for women and men from the 1920s to the 90s. Conveniently occurs every Friday, Saturday and Sunday so you can make a weekend of it, if you've got the stamina. Don't miss the nearby Sunday Upmarket at Elys Yard for more fashion, art and design (takes in some new vintage) or the adjacent Backyard Market that showcases young designers with a focus on arts, crafts and kitsch.

WIMBLEDON CAR BOOT SALE Ⓐ Wimbledon Greyhound Stadium, Plough Lane SW17 0BL Ⓣ 020 7240 7405 Two days a week, on Saturday and Sunday (except for Christmas, Easter and New Year) the stadium hosts a large car boot sale opening at 7.30am with half price admission after 8.30am by which time nearly all the very best bargains have been snapped up. Entrance is £2 for the first hour, 50p thereafter.

MOBILE VINTAGE CATERING

THE AFTERNOON TEA PARTY Ⓣ 020 8492 0031 Ⓦ www. theafternoonteaparty.co.uk Based in Highgate, the ATP specialize in hiring out their massive and lovingly preserved collection of vintage china, crockery and cutlery. They can also provide catering for weddings and picnics.

BETTY BLYTHE Ⓐ 73 Blythe Road W14 0HP Ⓣ 020 7602 1177 Ⓦ www. bettyblythe.co.uk A charming place to pop into for a cup of char, the Betty Blythe vintage tearoom in west London also provides catering of all kinds. Even – bravely or foolishly – offering kids' parties.

TRULY SCRUMPTIOUS Ⓐ 18 Phipps Hatch Lane EN2 0HL Ⓣ 01707 660371 Ⓦ www.trulyscrumptiouscatering.co.uk While plenty of caterers offer frou-frou afternoon teas with a vintage twist, the Scrumptious crew really live up to their name, with artisan chocolate cake and finger-food that's a cut above.

THE VINTAGE CATERING COMPANY Ⓐ 97 Camberwell Station Road SE5 9JJ Ⓣ 020 7738 7738 Ⓦ www.thevintagecateringcompany.com The VCC own a fleet of cute vintage ice-cream vans – Citroëns, Bedfords and Asquiths – fully kitted out to supply you with old-school snacks such as Ashmoor Hall Farm sausages or Cornish ice cream.

THE VINTAGE PATISSERIE Ⓐ 422a Mare Street E8 1HP Ⓣ 0800 955 1920 Ⓦ www.vintagepatisserie. co.uk Founded in 2007 by Angel Adoree, Vintage Patisserie is a classy operation providing customized tea parties (big or small) either at their Hackney HQ or at a venue of your own choosing. There are three possible time slots: Brunch High Tea in the mornings, Afternoon Tea and Evening Tea. All cost £45 per head.

VINTAGE STYLE TEAS Ⓣ 020 8643 2181 Ⓦ www.vintagestyleteas.com Vintage Style Teas offer a bespoke vintage afternoon tea service. They can serve you up homemade scones, cakes, cucumber sandwiches and typical "English village green" fare, all presented on vintage bunting and table linen. For weddings, they'll even organize vintage games for your guests.

VINTAGE TEA SETS Ⓣ 07540 293681 Ⓦ www.vintageteasets.co.uk This company assure you they can be "era-specific", and can provide a venue with vintage china, table linen, centrepieces and table styling, in addition to the food and catering staff you'd expect.

MOD

BAR ITALIA Ⓐ 22 Frith Street W1D 4RF Ⓣ 020 7437 4520 Ⓦ www. baritaliasoho.co.uk A family business since 1949, this Italian coffee bar has changed little since then and still uses the same secret blend of coffee. A slice of Little Italy "goodfellas-style", complete with a large poster of legendary boxer Rocky Marciano. A scooter club meets here every Sunday. *[See Central London]*

THE FACE Ⓐ 1 Marlborough Court W1F 7EE Ⓣ 020 7439 4706 Ⓦ www. carnaby.co.uk/store/the-face For over four decades The Face has stood just off Carnaby Street providing mods with iconic British clothing brands, footwear and three button tonic suits.

MENDOZA MENSWEAR 158 Brick Lane E1 6RU Ⓣ 020 7377 5263 Ⓦ www.mendozamenswear.com No less an authority than Ⓦ www.modculture.

co.uk has approved this "mod-friendly" menswear company. It uses mod designs and originals as inspirations for its modernist brand.

SCOOTERCAFFÈ Ⓐ 132 Lower Marsh SE1 7AE Ⓣ 020 7620 1421 Close to the back of Waterloo station, this bar offers arguably the best vintage coffee experience in London. Owned by a New Zealand scooter specialist and collector of vintage machinery. *[See South London]*

MUSEUMS AND GALLERIES

2 WILLOW ROAD Ⓐ Hampstead NW3 1TH Ⓣ 020 7435 6166 Ⓦ www. nationaltrust.org.uk/home/item236903 This classic modernist house was designed in 1939 by architect Ernö Goldfinger as his family home. Many locals objected at the time but its simple brick exterior and clean lines make it a surprisingly unobtrusive addition to the neighbourhood. It's now owned by the National Trust and still contains the Goldfingers' art collection and much of the original furniture. The house is closed over the winter.

DAS PROGRAMM Ⓣ 07908 710968 Ⓦ www.dasprogramm.org Not exactly a museum, Das Programm celebrates (and sells) the work of cult German product designer Dieter Rams (b.1932), specifically his Braun electrical goods and the furniture he designed for Vitsœ. Based in Highgate, viewings of the work can be made by appointment. Das Programm also hire and ship goods.

★ DENNIS SEVERS HOUSE ★

Ⓐ 18 Folgate Street E1 6BX Ⓣ 020 7247 4013 Ⓦ www.dennissevershouse.co.uk Ⓞ Mon noon–2pm, Sun noon–4pm

This immersive experience set in an 18th-century Spitalfields townhouse is the invention and legacy of the late artist Dennis Severs. It offers a unique tour in which you're invited to step back in time to several different periods within the history of the house.

The premise is that you've entered the home of a family of Huguenot weavers, the Jervises, and although you sense their presence, they remain just out of sight. As you move upwards through the candlelit halls, you embark on a sensory journey taking you from 1724 to 1914 with the help of ten atmospheric rooms. Sound and smell make for key companions, the silence punctuated with occasional audio accompaniment, the smells of various foodstuffs tickling the nostrils as you pace the old floorboards. Visitors will love all the little personal details, from the hand-painted tiles (old and new), to the cosmetics laid out on the dresser, to the freshly

made coffee and boiled egg by the bed. It all makes for a very effective installation, with many an anachronistic touch to bring you back up to date. Entrance costs £10 per person on Sundays, and £7 per person on Monday lunchtimes. The house is particularly glorious in the approach to Christmas – Silent Night evenings cost £17.50, or you can get the full Christmas experience for £45 per person, including mulled wine, mince pies and a chance to discuss the house with the curatorial team.

THE DESIGN MUSEUM Ⓐ 28 Shad Thames SE1 2YD Ⓣ 020 7403 6933 Ⓦ www.designmuseum.org This small but beautifully formed museum, housed in a former warehouse on the river, is industry-funded (rather than state) so there is an admission charge. A showcase for the best modern design from the 1900s onwards, it has a good permanent display but the temporary exhibitions – ranging from cutting-edge fashion to industrial design classics – are equally impressive. Other facilities include talks, podcasts and courses, and there is an online archive. There is also a good café and a shop.

ELTHAM PALACE Ⓐ Court Yard, off Court Road SE9 5QE Ⓣ 08703 331181 Ⓦ www.english-heritage.org.uk Henry VIII spent his childhood here and there's a well-preserved and impressive Great Hall but Eltham earns its vintage chops by virtue of the stunning Art Deco home built next to the hall for Stephen Courtauld in 1935. The *pièce de resistance* is the large, light-filled entrance hall, with its futuristic glass dome. This and all the rooms were designed by Rolf Engströmer, one of the unsung stars of Art Deco design.

★ FASHION AND TEXTILE MUSEUM ★

Ⓐ 83 Bermondsey Street SE1 3XF Ⓣ 020 7407 8664 Ⓦ www.ftmlondon.org
Ⓞ Tue-Sat 11am–6pm

For fashion historians and anyone interested in the cultural back-story behind vintage designs, this is a must-visit destination. Founded by designer Zandra Rhodes in 2003, the startling building – a riot of hot pink, orange and yellow – is the work of Mexican architect Ricardo Legoretta and a thing of wonder in its own right. Bermondsey is a neighbourhood on the up and near enough to Borough Market and Tate Modern, to make the museum – which hosts two or three ticketed exhibitions a year – a good starting point for a gastro-cultural day out.

The museum archives contain many rare pieces from British designers, including Rhodes herself – she manages to slip one or two of her creations into museum shows, but as an influence on the London design scene since founding her first boutique in 1966, she's earned the right. Now managed by Newham College, the museum also offers programmes of talks, and courses and one-off workshops in sewing, haberdashery, textile design, and pattern making as well as in digital design skills.

THE GEFFRYE MUSEUM Ⓐ Kingsland Road E2 8EA Ⓣ 020 7739 9893

Ⓦ www.geffrye-museum.org.uk Hoxton's renowned museum, located in what used to be 18th-century almshouses, is an arrangement of eleven domestic interiors, displayed chronologically from 1630 to the present day. There's a 20th-century extension to the mostly antique displays starting with an Edwardian Arts and Crafts drawing room and rooms re-creating spaces from 1935, 1965 and 1998. A good place to include in a Hoxton vintage weekend itinerary.

THE IMPERIAL WAR MUSEUM

Ⓐ Lambeth Road SE1 6HZ Ⓣ 020 7416 5000 Ⓦ www.iwm.org.uk The IWM may seem a slightly grisly recommendation for vintage aficionados, but in addition to all the weaponry the museum also shows how modern warfare has impacted on ordinary people's lives, in displays such as the Blitz Experience. Punters especially interested in World War II should also consider visiting the Churchill War Rooms in Whitehall which are also run by the IWM.

LEIGHTON HOUSE MUSEUM Ⓐ 12

Holland Park Road W14 8LZ Ⓣ 020 7602 3316 Ⓦ www.rbkc.gov.uk/museums For lovers of late-Victorian aestheticism (think intense women and soulful men), Leighton House is a must-see. The home of leading 19th-century painter Frederick Leighton, it is one of the finest examples of a custom-built artist's house and studio. The high point is the magical Arab Hall, decorated with hundreds of tiles from Syria, and with a pool and fountain at its centre.

LONDON TRANSPORT MUSEUM Ⓐ Covent Garden Piazza Ⓣ 020 7379 6344 Ⓦ www.ltmuseum.co.uk A popular museum with plenty of vintage buses and tubes from Victorian times to the golden age of London Transport (1920–60), when branding and design were overseen by Frank Pick who hired some remarkable talents such as graphic artist E. McKnight Kauffer and architect Charles Holden. The excellent shop has plenty of vintage-style items, including furniture upholstered with the type of moquette fabric used for old train and bus seats. For those bitten with by LT bug, the finest surviving Holden-designed tube station is the circular Arnos Grove of 1932 on the northern section of the Piccadilly Line (Wood Green on the same stretch of line is also pretty good).

MUSEUM OF BRANDS, PACKAGING AND ADVERTISING Ⓐ 2 Colville Mews, Lonsdale Road W11 2AR Ⓣ 020 7908 0880 Ⓦ www. museumofbrands.com Consumer packaging and advertising of all "aspects of daily life" from Victorian times to the present day. A fascinating slice of social history and a nostalgia-fest for many visitors.

MUSEUM OF LONDON Ⓐ 150 London Wall EC2Y 5HN Ⓣ 020 7001 9844 Ⓦ www.museumoflondon.org.uk Of the nine galleries covering the whole of London's history, the most relevant for vintagistas are the People's City (1850–1940s) and World City (1950s–today). There's a vast amount of interesting material on show including the original Art Deco lift from Selfridges department store. The museum also has a Docklands branch at Canary Wharf.

POLLOCK'S TOY MUSEUM Ⓐ 1 Scala Street W1T 2HL Ⓣ 020 7636 3452 Ⓦ www.pollockstoymuseum.com Tucked away close to Goodge Street tube above a working toyshop is a museum of six small rooms. This is the place to go to ogle vintage teddy bears, dolls' houses, mechanical toys and folk toys. Closed Sundays and bank holidays.

★ VICTORIA AND ALBERT MUSEUM ★

Ⓐ Cromwell Road, SW7 2RL Ⓣ 020 7942 2000 Ⓦ www.vam.ac.uk Ⓞ Daily 10am–5.45pm (Fri 10am–10pm)

The V&A is one of the world's greatest museums of applied art and design, offering an extraordinary survey of beautiful things from every corner of the globe and every period of human civilization. The museum is enormous, and it's a good idea to focus on just a small part of it at a time. Inevitably there is a great deal that might be thought of as "vintage". Bear in mind that objects can be arranged by period, nationality or by material, so that, for example, you can experience a broad survey of modernist design in Rooms 74 and 76 but can also look separately at 20th-century studio pottery in Room 142. If there is something specific that you want to see always check in advance that the particular room is open on the day of your visit. Temporary exhibitions often have a 20th-century focus and a strong vintage flavour, such as the recent "British Design 1948–2012" and "Ball Gowns – British Glamour since 1950."

The Modern galleries (Rooms 74 and 76) are very manageable and offer a quick tour of the last century, dividing at 1945. As with so much of the V&A it's an incredible mélange of objects, everything from teapots and candlesticks to furnishing fabrics and advertising materials. "Design since 1945" is even more sparing in its selection of objects, and carries less authority as a survey, but is full of interesting one-offs. It's displayed in a much brighter space, giving an immediate sense of jumping forward in time – and to a different set of design values. It's the shock of the familiar: objects that you remember using yourself, or seeing at relatives' houses.

The Fashion Galleries are housed within an imposing circular space (Room 40) and provide a remarkable survey of both clothes and accessories from 1750 to the present day. Displays are both chronological and thematic, and the collection is particularly rich in 20th-century material. The revolutions in style since the 1950s are sampled with pieces by all the great names, from Christian Dior to Alexander McQueen. Because fashion is one of the museum's strongest draws, temporary exhibitions are held pretty regularly and are staged in the two-storey central display area of the gallery. There's usually an entrance charge to temporary exhibitions but the museum itself is free. *[See West London]*

NIGHTS OUT

....

[See also Burlesque]

ALL STAR LANES
Ⓐ Victoria House, Bloomsbury Place WC1B 4DA ☎ 020 7025 2676 Ⓦ www. allstarlanes.co.uk Ⓞ Mon–Wed 4pm–11.30pm, Thurs 4pm–2am, Fri noon–2am, Sat 11am–2am, Sun 11am–11pm

Goodness knows what Virginia Woolf or Lytton Strachey would make of it, but American retro-style bowling has taken over Bloomsbury, with two venues

competing to be the area's king of the pins: All Star Lanes and Bloomsbury Bowling Lanes. Both are carefully styled venues, beyond the usual multi-lane experience – more high jinx than high scores – with diners serving burgers and classic American eats. All Star Lanes is the slicker outfit, a combination of white walls and pink-frocked waitresses which has been successfully exported to three more venues around the capital. On Saturday nights "Shake, Rattle and Bowl" pulls in the crowds, the soundtrack a happy mix of Northern Soul, ska and Motown as well as solid rock'n'roll.

★ BETHNAL GREEN WORKING MEN'S CLUB ★

Ⓐ 42–44 Pollard Row E2 6NB Ⓣ 020 7739 7170 Ⓦ www.workersplaytime.net
Ⓞ Hours vary according to event

For a fun-filled retro night out in the east, take your pick from the many throwback soirées at this working men's club. Fifties prom nights, sleazy sixties discos (replete with go-go dancing demoiselles), madcap theme-park bashes and eighties dance parties are among the many delights on offer. The unapologetically dated decor plays its part in giving you that yesteryear feel from the moment you step through the door.

Most events follow a club-night formula punctuated with cheerful burlesque performances and live music, but often it's a case of anything goes, so don't be surprised if an octogenarian club member takes to the stage to sing a few Sinatra-style solos. Punters can get involved too, whether it's playing old-

fashioned party games for dubious prizes, learning a few moves in a swing class or cheering on a dance troupe. And at some point in the proceedings, someone will inevitably bring out a limbo stick or pass around a stack of hula hoops.

Retro DJs expertly set the scene, creating soundtracks from the 1940s up to the 1980s to fit the theme. Dressing up can be a serious affair and while you don't need to be one hundred percent authentic, it's unwise to turn up in shop-bought fancy dress. It's a good idea to arrive early as the place fills up later on, as does the queue for the understated bar and its buckets of mercifully cold Peroni bottles. Keep an eye on the website for regular new developments and for the occasional daytime jumble sale or craft event.

THE BLUES KITCHEN Ⓐ 111–113 Camden High Street NW1 7JN
Ⓣ 020 7387 5277 Ⓦ www.theblueskitchen.com Look out for music events at this bar restaurant serving Southern BBQ food. There are soul nights, boogie woogie, Sunday blues jams, Motown and guest turns from the Stumblin' Slims Rock 'n' Roll Club. Music is both live and DJ-led with most retro genres catered for.

★ BLOOMSBURY LANES ★

Ⓐ Lower level, Tavistock Hotel, Bedford Way WC1H 9EU Ⓣ 020 7183 1979
Ⓦ www.bloomsburybowling.com Ⓞ Mon–Weds noon–1am, Thurs noon–2am, Fri & Sat noon–3am, Sun 1pm–1am

Of Bloomsbury's two bowling joints, Bloomsbury Lanes is, arguably, the more atmospheric with a bar crafted from an old New York bowling lane and its

delightfully youth-club-like carpeted dance floor. It is also the slightly larger
venue with eight lanes for bowling, compared to All Star's four, and has
additional karaoke rooms, for striking notes as well as pins.

Their club nights are big hitters too. Bloomsbury pulls in some impressive
names like Norman Jay and Trojan Sound System as well as hosting nights
themed around things as disparate as retro video games and John Hughes. Book
ahead if you want a lane; there seems to be no lack of people in Bloomsbury
looking to strike it lucky.

BROKEN DOWN DOLL BAR BOUTIQUE Ⓐ 72 Chamberlayne
Road NW10 3JJ Ⓦ www.brokendowndollboutique.blogspot.com Early evening
cocktails with vintage clothing and accessories until 10pm, Thursday to
Saturdays. Ideal for those who like to mash up their fashion with rest, recreation
and socializing.

THE DIRTY WATER CLUB Ⓦ www.dirtywaterrecords.co.uk 1960s and
70s garage rock nights run by Dirty Water Records and featuring such outfits as
The Fleshtones and The Cannibals. Gigs used to be held at The Boston Arms in
Tufnell Park (and sometimes still are), but now the venue of choice seems to be
The Shacklewell Arms in Dalston.

THE GOOD FOOT Ⓐ 8–10 Brewer Street W1F 0SE Ⓣ 020 7734 3040
Ⓦ www.madamejojos.com/club_nights/the_good_foot/about Held at Madame
Jojo's, there has been a nightclub on this spot in Brewer Street since at least
the early 1950s. Named after the James Brown classic "Get on the Good Foot",
Madame Jojo's dance floor is for anyone and everyone who loves the all-out party
euphoria created by vintage sounds.

★ GYPSY HOTEL ★

Ⓐ The Lexington, 96–98 Pentonville Road N1 9JB Ⓦ www.facebook.com/
GypsyHotel Ⓞ Date varies, 8pm–4pm

Not for the faint of heart or the weak of liver, Gypsy Hotel describes itself
as "Bourbon soaked, snake charmin' rock'n'roll cabaret". Well, that's a start.
It's the kind of night when you feel like anything could happen, and it usually
does. One moment you're dancing to some Balkan jazz punk and the next
you're watching a fire-eating burlesque artist. Throw in some dirty ol' blues
and a 40s-style crooner and you're getting closer to the madness. It's not clear
what holds it all together, some black magic possibly? The night's founder, Paul
Ronney Angel, does front the Urban Voodoo Lounge band after all.

There are some stiffer spirits at work in the Gypsy Hotel too. After moving
around venues for a while, the night finally seems to have found a suitable home

at The Lexington, whose red velvet-draped decor and extensive whisky and bourbon selection make a perfect bedfellow for this decadent and drunken night.

The crowd is as varied as the performances are. Rockabilly rebels, punk rockers, vintage princesses and Americana aficionados all hang out here, and can be guaranteed to rise to the occasion in style, whatever's required of them, whether that's cheering, heckling, dancing or cavorting. It's a combination that definitely works: Gypsy Hotel celebrated its sixth anniversary in 2012.

HAPPINESS FORGETS Ⓐ The Basement, 8–9 Hoxton Square N1 6NU Ⓣ 020 7613 0325 Ⓦ www.happinessforgets.com Dimly lit by 1950s onion lamps, this joint calls itself a "high-end cocktail bar [in a] low-rent basement" and is part of a new breed of British drinking establishments for grown-ups. Feel free to talk to the bartender and learn about artisan British spirits.

LA BELLE EPOQUE PARTY Ⓣ 020 7724 1617 Ⓦ www. belleepoqueparty.com Tuning in to the decadent aesthetic of *fin de siècle* Paris (think absinthe and the Moulin Rouge), Belle Epoque periodically conjures a world of circus and courtesans, music hall and cocktails, velvet, feathers and top hats.

LADY LUCK CLUB Ⓦ www.ladyluckclub.co.uk Dress-up nights, rock music and swing, and lots of dancing. Probably the busiest (and hottest) vintage night out organizer in London with something always going on at a variety of venues. Also responsible for a radio show on Shoreditch Radio featuring underground sounds from the 1920s to the 60s.

★ MOUSETRAP ★

Ⓐ Orleans, 259 Seven Sisters Road N4 2DD Ⓦ www.newuntouchables.com Ⓞ Monthly, Sat 10pm–6am

Round the corner from Finsbury Park bus station, amidst some rough and ready pubs and chicken bars, isn't really where you'd expect to find a club night catering to discerning 60s music fans. But that's one of several quirks of Mousetrap, which has been running in the same location since 2001. And it's a club night with a music policy set to please the most particular kind of enthusiast, alternating between two different nights: Fuzz for Freaks, where garage, psychedelia and freakbeat are the order of the day, and Soul Shakers which is flavoured by ska, Motown and R&B sounds. Organized by the New Untouchables, promoters of 60s and mod culture, the nights attract a young, friendly and fiercely passionate crowd, as exacting about the clothes they wear as they are about the music policy. Their fabulous array of authentic looks provides the colour for the evening in this small and unglamorous venue. Its main selling point, especially for the soul dancers, is the wooden dance floor.

Things officially kick off at 10pm but activity on the dance floor really gets going later on, with tired feet almost guaranteed with the £10 entrance fee by the time the 6am closing time comes. Stumbling out amongst Finsbury Park's early risers and lost souls, the immaculately coiffed gentlemen and ladies disperse back across the city. Ears ringing and feet still tapping, there's always the guarantee they'll see each other again same place, same time next month.

PERIOD COSTUME HIRE

ANGELS Ⓐ1 Garrick Road NW9 6AA Ⓣ 020 8202 2244 Ⓦ www.angels. uk.com With the largest collection of costumes and accessories in the world, Angels can supply you with anything you could possibly imagine wearing. While you can't just turn up to their vast warehouse, you can book a tour, and there's also a well-stocked fancy dress shop on Shaftesbury Avenue.

ANTOINETTE COSTUME HIRE Ⓐ High Street Buildings, 134 Kirkdale SE26 4BB Ⓣ 020 8699 1913 Ⓦ www.costumehirelondon.com Describing themselves as "vintage costumiers with a fancy dress heart", Antoinette's south London base holds a large selection of fancy dress, theatrical costumes and period evening wear for him and her.

THE COSTUME STUDIO Ⓐ Montgomery House, 159 Balls Pond Road N1 4BG Ⓣ 020 7923 9472 Ⓦ www.costumestudio.co.uk Though it's aimed more at the TV and film industry than the dedicated partygoer, non-entertainment-professionals can still hire from this east London costume company.

NATIONAL THEATRE COSTUME HIRE STORE Ⓐ Chichester House, Kennington Park Business Estate, 1–3 Brixton Rd SW9 6DE Ⓣ 020 7735 4774 Ⓦ www.nationaltheatre.org.uk/costume-and-props-hire The NT's archive of costumes from bygone productions has a seemingly endless amount of racks

to browse. You'll need to book an appointment, but once you're there you'll want to stay all week.

PRANGSTA Ⓐ 304 New Cross Road SE14 6AF Ⓣ 020 8694 9869 Ⓦ www.prangsta. co.uk It's not surprising that this is the steampunk scene's costume hire place of choice:

the weird and wonderful stock here moves from the 1920s and 30s to the truly eccentric and outrageous. *[See South London]*

VIOLET'S BOX Ⓦ www.violetsbox.com Violet's Box contains a glamorous selection of outfits and accessories browsable by decade from the 1920s to the 80s, as well as by quirky costume categories ranging from "burlesque" to "Bavarian". Online-only, though trying-on appointments can be booked.

REPAIRS & RESTORATION

[See also Dressmaking, Tailoring & Alterations]

AFTER NOAH Ⓐ 121 Upper Street N1 1QP Ⓣ 020 7359 4281 Ⓦ www. afternoah.com This Aladdin's cave of vintage and antique furniture, homeware (and much more beside) also has a furniture restoration service. Though adept at fixing classic 20th-century items, they will not touch any modern or cheap stuff. *[See North London]*

CLASSIC SHOE REPAIRS Ⓐ 23–25 Brecknock Road N7 0BL Ⓣ 020 7485 5275 Ⓦ www.classicshoerepairs.com Designers such as Versace, Russell & Bromley and Gucci send their repairs here, as do a number of celebrities. Don't miss the many celebrity autographs which can be seen in the shop.

ELLIOTT & TATE Ⓐ 55 Dalston Lane E8 2NG Ⓣ 07947 764521 / 07840 003027 Ⓦ www.elliottandtate.com A quality outfit dealing in classic Danish furniture, the company also offers a restoration service for 20th-century furniture in general. Free estimates are provided.

FENS RESTORATION Ⓐ 46 Lots Road SW10 0QF Ⓣ 020 7352 9883 Ⓦ www.fensrestoration.co.uk Established twenty years ago, Fens restores furniture and metal objects of all kinds with a variety of different finishes possible. The shop also sells one-off pieces of French furniture and fittings.

JOHN ALVEY TURNER Ⓐ Unit 9, 43 Carol Street NW1 0HT Ⓣ 07986 285584 Ⓦ www.johnalveyturner.co.uk This musical instrument firm, founded in 1793, now specializes in every kind of fretted string instruments. As well as buying and selling instruments, they also do quality restoration and repair work.

LONDON ANTIQUE CLOCK CENTRE Ⓐ 87 Portobello Road W11 2QB Ⓣ 020 7985 0374 Ⓦ www.clockcentre.com Dating back to 1963, this shop sells all types of vintage time pieces from pocket watches to skeleton clocks. It's equally well known for its team of specialist repairers, with estimates provided free of charge.

LONDON SOUND ⓐ389b Alexandra Avenue HA2 9EF ⓦwww.
londonsound.org Set up in 1969, London Sound specializes in repairs of vintage
radios and radiograms as well as any hi-fi you care to mention. A free estimate is
available and all restored equipment gets an impressive twelve-month gaurantee.

SHOESHINE.CO ⓐTerminal 5 Heathrow Airport TW6 2GA Seriously old-
fashioned shoeshine while you wait. They don't so much restore your shoes (too
bad if a heel has dropped off) as buff them up like never before.

SPIT'N'POLISH SHOESHINE ⓐMarylebone Station NW1 6JJ Modern
take on the traditional shoeshine at one of London's most appealing and
vintagey railway stations. For details of other locations visit Shoeshine Express
at ⓦ www.shoeshine.net

TIM MARTEN GUITAR & AMP REPAIRS ⓐ9 Denmark Street
WC2H 8LS ☎07780 771673 / 07964 174387 ⓦ www.timmartenrepairs.co.uk
Tim Marten is the doyen of electric guitar repairers. If he's good enough for the
likes of Jimmy Page, Ray Davies and Roger Waters, he's surely good enough for
you. Based in the heart of Tin Pan Alley, where he's been, on and off, since 1977.

REPRODUCTION VINTAGE

BEGGARS RUN ⓐ2nd Floor, 47 Approach Road E2 9LY ☎020 8133 3466
ⓦwww.beggarsrun.com Beggars Run's approach is not so much repro-retro,
as a modern stylish take on classic male attire. Plenty of natty suits to choose
from, or maybe a midnight blue velvet dinner jacket is more your line, or an
overcoat with a fur collar? Chic, elegant and hip, and simultaneously timeless –
what more could you want?

BETTYLICIOUS ⓦwww.bettylicious.co.uk BettyLicious is an online store
that specializes in "vintage-inspired, 1940s/50s faux fashion and Hollywood
glamour clothing for very special ladies". This includes dresses, skirts and tops
but also lingerie and swimwear.

FREDDIES OF PINEWOOD ☎07711 686096/07956 864064 ⓦwww.
freddiesofpinewood.co.uk Online shop specializing in 1940s and 50s reproduction
jeans for men and women made from high quality denim. They also offer a
range of other vintage-style clothes – not all denim – including dungarees, pedal
pushers and capris.

REVIVAL 2.11 Kingly Court W1B 5PW ☎020 7287 8709 ⓦ www.revival-
retro.com A company with a passion for the 1930s and 40s. They love the music,

the fashions, the films and most of all the dancing, and sell the very best in modern day reproductions and reinterpretations of original fashions from that era. *[See Central London]*

SPLENDID STITCHES Ⓣ 07766 801108 Ⓦ www.splendidstitches.co.uk If your favourite vintage dress is falling apart (or you simply fancy another one in a different fabric), it can be rescued here. Splendid Stitches will take your much-loved original and either fix it or make you an exact copy.

THE VINTAGE DRESSMAKER Ⓦ www.irmaromero.wordpress.com Irma Romero is a London-based designer with a passion for vintage. She makes clothes that are based on old patterns, using quality fabrics that are often vintage in origin. All her outfits are bespoke and made to measure.

VIVIEN OF HOLLOWAY Ⓐ 294 Holloway Road N7 6NJ Ⓣ 020 7609 8754 Ⓦ www.vivienofholloway.com As well as fabulous frocks and separates in limited edition fabrics and styles, the shop also carries a wide range of hair-flowers, jewellery, shoes, handbags and more. It even has some of Vivien's own new vintage collection for sale. *[See North London]*

VITRA LTD Ⓐ 30 Clerkenwell Road EC1M 5PQ Ⓣ 020 7608 6200 Ⓦ www.vitra.com Vitra is a Swiss company which produces high-quality home and office furniture, much of which uses the designs by some of the key figures of the mid-20th century, including Charles and Ray Eames, and Jean Prouvé. Vitra's Clerkenwell showrooms are like a museum of iconic design and is worth visiting for inspiration (even if you can't afford to purchase).

SECRET LOCATION EVENTS

THE CANDLELIGHT CLUB Ⓦ www.thecandlelightclub.com Pop-up 1920s-themed speakeasy cocktail bar with live period music, always in a cool secret London location. Illuminated entirely by candlelight, hence the name.

DIE FRECHE MUSE Ⓦ www.diefrechemuse.co.uk Burlesque-tinged pop-up events with a decadent feel from an experienced team. Whether it's a Halloween romp inspired by tragic Hollywood stars or a Warhol Factory party, these are the glamour events for both the beautiful and the damned.

THE LAST TUESDAY SOCIETY Ⓐ 11 Mare Street E8 4RP Ⓣ 020 7998 3617 Ⓦ www.thelasttuesdaysociety.org The shop is packed to the rafters with taxidermy and other weird and wonderful curiosities, including a stuffed mermaid. Its owner, Viktor Wynd, also hosts and organizes several bizarre and original events. The themed balls are the most popular but there are also seances, lectures and literary discussions. Expect the unexpected.

LONDON POP-UPS Ⓦ www.londonpopups.com Not all pop-ups are vintage but a decent proportion are and this directory/calendar is a good place to check up on surprises and happenings.

THE PALE BLUE DOOR Ⓦ www.tonyhornecker.wordpress.com Occasional pop-up dining experience organized by artist Tony Hornecker at secret locations (but usually in Dalston). Dinner served with dashes of camp and drag artistry in a space reminiscent of surreal retro animation half *Belleville Rendezvous* half Jan Svankmajer.

PROHIBITION Ⓣ 020 7724 1617 Ⓦ www.prohibition1920s.com Prohibition nights at secret venues with cocktails in teacups, live music, gambling tables and general all-round glamour. The dress code is strict so it's top hats, spats and flapper dresses and absolutely not jeans and trainers. Be warned, tickets sell fast.

SECRET CINEMA Ⓦ www.secretcinema.org Immersive live cinematic experiences brought to you by an innovative events company that wants to re-create the awe and wonder of social cinema going. With costumes, surprise locations and sometimes even a secret choice of film there's a big buzz building around Secret Cinema and London is the perfect place for this venture to take root. Tickets are not cheap but, by most accounts, worth the investment.

VENUES

THE HORSE HOSPITAL Ⓐ Colonnade WC1N 1JD ☎ 020 7833 3644
Ⓦ www.thehorsehospital.com Avant-garde arts and fashion centre housed in
a two-floor purpose-built stable with several original period features including
iron pillars and tethering rings. The Contemporary Wardrobe Collection
is based here; they run occasional sales and also hire out clothes Ⓦ www.
contemporarywardrobe.com.

HOXTON HALL Ⓐ 130 Hoxton Street N1 6SH ☎ 020 7684 0060 Ⓦ www.
hoxtonhall.co.uk This gem of a small-scale music hall first opened in 1863. It
now functions as a community centre and performance space, but can also be
hired out for events. Not quite as stunning as Wilton's, this is still a wonderfully
atmospheric venue.

★ THE RIVOLI BALLROOM ★

Ⓐ 350 Brockley Road SE4 2BY ☎ 020 8692 5130 Ⓦ www.therivoli.co.uk
Ⓞ Sat 7.30pm–noon; Sun 7.30pm–11pm; Jive Party Sundays 8pm–1am. This
lost treasure has survived previous incarnations as a music hall and an early
picture palace before its revival as a 1950s ballroom, and traces from all of
these past lives remain in the Edwardian wall panelling, or the buffet area with
its burgundy vinyl-covered booths with grey geometric prints on the formica
tables.

Indeed, there is more burgundy and crimson decor here than in the entire
Angus Steak House chain, but put to infinitely more stylish use. Velvet-
cushioned chairs, strokable flocked wallpaper and tasselled Chinese lanterns
are the order of the day, along with chandeliers with flickering bulbs to
simulate gaslight. Every surface that can be, is covered with patterned tiles,
paisley brocade, and whatever flourishes will stick – even the walls of the
ladies' loos are pink marble.

Ultimately, it's about the dancing, and all are welcome on Saturday and
Sunday evenings. The Rivoli's clientele covers all ages, and children are allowed,
as long as they're with an adult (to prevent them sneaking into the bars). Jive
Party, on the third Sunday of each month, is the biggest draw of all, with live
big bands and the occasional full orchestra. Each evening begins with dance
classes for beginners before the floor fills with regulars, dressed to jive and
swing the decades away.

THE ROUNDHOUSE Ⓐ Chalk Farm Road NW1 8EH ☎ 08444 828008
Ⓦ www.roundhouse.org.uk Originally built in 1847 as a turning shed for

locomotives, The Roundhouse achieved its notoriously arty and radical
reputation back in the 1960s as the politically motivated Centre 42. What was
a rough and ready building then is now state-of-the-art music and arts centre.
The café attempts to conjure up something of the venue's both past with posters
evoking the glory days of The Who and Jimi Hendrix, who performed here.

★ WILTON'S MUSIC HALL ★

Ⓐ 1 Graces Alley E1 8JB Ⓣ 020 7702 2789 Ⓦ www.wiltons.org.uk Ⓞ Mahogany
Bar: Mon–Fri noon–11pm, Sat 5pm–11pm; Green Room Bar: Thurs–Sat from
6pm The jewel in Whitechapel's slightly tatty crown is the venerable Wilton's
Music Hall, a Victorian relic with a thriving arts programme, and also one of
the nicest places in London to have a drink. The auditorium is currently being
lovingly restored, but a programme of music, theatre, comedy, cinema and
cabaret continues in Wilton's other spaces, with historical tours of the building
taking place on Mondays and Saturdays.

The picturesquely dilapidated ground-floor Mahogany Bar, which is even older
than the theatre, serves delicious free snacks between 6pm and 8pm on weekday
evenings, often to free live musical accompaniment. Upstairs is the Green
Room, a speakeasy-style cocktail bar, initially opened to the public as part of
an immersive *Great Gatsby* theatre performance, and so popular that it's now a
flourishing little space with a sophisticated cocktail list. This is a more intimate
area, with the bar concealed behind its own mini set of stage curtains – book in
advance to secure a table.

VINTAGE FAIRS

ANITA'S VINTAGE FASHION FAIRS ⓦ www.vintagefashionfairs.com
Anita's fairs are held in Notting Hill and Battersea, and have attracted a strong
and devoted following with roughly one fair a month.

CLERKENWELL VINTAGE FASHION FAIR ⓐ The Old
Finsbury Town Hall, Rosebery Avenue EC1R 4RP ⓣ 020 7254 4054 ⓦ www.
clerkenwellvintagefashionfair.co.uk Regular, high-profile and upmarket vintage
fair with around fifty traders in evidence. Typically £4 for entry with tearoom
and other attractions. Located centrally close to Farringdon and Angel tubes.

ELVIRA VINTAGE ⓣ 020 3302 5748 ⓦ www.elviravintage.com Elvira,
the brainchild of former Central St Martin's students Tori Steinberg and Sophie
Scrimgeour, is an occasional pop-up shop selling high-end, carefully selected
vintage pieces at affordable prices.

FROCK ME ⓐ Chelsea Town Hall, King's Road SW3 5EE ⓣ 020 7254 4054
ⓦ www.frockmevintagefashion.com One of the very first vintage fashion fairs
in London. With over fifty exhibitors selling a complete cross section of vintage
clothing and accessories from the 1900s right up to the 80s. Emphasis is on
designer fashion, but you can still find a real bargain if you are prepared to browse.

HAMMERSMITH VINTAGE FASHION FAIR ⓐ Hammersmith
Town Hall, King Street W6 9JU ⓦ www.pa-antiques.co.uk One of London's
leading fairs is held every five or six weeks. This is a big event and you are
likely to find a good cross-section of vintage clothing covering the tastes and
changing fashions of over a century. Admission is £10 between 8am and 10am, £5
thereafter.

★ JUDY'S AFFORDABLE VINTAGE FAIR ★

ⓐ York Hall, 5 Old Ford Road E2 9PJ ⓦ www.judysvintagefair.co.uk

Shopping for vintage finds is always interesting for the element of treasure-
hunting involved but it's nice to go somewhere where you're guaranteed to find
something special at a price you can afford. Enter Judy's Affordable Vintage
Fair, a champion of good-value second-hand shopping since 2005. Judy's fashion
market travels up and down the UK, taking its handpicked traders and wares
around the major cities and towns. This is vintage shopping with a fair price tag, a
nice change from the inflated prices you often find in more conventional outlets.

Judy's sets up five times a year at Bethnal Green's York Hall, and sometimes at
Spitalfields Market, always with a mini tearoom and beauty parlour in operation,

as well as packed stalls of clothing and accessories from the last century. The fun doesn't stop there: there's also the regular Vintage Furniture Flea, with a raft of ceramics, fabrics, well-preserved retro furniture and kitchen items; and the child-centric Junior Vintage & Craft Fair, selling toys, books, clothing and more, with special entertainment laid on for when the kids are all shopped out. Entry at Bethnal Green is £2, Spitalfields is free.

THE LONDON ANTIQUE TEXTILES, VINTAGE COSTUMES, CARPETS & TRIBAL ART FAIR ☎020 8543 5075 Ⓦwww.pa-antiques.co.uk Brought to you by the organizers of the Hammersmith Vintage Fair, this event usually takes place at Hammersmith Town Hall or at the Olympia Hilton Hotel. It casts its net wide, though only some of the fifty or so dealers, are offering vintage wares.

THE LONDON VINTAGE FASHION, TEXTILES & ACCESSORIES FAIR ☎020 8543 5075 Ⓦwww.pa-antiques.co.uk With over nineteen years' experience of organizing specialist events, it has been described as the "Rolls Royce of Vintage Fashion Fairs". Delivers an exciting, enjoyable experience to shoppers.

LONDON VINTAGE WEDDING FAIR *[See Lifestyle: Weddings]*

NORTH LONDON VINTAGE MARKET ⒶSt Mary's Parish Hall, Cranley Gardens N10 3AH Ⓦwww.northlondonvintagemarket.blogspot.co.uk Regular market fairs in Crouch End, selling a mixed bag of stuff including furniture, kitchenware, and ephemera as well as fashion items. Entrance costs £1.50.

POP UP VINTAGE FAIRS LONDON Ⓦwww.facebook.com/popupvintagefairs A movable feast of vintage fashion. Pop Up appear at regular intervals usually at Hampstead Town Hall or the nearby St Stephen's Church in Pond Street (recently restored for community and public use).

SAMAYA LING VINTAGE ☎07877 057082 Ⓦwww.samayalingvintage.com This vintage retailer specializes in high end fashion and accessories from the 1920s and 30s, right up to the 80s. Available to view by appointment or you can visit her stand at The London Vintage Fashion Fair or at Frock Me Vintage in Chelsea.

THE VINTAGE EVENT ⒶBalham Bowls Club, 7–9 Ramsden Road SW12 8QX Ⓦwww.thevintageevent.com Events take in live music, performers and even a vintage gin (and tea) room. Usually held in Balham but also sometimes at The Dogstar in Coldharbour Lane, Brixton.

★ THE VINTAGE FAIR ★

ⓐShoreditch Town Hall, 380 Old Street EC1V 9LT Ⓦwww.thevintagefair.com

The Vintage Fair, which pops up in different venues across the UK, is another great gathering of men's and women's vintage wares. Its usual London location is the fantastic Shoreditch Town Hall, where the fair appears five or six times a year. It's a big crowd-puller, drawing huge queues of well-dressed shoppers along Old Street just before it opens.

There's usually between forty to sixty stalls in attendance at each fair, so there's always plenty of material to choose from. Vendors come laden with clothing and accessories from the 1940s to the 80s, and you can also buy crafts and jewellery from up-and-coming designer-makers. Not bad for the £2 entry fee. No vintage shindig would be complete without the requisite tearoom, retro soundtrack and classic makeovers (care of expert stylists Lipstick and Curls); the Vintage Fair has all of this, plus games, live music acts and fun workshops to get visitors involved. There's something for every price bracket and it's easy to lose an entire day here.

VINTAGE FASHION FAIR LONDON ⓐCecil Sharp House, 2 Regent's Park Road NW1 7AY Ⓣ020 7485 2206 Ⓦwww.vintagefashionfairlondon.co.uk
Holding a number of fairs throughout the year at their usual venue in Primrose Hill. Fashion Fair dates are published on the website. You will be able to find very wearable vintage pieces at affordable prices and also designer labels if you are looking for something extra special.

VINTAGE KILO SALE Ⓦwww.judysvintagefair.co.uk/kilo/ Lots of quality mixed vintage from the 1970s through to the 90s. A hundred rails of clothing and accessories all in one pop-up shop. Payment is by weight, with one kilo of clothing costing a mere £15.

VINTAZIA FRIDAY NIGHT VINTAGE FAIRS ⓐSt Luke's, The Avenue TW9 2AJ Ⓣ07880 531958 Ⓦwww.vintaziavintagefairs.co.uk. A regular event in Kew, Vintazia is a bargain at £2 for entry. Their aim is to mix shopping with entertainment, fashion, accessories, furniture and lots more.

WANSTEAD VINTAGE FASHION AND BROCANTE FAIR
ⓐChristchurch Hall, Wanstead Place E11 2SW Ⓣ07860 214 009 Ⓦwww.lovevintage.co.uk This rising star in the Vintage Fair circuit has been going since 2010 and holds around four fairs a year. Brocante, for those with rudimentary French, roughly translates as secondhand.

WEBSITES & BLOGS

DIARY OF A VINTAGE GIRL Ⓦ www.diaryofavintagegirl.com The world's not short of vintage blogs with London connections but this is a particularly persuasive one from Fleur de Guerre, a multitalented freelancer, vintage girl-about-town and writer. With lots of links to fellow vintagistas.

RETRO CHICK Ⓦ www.retrochick.co.uk One of the UK's leading vintage lifestyle and fashion blogs with a particular passion for the 1930s to the mid-50s and a mild obsession with the styles and everyday life of World War II.

STYLEEAST Ⓦ www.styleeast.blogspot.co.uk Showing some stylish places and faces in east London, focuses on the area's wackier residents. Behind the camera is Jennifer X, by day a besuited financier, by night a dedicated fashion hunter.

SWELL VINTAGE Ⓦ www.swellvintage.blogspot.co.uk A blog with an online jewellery store attached to it, Swell Vintage was born out of a love for history, jewellery and all things handmade. This is jewellery that celebrates the past, but is also fun, unique and wearable.

THRIFTMYSTYLE Ⓦ sharonrosepixie.blogspot.co.uk A diary of vintage pieces discovered more or less everywhere they can be found. The blogger's obsessions are eclectic and wide-ranging – everything from Ossie Clark to leopardprint. Her intention is to inspire.

TIME OUT Ⓦ www.timeout.com/london The old lady of London listings has kept a beady eye on the rise of vintage activity in London and is well worth checking out, even if she cannot keep abreast of every development.

TUDERHOFF Ⓦ www.tuderhoff.com Diana (a clothes designer) and Ves (an engineer) are Tuderhoff: suppliers of high quality 20th-century furniture, ceramics and lighting, with a bias towards classic modernist designs. Viewing at their Walthamstow base is by appointment only. Prices reflect the quality but they also hire out furniture for photo shoots.

TWENTIETH CENTURY SOCIETY Ⓐ 70 Cowcross Street EC1M 6EJ Ⓣ 020 7250 3857 Ⓦ www.c20society.org.uk Originally called the Thirties Society, the Twentieth Century Society is a lobby group and educational body celebrating (and campaigning to preserve) significant examples of British architecture and design from 1914 onwards. The society organizes regular lectures and walks, and there are plenty of other perks if you become a member.

VINTAGE FASHION CLUB Ⓦ www.vintagefashionclub.com Internationally curated website with London contributors. Fun, listy and with lots of informative content and several London-orientated features and articles. It might not be completely up to date but its content is rich and informative.

THE VINTAGE GUIDE TO LONDON

Ⓦ www.thevintageguidetolondon.com If there is one website you need to bookmark, this is it. Its wide coverage of stores and categories is organized within a clear structure. The site also takes advertising and is excellent for catching up with the latest news and events.

THE VINTAGE PATTERN FILES Ⓦ thevintagepatternfiles.blogspot.co.uk

Vintage knitting and sewing enthusiast Wendy, (who also blogs at Ⓦ thebutterflybalcony.blogspot.co.uk) has set up a fantastic link library of free old-style knitting and sewing patterns sourced from across the web.

VINTAGE VIXEN Ⓦ www.vintagevixon.blogspot.co.uk

Vintage Vixen is a hippy chick with a sprinkling of rock star glam heavily accessorized with tribal jewellery. Her thing is the late 1960s through to the early-70s. She buys second-hand as it's more ethical and gets a little buzz out of finding something fabulous that no-one else will have. Vintage Vixen is listed as one of the top ten vintage clothing blogs in the UK by PR firm Cision.

YESTERDAY GIRL Ⓦ www.jennyjenny-yesterdaygirl.blogspot.co.uk

Piles of enthusiasm from a London-based lady hugely into the 1940s and 50s with masses of links to other like-minded souls.

WEDDINGS

FUR COAT NO KNICKERS Ⓐ Top Floor, Kingly Court W1B 5PW
Ⓣ 07814 002295 Ⓦ www.furcoatnoknickers.co.uk Popular vintage clothes store also specializes in wedding wear. The brides blog spot linked to the Fur Coat website inspires confidence. Definitely worth a look, should you find yourself near Carnaby Street with the nuptial day fast approaching.

HARLEQUIN FOX Ⓣ 07891 052956 Ⓦ www.harlequinfox.com Hand-crafted bespoke bridal wear inspired by classic vintage designs. Prices start at £950 for dresses and £150 for bridesmaids. Dressmaker Natasha Shaw is based in Camberwell but is prepared to go anywhere in London or its outskirts.

HEAVENLY VINTAGE BRIDES Ⓐ 20 Westbourne Avenue W3 6JL
Ⓣ 07814 020319 Ⓦ www.heavenlyvintagebrides.co.uk Unique wedding dresses, starting at £400 and with most under £1000. Their own brand, reproducing classic designs from the 1940s to the 70s, was launched in 2012.

JANE BOURVIS Ⓐ89 Golborne Rd W10 5NL Ⓣ020 8964 5603 Ⓦ www.janebourvis.co.uk A studio specializing in weddings and special occasions, sourcing outstanding garments from 1900 onwards. Think corsets, antique textiles, lace and the understated elegance of a bygone age.

MISS VINTAGE WEDDING AFFAIR Ⓣ07759 848813 Ⓦ www. missvintageaffair.co.uk Occasional London wedding fair held at the Battersea Arts Centre (which is also a great venue for the big day itself). Intended for creative, adventurous and imaginative brides looking for inspiration.

A MOST CURIOUS WEDDING AFFAIR Ⓣ07852 150285 Ⓦ www. amostcuriousweddingfair.co.uk Cool design-led bridal events for the style-conscious and vintage-curious. York Hall was the venue for their London event and they also pop up in Norwich.

LONDON VINTAGE WEDDING FAIR Ⓐ The Old Finbsury Town Hall, Rosebery Avenue EC1R 4RP Ⓦ londonvintageweddingfair.co.uk Another occasional event that gathers the very best UK vintage wedding dealers. Plenty of beautiful pieces in great condition – wonderful dresses, antique lace, jewellery and shoes.

ROCKN'ROLL BRIDE Ⓦ www.rocknrollbride.com Popular wedding blog for brides looking for a little "kick ass weddingness" and who don't want to go all decorous, demure and boring on the big day. Lots of ideas from Kat Williams and her many fans.

VINTAGE WEDDING FAIR Ⓦ www.vintageweddingfair.co.uk A venture by Discover Vintage Ltd which runs fairs throughout the UK including about two a year in London, usually at Chiswick Town Hall. Entry is £6 on the door.

VICTORIA MILLÉSIME DESIGN LONDON Ⓦ www.victoriamillesime.co.uk Online vintage store strong in wedding accessories, jewellery and headpieces and tiaras. A great site if you're looking for that finishing touch to an amazing wedding outfit. Vicky's blog is worth a browse too.

THE VINTAGE WEDDING DRESS COMPANY Ⓐ 33 Tottenham Street W1T 4RR Ⓣ 020 7637 4898 Ⓦ www.thevintageweddingdresscompany.com Private appointments can be made for a look round the showroom (no buggies, babies or small kids) which houses collections of unique original dresses (from £650) and the decades collection (from £1280).

ZOE LEM'S VINTAGE WEDDING FAIR Ⓦ www.zoelem.co.uk Less "aprons and teacakes" and more Hollywood glamour is the keynote to this wedding fair from the self-styled "vintage shape mistress". The venue is usually the Old Sessions House in Clerkenwell and Zoë also offers all sorts of high-end wedding fashion consultation by private appointment.

WANT TO KNOW THE BEST
KEPT SECRET OF DESIGNERS
AND INTERIOR JOURNALISTS?

LOOKING FOR ORIGINAL
C20 DESIGN CLASSICS AT
GREAT PRICES FROM 100 TOP
DEALERS AND DESIGNERS?

SHOP 'BUY VINTAGE' AT
WWW.MODERNSHOWS.COM

Modern Shows

CURATORS OF MIDCENTURY MODERN AND THE MIDCENTURY SHOW

INDEX

Picture credits

All pictures in this guide are © Rough Guides, except those listed below.

Rough Guides photographers: Frances Ambler, Marta Bescos, Emily Bick, Samantha Cook, Diana Jarvis, Nicholas Jones, Lara Kavanagh, Natascha Sturny, Ed Wright

Front cover: © The Land of Lost Content Museum and Library

Inside Back Cover: Wayne Hemingway at the Southbank Centre © Rebecca Reid/ Eyevine

Photography: p.v Wayne Hemingway © David Jones Photography; p.16 Ed's Easy Diner © Ed's Easy Diner; p.29 The Vintage Showroom © Nic Shonfeld; p.34 Absolute Vintage © David Yeo; p.43 Elemental © Elemental; p.44 Fatboy's Diner © Alex Winn; p.48 House of Vintage © Marcia Cooper; p.50 Labour and Wait © Labour and Wait; p.52 Maison Trois Garcons © Maison Trois Garcons; p.53 Samurai cocktail at Nightjar © Nightjar; p.54 Paper Dress Vintage © Katy Tuck Photography; p.57 Speedie's © Speedie's; p.61 Vintage Heaven © Marek Neumann; p.68 Annie's © Annie's; 72 Can't Buy Me Love © Can't Buy Me Love; p.74 Drink, Shop & Do © Daniel Gianini; p.78 Judith Michael & Daughter © Judith Michael & Daughter; p.84 Pelicans & Parrots © Elisabeth Blanchett; p.103 Lassco © Stefan Loret; p.114 What the Butler Wore © Bridget Duffy; p.119 Alfie's Antique Market © Alfie's; p.124 Dodo Posters © Dodo Posters at Alfie's; p.125 Dolly Diamond © Dolly Diamond; p.126 Gallery 1930 © Gallery 1930; p.132 The Old Cinema © The Old Cinema; p.138 The Prince Alfred © Peter Hamblin; p.141 Retro Woman © Mariann Metsis; p.143 The Troubadour © Jacek Niewadzi; p.144 The V&A shop © Courtesy of the V&A shop; Victoria & Albert Museum; p.145 Victory Vintage © Elisabeth Blanchett; pp.146–147 Fatboy's Diner © Alex Winn Photography; p.161 The Powder Room © The Powder Room; p.172 The Chap Olympiad © The Chap Olympiad; p.174 The Vintage Festival © Chris Jackson/The Vintage Festival; p.186 Denis Severs House © James Brittain/ Denis Severs House; p.190 All Star Lanes © All Star Lanes; p.195 Prangsta © Ollie Harrop/Prangsta; p.200 Wilton's Music Hall © Gill Allen/The Times

Illustrations and vintage posters: p.i, 148, 150, 151, 153, 157, 159, 166, 168, 169, 170, 172, 175, 178, 180, 184, 187, 197, 206: all © The Land of Lost Content Museum and Library

Every attempt has been made to trace the copyright holders of the images used in this book and we apologize for any omissions. We would be pleased to insert the appropriate acknowledgements in any subsequent editions.